Education in National Politics

Educational Policy, Planning, and Theory
SERIES EDITOR: Don Adams, *University of Pittsburgh*

Analytical Models in Educational Planning
and Administration
Hector Correa

Contemporary Educational Theory
Robert E. Mason

Education as Cultural Imperialism
Martin Carnoy

Education and Emigration:
Study Abroad and the Migration of Human Resources
Robert G. Myers

Education in National Politics
Norman C. Thomas

The Possibilities of Error:
An Approach to Education
Henry J. Perkinson

The Public School Movement:
A Critical Study
Richard Pratte

Schooling and Social Change in Modern America
Don Adams with Gerald M. Reagan

Schooling in a Corporate Society:
The Political Economy of Education in America
Martin Carnoy

Social Forces and Schooling:
An Anthropological and Sociological Perspective
Nobuo Kenneth Shimahara and Adam Scrupski

EDUCATION IN NATIONAL POLITICS

Norman C. Thomas
Department of Political Science
University of Cincinnati

DAVID McKAY COMPANY, INC.
NEW YORK

In Memoriam

James K. Pollock
1898–1968

Lionel H. Laing
1905–1973

Education in National Politics
COPYRIGHT © 1975 BY DAVID McKAY COMPANY, INC.

International Standard Book Number: 0–679–30267–0
Library of Congress Catalog Card Number: 74–83092
MANUFACTURED IN THE UNITED STATES OF AMERICA
Design by Bob Antler

PREFACE

This is a study in public policy making. It represents an attempt to further the understanding of the processes through which policies are formulated, adopted, and implemented at the national level of government. My objective in conducting the study was to provide an empirically based description which would lend itself to the testing of certain hypotheses and the development of generalizations regarding the making of domestic policies. This meant that the study would have to adopt a focus that encompassed more than a single policy decision and yet was sufficiently limited that the behavior of the participants could be observed and analyzed.

I decided to concentrate on a specific policy area: education. In addition to being a subject of great personal interest and concern, education was one of the principal sectors of President Johnson's Great Society; consequently, important new national policies had been adopted in recent years. This suggested that relationships between governmental decision makers and individuals and groups seeking to influence them were likely to be dynamic and flexible. A study conducted in an area of great presidential emphasis seemed more likely to provide information regarding the nature of policy change and development than, say, the examination of policy making in a more established area such as antitrust or agriculture.

Educational policy making at the national level proved to be too broad and comprehensive a subject for one person to investigate and analyze in a limited time. I therefore narrowed the focus of inquiry to the making of policies underlying the programs administered by the U.S. Office of Education and I imposed a rough time limit of the period covering the 90th Congress (1967 and 1968). I defined the subject, then, in terms of substance, governmental level, institutions, and time period.

My primary concern is with the policy-making process; however, I have given considerable attention to the substantive issues that concern policy makers and to the alternatives that confront them. Without passing judgment on the wisdom of past decisions, I have attempted to assess the probable consequences of specific courses of action. I freely admit, however, that after a sustained investigation of the subject, I have formed definite opinions regarding education and federal educational policies. But I am not an educational expert. My stance is empirical rather than normative with respect to the policies under study.

In addition to examining the process of national educational policy making, it is my hope that this study will be of interest and value to government officials, persons in the education community, and members of the general public who are concerned with the present condition and the future of American education. It is my conviction that research in political science must try to have both theoretical significance and social relevance. In policy analysis more than any other area of inquiry is this a difficult objective.

Research for this study was conducted during the academic year 1967–68 when I was on sabbatical leave from the University of Michigan. During that period I received additional support in the form of a fellowship grant from the Relm Foundation, Ann Arbor, Michigan, and an appointment as a guest scholar at the Brookings Institution. In the summer of 1968, an appointment as a research associate in the Institute of Public Administration of the University of Michigan enabled me to conclude my interviews and to begin analyzing the data I had collected. My thanks go to all the aforementioned institutions.

It is almost impossible to extend thanks to all those persons who aided in the conduct of the study. Some, however, are deserving of a special note of appreciation. My former student Harold L. Wolman provided countless helpful suggestions and comments in a multitude of ways. Another former student, Mrs. Cora Beebe of the U.S. Office of Education, provided invaluable advice and assistance. Samuel Halperin, former deputy assistant secretary of Health, Education, and Welfare, was a storehouse of information, a constructive critic, and a valuable sounding board for my ideas and interpretations. Miss Helen Miller, specialist in education at the Legislative Reference Service of the Library of Congress, provided indispensable aid in the collection of government documents and other published information. Ben Reeves, director of publications for the House Committee on Education and Labor, was always willing to explain its latest actions. I am also indebted to all those persons who permitted me to interview them.

Responsibility for the information presented in the following pages and the conclusions drawn from it is, of course, mine alone.

Norman C. Thomas
Cincinnati, Ohio
1974

CONTENTS

Part I **INTRODUCTION**

1 The Educational Policy Process   3

Part II **THE POLITICS OF EDUCATION**

2 The Development of the Federal Role in Education   19
3 Issues and Problems: The Substance of Expectations
   and Demands   37
4 Educational Policy and the 90th Congress   72

Part III **THE POLICY PROCESS**

5 Institutions, Individuals, and Their Roles   113
6 Communication Patterns and Information Sources   154
7 Policy-Making Stages   172

Part IV **CONCLUSION**

8 The Educational Policy Process in Retrospect   221

   Index   241

Education in National Politics

INTRODUCTION

1

THE EDUCATIONAL POLICY PROCESS

Throughout the 1950s and the early 1960s one of the most controversial domestic political issues was federal aid to education. Efforts by the National Education Association and other professional groups, organized labor, and political liberals to secure passage of legislation authorizing general federal aid to elementary and secondary education foundered in Congress. There, conservative opponents of any substantial federal role in education were able to prevent the formation of a winning coalition by invoking three related issues known as the three Rs: Race, Religion, and Reds (or federal control).[1]

During those years, federal educational programs were modest in their objectives and in the level of funds appropriated for them. The principal education agency, the U.S. Office of Education (USOE), functioned mainly to furnish statistical information and consultative services to state and local education officials and their professional associations. Those federal educational programs in existence were narrow in scope and additive in their effects. Education was a relatively minor policy area in which the relationships between the education community and governmental decision makers were stable and predictable.

The first major breakthrough in this pattern came in 1958 when Congress, with the support of President Eisenhower, passed the National Defense Education Act (NDEA) in response to the challenge presented by the successful orbiting of the Russian sputnik in October 1957. NDEA authorized a variety of categorical aid programs for higher and secondary

3

education. Although it resulted in a substantial expenditure of federal funds, NDEA hardly amounted to massive general aid to education. It tended to place heavy emphasis on those aspects of education that could be related to defense: natural science, mathematics, and foreign languages.

The next major developments in the expansion of the federal role in education followed closely the assassination of President Kennedy. In December 1963 Congress passed the Higher Education Facilities Act and an omnibus bill providing for aid to vocational education, an expansion of NDEA, and a continuation of aid to federally impacted areas. 1964 witnessed the enactment of the Library Services and Construction Act. The logjam had begun to break. In 1965, following President Johnson's landslide victory in the 1964 election, which also produced heavy Democratic majorities in Congress, two additional education assistance bills became law. The Elementary and Secondary Education Act (ESEA) is the most important piece of federal education legislation enacted to date. Although the federal government's contribution to the financing of elementary/secondary education is proportionally small (around 7 to 8 percent), it is large enough in absolute dollar amounts to have a substantial, if not critical, effect. The categorical assistance programs of the five titles of ESEA sought to improve the quality of American education through the leverage of that marginal impact. The Higher Education Act had similar objectives, but with a lower level of expenditures authorized for its programs.

In the space of two years, then, Congress enacted five major statutes authorizing a wide range of programs which catapulted the federal government into the American educational system as a major source of funds and a potential force for substantial changes in that system.

By January 1967, when the 90th Congress convened, most of the new programs had been implemented and their effects were beginning to be felt. The USOE had assumed a greatly expanded role, and new relationships had developed or were forming between federal officials and the individuals and groups in American education who were affected by their decisions and actions. It is the process of national educational policy making in this altered environment that is the object of inquiry in this study.

The Study of Public Policy Making

In discussing how to study public policy making it is first necessary to define the term "policy." It has always seemed to me that policy is a concept which is employed frequently and the meaning of which is generally understood. Yet it is seldom defined explicitly. For the purposes of this study, I have defined policy as a course of action (or inaction) pursued by an actor or a group of actors with regard to a subject.[2] A public policy is one which is made by government officials, affects all members of the community, and is recognized by them as binding. Public policy making refers, then, to the activities of government officials and agencies leading to the selection of authoritative courses of action. Public policy making is primarily allocative in that the choices made relate to subjects which involve the enhancement of certain values and the rejection of others.

Salisbury has offered a broader definition of policy which encompasses "authoritative outputs of the political system, actions aimed at affecting those outputs, and the goals or purposes or interests at stake in authoritative decisions." [3] This formulation is quite consistent with the one offered here and is indicative of the concerns of this study. The scholar who sets out to study public policy making must examine its content, the actions which determine content, and the values at stake.[4] A major objective of this study is to maintain a reasonable and discreet balance between these concerns.

Perhaps the most frequently employed approach to the study of public policy making has been case analysis. Individual case studies have provided a wealth of empirical evidence of the behavior of policy makers in a wide variety of settings. While case studies have been useful for developing limited generalizations and testing certain theoretical propositions,[5] they have not produced anything resembling a substantial body of theory.[6]

A number of empirical studies of policy have attempted to explain the variation in policy outputs, as measured by expenditures in the American states, in terms of the economic, social, and political characteristics of state political systems.[7] The most striking finding of these studies is that structural characteristics of state polities, i.e., political variables such as party competition, patterns of legislative apportionment, and the strength of the governorship, do not "explain" (in the statistical sense) much of the variation in policy output between states. Rather, the critical independent variables are the economic and social characteristics of the states, e.g., income level, urbanization, and the like, which are indicative of the resources of state polities. These findings seem strongly to imply, as Salisbury points out, that the analysis of political processes and of policy-making activity cannot explain policy outputs.[8] This line of argument also appears to be buttressed by the incrementalist view of American politics. The incrementalists have argued that the prevailing pattern is for policies to vary only marginally from what has been done in the past.[9] Since past expenditures are the best predictor of future expenditures, there would appear to be but very narrow range for the operation of political variables.[10]

However, both the system characteristics analysts and the incrementalists have focused on expenditures. Their findings fail to account for decisions concerning the purposes for which money will be spent. Nor do they offer any explanations of individual, group, or institutional policy-making behavior. They do not come to grips with questions such as why certain groups benefited and others did not, why the decision makers pursued one course of action rather than others, and how innovation and change occur in policy. As significant as the findings of these studies have been, they do not obviate the need for, or the value of, examinations of the dynamics of choice in politics.[11]

Other scholars, most notably Fenno, have examined policy-making behavior in congressional committees.[12] Their research has shed light on the dynamics of a key sector of legislative policy making, and Fenno's conception of the committee as a political system has provided a valuable framework for analysis. Nevertheless, a detailed examination of the workings of a congressional committee illumines only a small sector of the full scope of policy-making activity. If one wishes to examine policy making beyond the structure of relationships that exist within a single institution and between the institution and its environment, committee-centered or agency-centered research will not be sufficient.

Wildavsky overcame this problem in his study of the budgetary process.[13] He analyzed this highly significant form of policy making in terms of the role perceptions and strategies of individuals located in the Budget Bureau, the agencies, and the appropriations committees. Appropriations politics, however, constitutes a special type of policy making. The policy choices involve the distribution of resources among previously authorized programs. The units of decision are uniform and the analyst can compare and quantify them with ease. But the crucial decisions are those unmeasurable actions which establish or terminate programs including the rules and structures which determine the allocations yet to come. There is a "fundamental distinction to be made between" policies that affect the "*amount* of expenditure" and those that determine the "*kind* or the *distribution* of the amount." [14]

This difference becomes apparent in the development of a research strategy for the analysis of policy decisions regarding substantive programs in areas such as education. The choices confronting policy makers include basic value questions: What should the federal role be? What kinds of programs are needed? To what extent should resources be devoted to education rather than other areas such as housing? These choices are likely to be more comprehensive and less incremental than those involved in making appropriations. The substantive issues up for decision and the pattern of policy-making activity are likely to vary much more from year to year depending on the circumstances.

If this distinction between decisions involving the level of expenditures, i.e., the direct allocation of tangible benefits, and those which establish rules, structures, and programs, is valid, and if one wishes to proceed beyond the limits imposed by the study of a single decision, however important it may be, what can be done? The strategy employed here follows a path suggested by several scholars. Griffith has called attention to "whirlpools" or centers of activity which focus on particular problems.[15] Freeman has referred to the same phenomena as the "subsystems" of government and has studied the interactions of participants in a setting formed by "an executive bureau and congressional committees, with special interest groups intimately attached." [16] Cater referred to them as the "subgovernments of Washington." [17] A recent text speaks of "policy clusters" and defines them as "coalitions of officials and non-officials . . . who decide the final terms of policy in specialized areas." [18]

These observations suggest that a fruitful approach to the study of public policy making lies in the analysis of a specialized policy area. Such an analysis should provide an empirical description of policy making in the specific substantive area and identify some of the major determinants of policy-making behavior. It should also have implications for theories concerning the operation of the general political system. Finally, the analysis should focus on the objectives, behavior, and interrelations of the individuals—legislators and their staffs, bureaucrats, lobbyists, and educators—who make policies.

The policy-making process in the area of education is particularly appropriate for analysis because of recent comprehensive changes in national educational policy. Legislation enacted since 1963, and particularly in 1965, has revolutionized the federal role in education. In terms of Lowi's typology, redistributive policies have been adopted in education.[19] Most studies of policy making have focused on distributive or regulatory policies. The study of an area in which redistributive policies have recently been or are being made is of considerable importance because of the growing significance of such areas and the relative lack of interest shown in them to date.

This is not to say, however, that education is important primarily because it involves redistributive policy making or that all educational policy making is redistributive. In fact, much of the activity analyzed herein is distributive or regulatory. Furthermore, the importance of education stems from its function as a fundamental underpinning of the economic and social systems. In times of rapid change accompanied by social and political turbulence such as the United States has experienced since 1965, education has a critical role to play in helping new generations adapt to the change. To accomplish this task education itself must change. Much of the dynamics of educational policy making in recent years centers on recognition of this phenomena and involves efforts to change education so that it might be a more effective change agent.

The Educational Policy Process

The educational policy process* included key individuals located in the U.S. Office of Education (USOE), the Health, Education, and Welfare (HEW) hierarchy, the presidential staff, the Budget Bureau, the House and

* Hereafter I will refer to the policy process rather than the policy-making process.

Senate subcommittees having jurisdiction over education, the Labor–HEW appropriations subcommittees in the two houses, educational interest groups, other groups with an interest in education, and a number of important individuals in the education profession and the general community who are frequently consulted by government officials. The major entities in the external environment included the remainder of Congress, other government agencies with educational program responsibilities, the education profession, state and local education authorities, and other systems in the polity. Some elements, the federal judiciary being a prime example, move in and out of the educational policy process depending on the circumstances.[20] Because of the relative isolation of the courts from other major participants in the political process and because the decisions of the courts affecting education tend to involve fundamental issues of constitutionality, I have not included the Judiciary within the framework of the policy process.

The policy process involves three stages which are serial with respect to single policies, but which occur simultaneously with respect to all educational policies. The stages include:

1. Innovation and formulation—ideas are generated, demands based on them articulated, certain demands are accepted and advanced by government officials as specific proposals for action.
2. Adoption—policy proposals are formally authorized through legislative enactment and funded through the appropriations process.
3. Implementation—administrative action is taken to implement funded programs. This stage involves the determination of organizational arrangements, drafting of guidelines and regulations, and expenditure of funds. It also involves interpretation of legislation by administrative officials and, if necessary, by the courts.

It should be noted that with the exception of budgeting and appropriating, much policy-making activity is substantively nonrecurrent. Procedures, however, are likely to reflect patterned behavior and they are my principal concern.

Using this approach, my analysis of the educational policy process will attempt to answer a number of questions. Some of the more important points to be raised include:

Where do ideas originate?
What means are used to obtain and evaluate ideas?
What are the issues, or what is at stake?
Who makes demands?
Who has access to the decision makers?

Are there interests who do not appear to be able to make demands? Why
    are they unable to do so?
Who are the principal policy makers?
At what stage (or stages) of the process are they active?
What are their role orientations?
What are their expectations regarding the process?
What are the major sources of information on which they rely?
What are their relationships with other policy makers?
What kind of communications network exists among the policy makers?
What is the impact of individual personalities?
What are the policy-makers' attitudes toward educational policy issues?
How are choices made among competing alternatives for resource
    allocations within the education program area?
How are conflicts resolved?
What effect do institutional factors have on policy-making activity?
To what extent is educational policy making incremental?
Under what conditions does policy innovation occur?
What are the consequences of the application of Program Planning
    Budgeting and cost-benefit analysis to educational policy making?
What are the major educational programs of the USOE?
I.e., who gets what?
Who doesn't get what?
What new demands arise as feedback from the programs?
How do present policies affect the policy process?

The study will not furnish answers to all these questions, but they indicate the
direction in which the analysis will move.

Research Strategy

The initial problem in studying the educational policy process was to
identify the policy makers. Once the institutions encompassed in the policy
area were defined (by the arbitrary criterion of what would be physically
manageable in the time available for data gathering) it was necessary to
determine who had actual or potential influence over the content of
educational policies. The technique I employed to identify the influentials
combined elements of the reputational and positional approaches.[21]

The initial step was to compile a list of potential influentials. To all those
persons holding formal positions of authority—appropriate congressional
committee chairmen and subcommittee members, USOE officials down to the
bureau chief level, HEW officials including the assistant secretaries, presiden-

tial staff members, Budget Bureau officials with responsibility for education, and the principal officials of education pressure groups with responsibility for federal relations—I added members of White House task forces on education and of major education advisory councils, and various individuals who frequently testified before congressional committees regarding proposed education bills. A series of background interviews with ten persons intimately acquainted with various aspects of the policy process yielded additional names, e.g., congressional committee staff members, foundation officials, and prominent educators and laymen. The names on the list totaled 175.

The next step involved interviews with 24 persons possessing substantial knowledge of the USOE or its programs. Eight of them had particular competence in the field of higher education programs, eight in the elementary/secondary field, and eight had general knowledge extending to both areas. These individuals included congressional staff members, USOE and HEW officials, Budget Bureau officials, pressure group members, and journalists. Five of them eventually were included on the panel of influentials who comprised the participants of the policy process. These 24 respondents were asked to examine the list of 175 potential influentials and check those whom they considered to be most important with respect to policy innovation and formulation, policy adoption, and policy implementation. Their responses, along with other information obtained from a more general background investigation, provided the basis for narrowing the list to a total of 77 influentials. The determination of the influentials was a subjective judgment, although the ratings of the 24 knowledgeable persons were a major factor in reaching it.[22]

The selections were made as objectively as possible, although another analyst might have added certain names and excluded some of those who were chosen. In fact, as the study progressed, I interviewed six persons not on the original list whom subsequent research revealed should have been, and I dropped two persons from it. Considering the methodological problems involved,[23] I am confident that the panel is a fairly accurate representation of the educational policy-making elite that functioned during the period of the 90th Congress.

The materials that serve as the basis of description and analysis are those suggested and used by Fenno in his study of the appropriations process: "the normative expectations of the various participants, the perceptions and attitudes, or images, of the participants, and the behavior of the participants." [24] Also, Murray Edelman has suggested that an essential factor in policy formation are the assumptions of the policy makers regarding the determinants of future political responses of the mass public.[25] The normative expectations of the policy makers are expressed in terms of their official role orientations. A comparison of these role expectations with behavior in these roles will greatly facilitate the explanation of the behavior. To the extent that role expectations and role behavior correspond, behavior patterns will be more stable and explanation made easier. The perceptions and attitudes of the policy makers reveal what they see in their situation and how they evaluate it. Fenno points out that while it is possible to distinguish perceptions from attitudes in theory, in practice they are inextricably intertwined. He resolves this problem by lumping them together as images. The images of the participants reveal how they and others behave and how they evaluate that behavior. This information is vital to identifying and understanding the relationships that exist in the policy process.

In his study, Fenno explicitly rejected the explanation of behavior through reference to specific individuals and their personalities. His approach was "to show how much generalization is possible short of heavy reliance on personality data." [26] The alternative, he suggested, is to undertake a sophisticated analysis of the personality variable using "meaningful psychological variables." [27] His results, while highly impressive, do not really resolve the basic problem. This is because individuals involved in the policy process tend to view it in terms of other individuals and their personalities. Indeed, much of the interview data which the Washington researcher gathers is personality-centered. Not to use it in some way is to leave untouched a substantial amount of potentially valuable explanatory information. Nor need one be a psychologist to assess the impact of personality on policy making. [28]

It is also true that the roles assumed by the participants in the policy process are the product of both position and personality. Personality is a many-faceted concept. I am using it here to refer to the sum total of the individual's life experiences; i.e., his background, past associations with other members of the system, his occupation, his values and policy preferences, his leadership style, and similar factors. Thus defined, personality is a conglomerate of many variables which is in large part determinative of the roles assumed by the participants in the educational policy process within limits or boundaries set by organizational or institutional forms.

Therefore, I do not reject the use of personality, and all that it entails, as an independent variable. Following Manley, however, the analysis will stress the "group-sociological" view of leadership rather than the "individual-personality" view. [29] This will involve an attempt to ascertain how and why certain policy makers are able to assume leadership roles rather than a search for the psychological determinants of their behavior.

The specific policy-making activity that will be examined includes the following actions taken during the period of the 90th Congress (1967–68): (1) the enactment and implementation of the Education Professions Development Act of 1967; (2) the enactment of the 1967 Elementary and Secondary Education Act Amendments; (3) the enactment of the Higher Education Act Amendments of 1968; (4) the enactment of the Vocational Education Amendments of 1968; and (5) the passage of the appropriations bills for fiscal years 1968 and 1969 for the Department of Health, Education, and Welfare. In the course of examining these major policy developments, the resolution of related minor issues will also be analyzed.

The sources of data include interviews, public documents, and secondary materials. The principal interviews were conducted with 71 influential participants in the educational policy process. A supplementary series of interviews with 22 USOE division directors and at least 35 background interviews were also conducted. The primary interviews sought to obtain information in three basic categories: role orientations, perceptions, and attitudes. They were semistructured in that each respondent was asked the same set of general open-end questions, although it was not always possible to complete all of them in the time available. Frequently, promising avenues of inquiry opened and were explored at the expense of obtaining other data. In this manner, I was able to obtain a considerable amount of valuable information relating to policy-making activity.

Because the interview procedures were eclectic, as elite interviewing tends to be, the data are for the most part nonquantitative and the analysis will be conducted in qualitative terms. The objective of the study, stated again, is to describe and explain the educational policy process as accurately as possible. It is unlikely that the analysis will have great predictive value, but it should lead to a better understanding of the relationships involved in making national educational policy.

Notes

1. This description follows Stephen K. Bailey and Edith K. Mosher, *ESEA: The Office of Education Administers a Law* (Syracuse: Syracuse University Press, 1968), chaps. 1 and 2. A more extensive background discussion appears in chapter 3 herein.

2. Cf. James E. Anderson, *Politics and the Economy* (Boston: Little, Brown, 1966), p. 50.

3. Robert H. Salisbury, "The Analysis of Public Policy," in Austin Ranney, ed., *Political Science and Public Policy* (Chicago: Markham, 1968), pp. 151–75.

4. For somewhat differing views concerning the appropriate distribution of emphasis between content and process in public policy research, see Austin Ranney, "The Study of Policy Content: A Framework for Choice," in Ranney, *Political Science and Public Policy*, pp. 3–22; and Vernon Van Dyke, "Process and Policy as Focal Concepts in Political Research," ibid., pp. 23–40.

5. See, for example, Martin Meyerson and Edward C. Banfield, *Politics, Planning and the Public Interest* (Glencoe, Ill.: Free Press, 1955); E. C. Banfield, *Political Influence* (New York: Free Press of Glencoe, 1961); Jason L. Finkle, *The President Makes a Decision: A Study of Dixon-Yates* (Ann Arbor: Institute of Public Administration, University of Michigan, 1960); Raymond A. Bauer, Ithiel deSola Pool, and Lewis A. Dexter, *American Business and Public Policy* (New York: Atherton Press, 1963); Norman C. Thomas, *Rule 9: Politics, Administration and Civil Rights* (New York: Random House, 1966); and Philip Meranto, *The Politics of Federal Aid to*

Education in 1965: A Study in Political Innovation (Syracuse: Syracuse University Press, 1967).

6. Attempts to tease theory out of case literature are quite rare. See, however, Morris Davis, "Some Aspects of Detroit's Decisional Profile," *Administrative Sciences Quarterly* 12 (September 1967): 209–24; and Lewis A. Froman, Jr., "An Analysis of Public Policies in Cities," *Journal of Politics* 29 (February 1967): 94–108. For a good discussion of the problems involved in developing policy theory, see Froman, "The Categorization of Policy Contents," in Ranney, *Political Science and Public Policy*, pp. 41–52.

7. The principal studies include Richard E. Dawson and James A. Robinson, "Inter-Party Competition, Economic Variables, and Welfare Policies in the American States," *Journal of Politics* 25 (May 1963): 265–89; Richard I. Hofferbert, "The Relation between Public Policy and Some Structural and Environmental Variables in the American States," *American Political Science Review* 60 (March 1966): 73–82; Hofferbert, "Ecological Development and Policy Change in the American States," *Midwest Journal of Political Science* 10 (November 1966): 464–85; Thomas R. Dye, *Politics, Economics, and the Public: Policy Outcomes in the American States* (Chicago: Rand McNally, 1966); Ira Sharkansky, "Economic Development, Regionalism and State Political Systems," *Midwest Journal of Political Science* 12 (February 1968): 41–62; *Spending in the American States* (Chicago: Rand McNally, 1968); and Sharkansky and Hofferbert, "Dimensions of State Politics, Economics, and Public Policy," *American Political Science Review* 63 (September 1969): 867–79.

8. Salisbury, "Analysis of Public Policy," p. 164.

9. See David Braybrooke and Charles Lindblom, *A Strategy for Decision* (New York: Free Press, 1963); Lindblom, *The Intelligence of Democracy* (New York: Free Press, 1965); Aaron Wildavsky, *The Politics of the Budgetary Process* (Boston: Little, Brown, 1964); Otto A. Davis, M. A. H. Dempster, and A. Wildavsky, "A Theory of the Budgetary Process," *American Political Science Review* 60 (September 1966): 529–48; and Richard F. Fenno, *The Power of the Purse: Appropriations Politics in Congress* (Boston: Little, Brown, 1966).

10. Salisbury, "Analysis of Public Policy," p. 164.

11. See Salisbury and John P. Heinz, "A Theory of Policy Analysis and Some Preliminary Applications" (Paper delivered at the 1968 Annual Meeting of the American Political Science Association, Washington, D.C.), p. 2.

12. See *The Power of the Purse*; Fenno's "The House Appropriations Committee as a Political System: The Problem of Integration," *American Political Science Review* 56 (June 1962): 310–24; Charles O. Jones, "Representation in Congress: The Case of the House Agriculture Committee," *American Political Science Review* 55 (June 1961): 358–67; James A. Robinson, *The House Rules Committee* (Indianapolis: Bobbs-Merrill, 1963); H. P. Green and Alan Rosenthal, *Government of the Atom* (New York: Atherton Press, 1964); and John F. Manley, "The House Committee on Ways and Means: Conflict Management in a Congressional Committee," *American Political Science Review* 59 (December 1965): 927–39.

13. *Politics of the Budgetary Process*.

14. Salisbury and Heinz, "Theory of Policy Analysis," p. 2.

15. Ernest S. Griffith, *The Impasse of Democracy* (New York: Harrison-Hilton Books, 1939), p. 182.

16. J. Lieper Freeman, *The Political Process: Executive Bureau-Legislative Committee Relationships* (New York: Random House, 1955), p. 5.

17. Douglass Cater, *Power in Washington* (New York: Random House, 1964), pp. 3–48.

18. Dan Nimmo and Thomas D. Ungs, *American Political Patterns* (Boston: Little, Brown, 1967), p. 298.

19. According to Lowi, policies are either regulatory, distributive, or redistributive. See Theodore J. Lowi, "American Business, Public Policy, Case Studies and Political Theory," *World Politics* 16 (July 1964): 677–715. The basis of the classification is the nature of their impact. Distributive policies are easily "disaggregated" down to the individual or group level. Because they are easily dispensed in small amounts they do not generate a high degree of conflict. Examples would include farm subsidies, public works projects, and the tariff.

Regulatory policies can be disaggregated only to the level of the sector of the economy in which they occur. They impose restraints on the alternatives open to certain groups. Examples include antitrust policy, public-utility rate regulation, and acreage allotments.

Redistributive policies have broad categories of impact and cannot easily be disaggregated. They involve conferring material benefits (property) on one group through the deprivation of another. Redistributive issues give rise to considerable conflict. Income taxation and decisions to institute new welfare sector programs provide examples of redistributive policies.

Salisbury has modified this typology by establishing self-regulatory policies as a separate category. Such policies "also impose constraints upon a group, but are perceived only to increase, not decrease, the beneficial options to the group." The distinguishing feature is that those making demands also take part in the decisional process. Usually only a small group makes demands and the level of conflict is low. See "Analysis of Public Policy," p. 158. Examples include professional licensing and fair-trade legislation.

20. The principal instance of judicially made educational policy was, of course, the Supreme Court's 1954 decision in *Brown v. Board of Education*. Since then the federal courts have been involved in the implementation of the original decision and the application of the equal protection clause of the Fourteenth Amendment to public schools. Other areas in which judicial decisions promise to have a critical impact on education involve the constitutionality of public aid to private sectarian schools and of the financing of public education by means of local property taxes.

21. My approach is similar to but somewhat less complex than that outlined by Kenneth J. Gergen, "Assessing the Leverage Points in the Process of Policy Formation," in Raymond A. Bauer and Kenneth J. Gergen, eds., *The Study of Public Policy Formation* (New York: Free Press, 1968) pp. 182–203. Undoubtedly the precision of my procedures could have been improved had I had the opportunity to read Gergen's discussion prior to conducting my research. Nevertheless, I believe that we recognize the same problems in the identification of influentials, that we have the same basic objectives, and that our techniques would yield similar results.

22. Originally, I had hoped to make the selections automatically on the basis of the ratings. Many of the persons who made ratings, however, were either too indiscriminate in that they could not or would not make choices, or they nominated only a few persons. The principal value of these interviews was to indicate which persons were not influentials rather than to point out those who were.

23. See Gergen, "Assessing the Leverage Points," for an extended discussion.

24. *Power of the Purse*, p. xx.

25. Murray Edelman, *The Symbolic Uses of Politics* (Urbana: University of Illinois Press, 1964).

26. *Power of the Purse*, p. xxiii.

27. Ibid.

28. See John F. Manley, "Wilbur D. Mills: A Study in Congressional Influence," *American Political Science Review* 63 (June 1969): 442–64; Ralph K. Huitt, "Democratic Party Leadership in the Senate," *American Political Science Review* 55 (June 1961): 333–44; idem, "The Outsider in the Senate: An Alternative Role," *American Political Science Review* 55 (September 1961): 566–74. A good discussion of the problems involved in analyzing the political process from the perspective of the individual participant is Lewis J. Edinger, "Political Science and Political Biography: Reflections on the Study of Leadership," *Journal of Politics* 26 (May 1964): 423–39. An argument for the systematic analysis of personality, largely in terms of psychological variables, appears in Fred I. Greenstein, "The Impact of Personality on Politics: An Attempt to Clear Away Underbrush," *American Political Science Review* 61 (September 1967): 629–41.

29. "Wilbur D. Mills," p. 442.

II

THE POLITICS OF
EDUCATION

2

THE DEVELOPMENT OF
THE FEDERAL ROLE IN EDUCATION

It has often been asserted that "education is a local responsibility, a state function, and a national concern." For most of American history this statement has been factually accurate. Historically, public education as a local responsibility and a state function can be traced to two statutes of the Massachusetts Bay Colony: the Massachusetts Bay Colony Act of 1642 and the "Old Deluder Satan Act" of 1647. These laws required that local communities establish schools (in which Bible reading would naturally be a major activity), in order to prevent the Old Deluder, Satan, from corrupting the youth of the colony. The concern of the federal government with education dates from two ordinances enacted in 1785 and 1787 by Congress under the Articles of Confederation. Developments since then led to the point where, by the end of 1966, education had become a substantial responsibility of the federal government.[1]

Education Becomes a National Issue

In the period of federal "concern" with education, the federal government extended moderate support to state and local educational efforts. Initially that support was limited to land grants, but in the late nineteenth and early twentieth centuries modest grants for specific educational objectives which were subject to limited federal controls were made. The most important

19

federal contribution to education during this period was not in sustained support for substantial education activities, but rather as a stimulus for the development of state and local efforts. The only attempts to obtain general federal aid to elementary and secondary education in this period occurred shortly after the Civil War, and they were unsuccessful. The issue of general federal aid did not arise again until the mid-1940s, although during the depression years a number of the emergency agencies carried out educational activities as a part of the overall relief program.[2]

World War II proved to be the major force propelling education into the national political arena as a major issue. The Lanham Act of 1940 authorized federal funds for the construction, maintenance, and operation of schools in communities confronted with increased populations as a result of the defense effort. Some form of assistance for federally "impacted" areas has been continued ever since.

In 1944 Congress, in response to war-generated conditions, passed the Serviceman's Readjustment Act, better known as the "GI Bill of Rights." Similar legislation was enacted in 1952 for Korean war veterans and in 1966 for Vietnam veterans. Technically these were not education measures; rather, they were laws designed to ease the readjustment of veterans to civilian life.

Nevertheless, "in terms of the number of persons receiving aid, the amount of money spent and the impact upon the nation's educational attainments, they were the most significant federal education programs ever enacted."[3] Under the World War II GI Bill approximately 7.8 million veterans received $14.5 billion in educational assistance. The broad extent of the aid and the fact that it went directly to the individual student were major features of the veterans education programs.

World War II had other effects on American education. One partial consequence of the war was a sharp rise in the birthrate and an expansion in school enrollment. The pressures of increased enrollment placed great strains on the nation's education system. The war, however, had adversely affected the capacity of the education system to respond to the anticipated growth. Capital outlays for school construction, which dropped sharply during the depression, were virtually suspended during the war. A further complication was the war-induced inflation which saw the value of the dollar decline by 40 percent between 1946 and 1953.[4]

The development of the federal role in education during the period 1945–61 was sporadic. Efforts to enact general aid legislation were unsuccessful and highly controversial.[5] There were, however, important special programs authorized which substantially increased the scope and extent of federal responsibility for education. These represented incremental responses to the demands of special educational publics.

The Battle for General Aid: 1945–1960

By the end of 1960, all attempts to pass general federal aid to education legislation had failed. The issue of federal aid, itself complex, had become intertwined with two broader social conflicts: public vs. private sectarian education, which reflected the ancient constitutional conflict over the separation of church and state; and integrated vs. segregated schools, which reflected the problem of race relations.

The effect of adding racial and religious dimensions to the controversy over federal aid to education was to increase the alternative forms which legislation might assume, thus greatly complicating the task of forming a majority coalition. Although the number of possible combinations was much greater, in practice three types of bills were under consideration at one point or another:

1. Aid to education with no restrictions as to religion or race
2. Aid to education limited to public schools with no limitations for segregated schools
3. Aid to education with no restrictions on aid to private sectarian schools, but denied to segregated school systems

A fourth possibility, which was very much alive but never formally considered, was a bill that confined aid to public schools and denied it to segregated school systems. Obviously, the strategy of dedicated opponents of federal aid was to support antisegregation provisions and to insist that aid be limited to public schools only. The question which the supporters of federal aid consistently faced was whether their commitment to racial equality and/or rigid church-state separation would override their desire to improve American education. For many of them it was a Hobson's choice—either cast a vote ostensibly against civil rights and/or for federal aid to sectarian schools, thus helping to kill federal aid legislation, or vote against their consciences and face possible constituency retaliation at the polls. For Catholic liberals one aspect of the problem was reversed, a bill which denied aid to parochial schools was either personally distasteful or politically dangerous or both.

Against the ideological argument that federal aid would lead to federal control, the practical arguments over whether aid should be for construction alone or for construction and salaries, and the economic argument over whether aid should be limited to loans or should include grants as well as loans, were juxtaposed the religious and racial controversies. The obstacles to designing legislation that would attract the support of a majority coalition that could sustain itself long enough to pass a bill seemed almost insurmountable. Yet mounting enrollments and growing public expectations and demands regarding education increased the pressure for some form of federal action. The states and local communities, in spite of greatly expanded revenues and increased expenditures for education in the years since World War II, were increasingly hard pressed to survive the fiscal "crunch" on their own. Federal aid was the most apparent solution, but it was, by virtue of its nature and its relationship to other conflicts, an explosive issue of major proportions.

Although Congress did not enact general federal aid legislation between 1945 and 1960, it did pass a number of laws whose approaches to the problem of education assistance, which when modified and combined, served as a basis for the legislation eventually adopted in the 1960s. For the most part these statutes were "expediential responses" [6] to emergency situations or to pressures in specific sectors of education. In a very real sense they represent "disjointed incrementalism" [7] in action. Unrelated to each other in conception or design, they constituted a series of steps which led to a substantially expanded federal role in education.

Two of these laws, both enacted in 1950, had their origins in conditions resulting from World War II. The National Science Foundation Act reflected recognition of the importance to national security of scientific research and development and of the training of scientific personnel at the graduate and undergraduate levels. The NSF Act, which became law in 1950 after unsuccessful attempts to pass similar legislation in 1947 and 1948, established the National Science Foundation (NSF) and authorized it to "promote scientific research, correlate and evaluate research supported by other government agencies, improve the teaching of science, mathematics and engineering . . . co-operate in international scientific exchange, and disseminate scientific information." [8] Originally, NSF was established to meet specific needs of higher education, which has indeed benefited greatly; but some of its activities, principally training institutes for science teachers and curriculum-revision projects, have had positive consequences for elementary and secondary education. Created in order to strengthen national security, NSF's significance for federal educational policy lay in the precedent it set for direct support of education research. The positive results achieved over the years by many of NSF's education programs suggested to high-level officials of the Johnson administration that federal assistance should not only ease financial pressures on education, but it should also lead to qualitative improvements in education.

The second major development in 1950 was the enactment of two statutes, Public Law 81-815 for school construction and Public Law 81-874 for operating expenses, authorizing grants to public school districts "impacted" by federal activity. Essentially continuations of the Lanham Act of 1940, the impact laws were based on the principle that the federal government had an obligation to make payments in lieu of taxes to local communities because federal property is nontaxable. The impacted-areas programs proved highly popular with Congress because they imposed no federal controls, were easy and inexpensive to administer, and were widely distributed.[9] Congress has steadfastly resisted the efforts of Presidents Eisenhower, Kennedy, Johnson, and Nixon to cut back the level of impacted-areas spending or to phase out the programs by replacing them with general federal aid. An informal but quite potent lobby of school superintendents whose districts receive impacted-areas aid watches all congressional actions which affect "their" programs, including appropriations. The extent of congressional support for the impacted-areas programs was demonstrated in 1968 when the administration's budget request of $410 million for the programs was increased to $520 million in the appropriation for fiscal year 1969.[10]

The impacted-areas programs, which have become almost sacrosanct, have had important effects on educational policies. The laws served as a model—substantial assistance for construction and operating expenses with no federal controls but limited to public schools—which the National Education Association (NEA) and its allies subsequently sought to extend to general aid bills. However, the impacted-areas laws were not general but categorical aid. The category was the "impact" of external factors (in this case federally related activity) on the environment but beyond the control of local school authorities. The impact concept was to be employed in another context in the 1960s.

In 1954 Congress passed the Cooperative Research Act (PL 83-531), which authorized USOE "to make contracts and cooperative arrangements with colleges and universities for joint studies of educational problems," [11] as part of President Eisenhower's limited education program for that year. The importance of the act was not the level of expenditures, which were quite modest, but the principle of federally funded educational research under the control of USOE.

The most far-reaching education policy development of the 1950s was the National Defense Education Act (NDEA) of 1958 (PL 85-864). NDEA was primarily a reaction to the Russian achievement of placing the first man-made satellite, *Sputnik I,* in orbit in October 1957. The implication drawn from this spectacular Soviet feat was that American education, especially in the areas of science and technology, was inadequate. The sense of emergency was sufficiently strong that Congress passed the act with minimal controversy after President Eisenhower sent a special message to Congress requesting a $1.6 billion program to improve education in science, mathematics, and foreign languages.

In signing the bill, President Eisenhower emphasized that its purpose was to strengthen the American education system so that it could "meet the broad and increasing demands imposed on it by considerations of basic national security." [12] The bill was able to obtain quick and favorable consideration because it was related to national security. The inclusion of the word

"Defense" in the title of the act was no accident; its congressional backers deliberately placed it there on the assumption that it would be difficult for a congressman to vote against a "Defense" education act.[13] In the rationale for NDEA, national security was the end, education the means. Using this approach, it was possible to design the bill so that some aid would go to private schools and to students attending them and to avoid a crippling antisegregation amendment.

The NDEA's substantive provisions reflect the broad categorical approach embodied in it:

Title II—authorized loans to college students with the provision that up to 50 percent of the amount would be "forgiven," at the rate of 10 percent a year for each year that the student taught in public schools

Title III—authorized matching grants for public schools and loans to private schools for the purchase of equipment used in teaching science, mathematics, and foreign languages

Title IV—authorized 5,500 three-year graduate fellowships for students enrolled in new or expanded programs

Title V—provided state education agencies with funds for guidance, counseling, and testing and for guidance and counseling training

Title VI—sought to improve foreign-language teaching by authorizing research centers and institutes and teacher-training institutes

Title VII—authorized a program for the development of educational utilization of television and related communications media

Title VIII—expanded vocational education by providing funds to the states for training skilled technicians in science-related occupations[14]

NDEA did not, however, come close to furnishing the comprehensive general aid to education sought by the NEA and its allies even though both higher and elementary-secondary education received substantial assistance. It neglected the humanities and social sciences and, for the most part, it failed to reach those sectors of education in greatest need of help: schools in central-city slums and depressed rural areas. Furthermore, in those areas it did reach, NDEA "tended to strengthen the superior and wealthier secondary schools that had the staff, the equipment, the matching funds and the students to profit from marginal infusions of federal money for science, mathematics and foreign language."[15] Yet NDEA has been very popular among educators and it has strong congressional support.

In spite of its limitations and its somewhat dubious (or should one say devious?) rationale, NDEA was a breakthrough of major proportions. Substantial categorical assistance was made available to both public and private institutions at all levels of education, and students received direct aid in the form of loans or grants depending on their situation. USOE received responsibility for the operation of major programs, adding a new dimension to its role. That a national emergency could furnish the occasion and the rationale for such a law was a fact not ignored by supporters of general federal aid to education.

By the end of the Eisenhower administration, then, a sizable federal role in education had developed. It was, however, limited categorical assistance which directly benefited some sectors of education and neglected others. Adopted under emergency if not crisis conditions, it was based on criteria other than achieving an overall qualitative improvement in American education and aiding directly those educational areas in which the needs were greatest.

The Struggle Renewed: Education on the New Frontier

In 1961 a new Democratic administration committed to a comprehensive program of domestic legislation was one of many factors which suggested to supporters of general federal aid to education that their goal was at last within reach. Prior to assuming office, President-elect Kennedy had commissioned task forces of experts to examine the major areas of domestic and foreign policy.[16] Among these was a six-man task force on education chaired by Frederick Hovde, president of Purdue University, which recommended a massive program of general aid to public elementary and secondary education, a program of support for the construction of academic facilities in public and private colleges and universities, and a general expansion of the NDEA including greatly increased loan funds for students.[17] Although the legislation that President Kennedy later proposed was scaled down from the ambitious design of the education task force, the thrust and direction of the report survived in it. The task force report received little attention initially except from officials of the Roman Catholic church. Francis Cardinal Spellman and Monsignor Frederick G. Hochwalt, director of education for the National Catholic Welfare Conference, issued statements which made clear the church's opposition to any program of aid to elementary and secondary education which did not include parochial schools.[18]

Aside from the prospect of Catholic opposition to a program that did not provide some assistance for parochial schools, however, the signs augured well for general aid legislation. The new President made it a major element in his domestic program and indicated that he would give it strong support. In Congress, Adam Clayton Powell, a supporter of federal aid to education, had succeeded an opponent of federal aid, Graham Barden (D.-N.C.), as chairman of the House Education and Labor Committee. Powell reorganized the subcommittee structure of the committee to expedite action and promised to provide more positive and forceful leadership as evidenced by his willingness to oppose efforts to attach antisegregation provisions to education bills.

In spite of Powell's help in defusing the explosiveness of the racial issue and the successful effort made early in 1961 to stifle the conservative roadblock in the House Rules Committee by enlarging it from twelve to fifteen members,[19] the Kennedy administration did not manage to secure passage of general aid to education legislation. The divisive issue proved to be the question of aid to parochial schools. It prevented House action in 1961 and deterred any attempt at passage in 1962.[20] It was apparent by the end of 1962 that a legislative strategy which filtered out the complications of the religious as well as the racial issue would have to be found because conflicts among the supporters of federal aid to education were prime weapons of its opponents.

The Kennedy administration adopted an alternative strategy in 1963, when the 88th Congress convened, of presenting a comprehensive program of legislation in an omnibus bill. This approach was designed to prevent conflict between educational interest groups and to facilitate the task of consensus building by reducing the number of bills. It was also a convenient device for directing public attention to the full range of the nation's educational needs. Its disadvantages were that it failed to set priorities and by requesting so much, it decreased rather than increased prospects of passage; and it would be a highly unwieldy bill to move through the tortuous processes of committee consideration and floor debate.

Chairman Powell of the House Education and Labor Committee recognized the defects of the omnibus strategy and dismantled the bill on the ground that it was unlikely that the House would ever pass it. Congress did enact a "minibus" bill extending the impact laws and NDEA in mid-August. By late fall, two additional education bills providing for expanded aid to vocational education and assistance for college construction were sent to a joint-conference committee. There a deadlock arose over the allotment formula, and the work-study and residential-schools programs of the vocational education bill. At the time of President Kennedy's assassination it appeared that the bills would die. Following that tragic event, the conferees reached an agreement on both pieces of legislation. The factors that broke the deadlock appear to have included a sense of shock, remorse, and atonement stemming from the assassination and the personal intervention of President Johnson.[21]

The enactment of the Higher Education Facilities Act (HEFA) and the Vocational Education Act of 1963 and the Library Construction and Services Act of 1964, which was signed on February 11, represent the contributions of the New Frontier to an expanded federal educational role. They were substantial in scope. The HEFA authorized a five-year program of grants and loans for the construction of college facilities. The legislation was particularly significant as it was not enacted in response to national security considerations, but rather to meet an explicit educational need. It also made private institutions eligible for grants and loans. The only stipulations which reflected the religious issue were that grants had to be for facilities used in teaching science, mathematics, engineering, or modern languages and that loan funds could not be used for facilities that were used for religious purposes.

The Vocational Education Act vastly expanded existing programs and instituted new work-study and residential-schools programs. It indicated recognition of the need to meet educational requirements of that segment of the population which least directly benefits from higher educational assistance and whom the elementary and secondary schools have served least effectively. The Library Services Act authorized a sizable program of grants for library construction and operation. The fact that these measures could be enacted after the intensity of the religious controversy in 1961 and 1962 gave encouragement to the new Johnson administration and to supporters of an expanded federal role in education that a way might yet be found to provide aid to elementary and secondary education.

Education as a National Responsibility

Two statutes that Congress passed in 1965, the Elementary and Secondary Education Act (ESEA) and the Higher Education Act (HEA), are the major contributions of the Johnson administration to the development of the federal role in education. Together they constitute the greatest expansion of that role which has ever occurred. The factors that combined to produce these major redistributive policy innovations are difficult to measure, but they include related legislative developments in the areas of civil rights and antipoverty legislation, the political leadership of President Johnson, the development of a new approach for channeling federal funds to elementary and secondary schools, and the results of the 1964 election. No doubt all these factors were in some way of critical significance.

The passage of the Civil Rights Act of 1964 (PL 88-352) helped to set the stage for the legislative triumphs of 1965. Title VI of what is the strongest civil rights law since the Reconstruction era prohibited racial discrimination in all federally assisted programs. This had the effect of removing the threat of racial complications in education legislation arising from antisegregation amendments.

Legislative Victory: Education, Poverty, and the Great Society

In 1964 President Johnson also launched an all-out "war against poverty." The major vehicle for waging the anti-poverty war was the

Economic Opportunity Act (PL 88-452) which authorized a number of new programs in areas such as education, health, welfare, manpower training, and urban development. The Economic Opportunity Act recognized the gross educational disadvantage of poor children and sought to respond to some of their special needs.[22] The "rediscovery of poverty" and the concept of using education as a means of alleviating both the causes and effects of poverty created a significant change in the climate for education legislation in 1965.[23]

Also in 1964, two congressional supporters of federal educational assistance introduced bills which reflected the concern with poverty and the educationally disadvantaged child.[24] Representative Carl Perkins (D.-Ky.) authored legislation designed to "improve educational quality" and which employed an allotment formula based on school-age children of families earning less than $1,000 a year. Senator Wayne Morse's bill sought to apply the impacted-areas concept to depressed regions "impacted" by poverty. Morse's formula included such criteria as unemployment, welfare payments, and income level. At the hearings on his bill, Morse pressed administration spokesmen, principally Commissioner of Education Francis Keppel and Assistant HEW Secretary Wilbur Cohen, for support of legislation employing the poverty-impact approach.

Another major development contributing to passage of the legislation occurred early in 1964 when a number of President Johnson's close advisers, including Budget Director Kermit Gordon, Presidential Assistant Bill Moyers, and Chairman Walter Heller of the Council of Economic Advisers, suggested that the President commission a series of task forces to study specific policy areas.[25] Directed to ignore questions of political feasibility and to develop new ideas and approaches, the education task force of thirteen members under the chairmanship of John W. Gardner, president of the Carnegie Corporation, contributed significantly to the development of the sections of ESEA which were designed to promote change in education.[26] The task force also helped to precipitate a shift in emphasis in federal educational policy. That shift, which also received impetus from the antipoverty war and the legislation introduced by Morse and Perkins, involved the abandonment of attempts to pass legislation authorizing general federal aid to elementary and secondary education and the adoption of an approach utilizing a broad range of categorical assistance programs designed to attack specific problems such as the education of economically disadvantaged children.

The new approach, although considerably less than general aid to elementary and secondary education, would channel a substantial amount of federal money into the nation's schools. It also furnished a means of avoiding potentially fatal complications arising from ideological objections and from the church-state controversy. The poverty rationale placed opponents of legislation designed to improve the education of poor children in the position of denying them an effective opportunity to escape from their condition and become economically productive rather than dependent citizens.[27] Also, the concept of providing assistance for the education of poverty-stricken children offered a solution to the impasse over aid to parochial schools.

The task of fashioning a viable piece of legislation employing the new approach fell primarily to Cohen, Keppel, and Samuel Halperin, Keppel's assistant for legislative liaison. Keppel played a key role as an "intermediary broker of ideas,"[28] who negotiated between the bureaucracy (HEW–USOE), the Budget Bureau and the White House staff, the key congressional leaders, the principal education associations, and other interest groups including the National Catholic Welfare Conference (NCWC). According to Keppel, his job was "to administer OE by passing legislation."[29] The key to Keppel's success in developing a bill which would attract and retain the support of a congressional majority lay in obtaining the approval of the NEA and the NCWC to the central features of the legislation as it was being developed. This he accomplished through individual and joint meetings with representatives of the two organizations.[30]

The willingness of both organizations to compromise—the NEA accepted less than general aid and it acquiesced in some form of assistance to sectarian schools, while the NCWC settled for substantial but less than equal participation in the various aid programs—was essential to the passage of the ESEA. Apparently the leaders of the NEA and the Catholic hierarchy both concluded after the 1961 and 1962 debacles that compromises were necessary if elementary and secondary schools were ever to receive substantial federal assistance. The coalition Keppel fashioned was a delicate one, however, and it could have easily collapsed if either side reasserted its old demands.

The success of the measure in avoiding previous pitfalls became apparent on January 12, 1965, when President Johnson proposed it to Congress in an education message. Monsignor Hochwalt of the NCWC gave the bill a qualified endorsement, and the NEA issued a restrained statement calling the President's proposals realistic and "politically feasible." The bill eventually became law with only minor changes. Its five substantive titles managed to fashion artful compromises that dodged the thorny problems of religion and federal control, and yet it retained the flavor of creative change and innovation that had characterized the report of the Gardner Task Force. Each title contributed to the development of the successful legislative strategy.[31]

Title I proposed a three-year program of grants to local education agencies for the education of disadvantaged children. The distribution formula would allocate 50 percent of each state's average expenditure per school-age (5–17) child to school districts in which at least 3 percent of the enrollment or 100 children came from families with an annual income less than $2,000. The formula provided for equalization on an intrastate rather than an interstate basis and favored the urban slum and impoverished rural districts. State education agencies would allocate the money after approving the proposals of local officials for aiding their educationally disadvantaged students with the local officials given wide discretion in drawing up their proposals. The balancing of responsibility among national, state, and local authorities was designed to meet objections of federal control. Title I dealt with the religious issue by leaving it to the states to determine the extent of aid to private school children and by requiring local authorities to include private school children in certain Title I projects through "shared time" classes.

Although the remaining four titles were of less importance in monetary terms, they all authorized substantial new programs and each represented an attempt to win for the bill the support of important interests. Title II would authorize a five-year program to purchase library resources, texts, and other instructional materials for the use of children and teachers in public and private schools. This title was the principal means whereby children in private, sectarian schools could benefit from the legislation. (The House later added a provision that materials purchased under Title II would remain under public ownership and could not be used for religious purposes.)

Titles III and IV reflected the influence of the Gardner Task Force and were responses to educational reformers who felt that federal programs ought to result in qualitative improvements in American education. Under Titles III and IV, the USOE would make grants directly to local and regional organizations for the establishment of supplementary educational centers and regional educational laboratories. Title IV also would provide for university-related research and development centers. The services of the supplementary centers established under Title III would be available to private as well as public school children, increasing the bill's attractiveness to Catholic interests.

Many state education officials objected to the direct federal grants authorized under Titles III and IV on the ground that they weakened the supervisory authority of state education agencies. The proposal in Title V for grants to strengthen state departments of education was in part an attempt to placate state officials and soften their opposition to other titles in the bill.

The Congress that received and considered the proposed ESEA differed substantially from its predecessors which had refused to enact general aid to education bills in the past. President Johnson's landslide victory over Senator Barry Goldwater in the 1964 election resulted in the largest Democratic majorities in Congress since the days of the New Deal. In the Senate, long favorable to federal aid to education, the margin rose to 68–32. Of even greater importance, however, was the net gain of 38 Democratic seats in the House, producing a 295–140 edge. In fact, on final passage of the bill in the House, "every one of the forty-eight newly elected Democrats . . . who filled a seat formerly occupied by a Republican voted for ESEA." [32] The election results also strengthened the hand of Perkins and Powell in the House and Morse in the Senate as they very nearly could command majorities among northern Democrats alone. Another consequence of the Democratic election triumph was the adoption of the "21 day rule," a procedure which greatly limited the capacity of the House Rules Committee to block legislation.

The strategy of the bill's managers, Perkins and Morse, was to move quickly through hearings in both houses and then, after passage in the House, to have the Senate pass the House bill intact, thus obviating any need for a conference committee. Quick action would limit attempts to consolidate the opposition and divide the supporters of the bill through controversial amendments. Avoidance of a conference would eliminate the possibility of unacceptable compromises, delay, and possibly defeat.

Hearings on the bill (H.R. 2362) before Perkins' General Education Subcommittee of the House Committee on Education and Labor ran from January 22 to February 2. At ten sessions during those twelve days witnesses from the NEA, other education groups, the NCWC, the AFL–CIO, and a number of prominent educators endorsed the bill. The executive secretary of the Council of Chief State School Officers (CCSSO), Dr. Edgar Fuller, objected to Title II on the ground that it provided federal funds to sectarian schools contrary to most state constitutions, laws, and educational policies. He also expressed disapproval of the direct federal administration of grants under Title III. Protestant, Jewish, and civil liberties spokesmen voiced objections to those provisions of the bill that permitted private, sectarian schools to receive benefits. In general, however, the coalition of groups opposing federal educational assistance legislation was weaker in 1965 and the coalition supporting it was stronger than at any time since 1945.[33] The Senate Education Subcommittee hearings began on January 26 and followed a pattern similar to the House hearings.

The House subcommittee reported the bill favorably on February 5 and the full committee, after making minor changes in "markup" sessions, reported the bill on March 8 by a vote of 23–8. Republican members of the committee were not happy with the rapid progress of the bill or with the majority's refusal to consider major amendments. They also objected to the bill's distribution formula as unduly favorable to urban-industrial states. The House Rules Committee held four days of hearings at which all points of view were aired, and the U.S. Chamber of Commerce, an old foe of federal aid to education, entered the picture with a statement attacking the bill. The Chamber's delayed-opposition technique had little apparent impact, however, for on March 22 the Rules Committee voted 8–7 on liberal-conservative lines to send the bill to the floor.

Action in the House on March 26 involved attempts to change the formula and to raise the religious issue. Perkins and Powell succeeded, however, in turning back all major amendments. The only successful amendment created a ten-member advisory council to the commissioner of education. By a vote of 263–153, the House passed the bill with the support of 97 percent of the northern Democrats, 41 percent of the southern Democrats, and 25 percent of the Republicans. The degree of partisanship in the vote was quite high (53 percentage points separated the level of Democratic [80 percent] from Republican [27 percent] support), but the heavy Democratic plurality was more than sufficient to carry the day.

On April 2, the Senate Committee on Labor and Public Welfare unanimously reported the House bill without amendments. The majority report was almost identical to the House committee report, which had been written by Perkins' staff and USOE personnel. The five Republican members of the Senate committee filed minority views in which they charged that the bill fell short both as an education measure and as an antipoverty measure, and they criticized reporting the bill without amendments as rule by presidential "decree" and executive "fiat." Their opposition on the floor was quite ineffectual, however, as the Senate rejected all amendments proposed during three days of debate and on April 9 passed the bill by a 73–18 vote. President Johnson, whose strong personal interest in education, extensive parliamentary knowledge, and forceful leadership contributed significantly to passage, signed the bill into law on April 11 in the one-room school he had attended as a boy in Stonewall, Texas.

The passage of the HEA (PL 89–329) later in 1965 came as an anticlimax after the drama of ESEA. In a spirit of bipartisan support, Congress authorized approximately $805 million in higher education programs for fiscal year 1966.[34] Particularly striking were the student-aid provisions. Federal undergraduate scholarships were authorized for the first time and a new loan program was instituted. The HEA also established a national Teacher Corps to provide skilled teachers and student interns for work in impoverished areas. In addition, HEA furnished institutional assistance for the purposes of developing university extension courses and services to help solve community problems, improving college library resources, strengthening "developing institutions," improving undergraduate instruction, and constructing additional classrooms under the HEFA.

Administrative Challenge: The Office of Education Assumes a New Role

Following the passage of ESEA, President Johnson moved to modernize USOE for the task of administering the large-scale new programs the act authorized. On April 15 he appointed a task force chaired by Dwight Ink, who was then the assistant general manager of the Atomic Energy Commission, to study the organization and procedures of the agency.[35] It was the President's feeling, which he based on information supplied by the Budget Bureau and the White House staff, that USOE was incapable of responding effectively to the challenge of administering the new legislation, and especially the ESEA. The prevailing view of USOE within the Executive Office of the

President was that of a hidebound bureaucracy, populated largely by older persons with backgrounds in state education agencies and schools of education. These officials were regarded as captives of the professional education associations who would be unable or unwilling to act creatively or to use imagination in program administration.

According to Ink, the task force quickly discovered that "things were bad; unbelievably bad." The task-force report found major weaknesses. Administrative services, particularly personnel administration and contract management, were not effectively supportive of operating programs. "In many instances the administrative operations had become an end in themselves." Further, they were excessively decentralized into operating divisions. Another major problem was the extent to which outsiders, either through advisory councils or through the activities of pressure groups, had assumed control over the internal operations of the agency. Consequently, the task force recommended a major reorganization rather than minor changes and the addition of personnel.

The principal changes implemented following the report of the Ink Task Force included: strengthening administrative services such as program planning and evaluation, legislative assistance, personnel and financial administration, information systems, etc., by placing them in six staff offices headed by assistant commissioners reporting directly to the commissioner; the reorganization of the operating units into bureaus of Elementary and Secondary Education, Higher Education, Adult and Vocational Education, and Research; and a massive reassignment of old personnel and the recruitment of many new top-level personnel. As Bailey and Mosher assessed it, "reorganization was important—less as an instrument to improve administrative rationality in some abstract sense than as a device for establishing new priorities and for reshuffling and dislodging old staff." The result was "new management controls, new long-range program and policy planning instrumentalities, and a tidier grouping of functions." [36]

In 1966 Congress amended both the ESEA and the HEA. The changes were more in the nature of perfecting improvements than substantive policy departures. The ESEA Amendments expanded the scope and increased the cost of Title I. This was accomplished by permitting states to use either the national average per pupil expenditure or its own average in computing entitlement, a move in the direction of greater equalization between states. In addition, the 1966 legislation provided for an increase in the poverty level to an annual income of below $3,000 beginning in fiscal 1968, a change which would add $300 million to funds authorized under Title I. Another change was the addition of a new title authorizing programs for the education of physically and mentally handicapped children. These programs would be administered by a new bureau with statutory status. The HEA Amendments extended the HEFA for three years, expanded and extended the developing-institutions assistance program, and increased national defense student-loan-program authorizations for fiscal 1968.[37]

To summarize, by the end of 1966 the Federal government was providing substantial assistance to all sectors of American education.[38] The long period of frustration over unsuccessful attempts to pass federal aid to education legislation was over. While Congress did not authorize general federal aid, it did firmly establish the expanded dimensions of the federal role in education through a wide variety of categorical assistance programs. The laws that authorized those programs, and especially the ESEA, were based on a fragile coalition of the major interests in American education, the NEA and its allied associations, the American Council on Education and the associations representing various types of higher educational institutions, the Catholic church as represented by the NCWC, and organized labor. Former Commissioner of Education Francis Keppel described the legislation as "a carefully constructed house of cards over which we sprayed cement in the hope that it won't come unglued." [39] Both religious and racial controversies could reassert themselves to "unglue" the delicate "house of cards."

As the 90th Congress considered federal educational policy and the Johnson administration sought to strengthen the administration of its programs so as to improve their effectiveness, policymakers still had to deal with questions of race relations, church-state separation, and the extent of federal control. But there was no longer serious debate over the propriety of a major federal role in education. New controversies surrounding the administration of federal assistance and its thrust, direction, and extent confronted them. It is to a consideration of the new issues and problems and the new implications of the old controversies that we turn in the next chapter.

Notes

1. Much of this information has been discussed in greater detail elsewhere. The principal sources include: Sidney W. Tiedt, *The Role of the Federal Government in Education* (New York: Oxford University Press, 1966), chaps. 2, 6, and 7; Congressional Quarterly Service, *Federal Role in Education* (2nd ed.; Washington, D.C.: Congressional Quarterly Service, 1967); Frank J. Munger and Richard F. Fenno, Jr., *National Politics and Federal Aid to Education* (Syracuse: Syracuse University Press, 1962), chap. 1; and Stephen K. Bailey and Edith K. Mosher, *ESEA: The Office of Education Administers a Law* (Syracuse: Syracuse University Press, 1968), chaps. 1 and 2.

2. Tiedt, *Role of the Federal Government.*

3. Congressional Quarterly, *Federal Role in Education,* p. 13.

4. Bailey and Mosher, *ESEA,* p. 11. For a discussion of the capacity of the states to support education, see Sidney C. Sufrin, *Issues in Federal Aid to Education* (Syracuse: Syracuse University Press, 1962), chaps. 2 and 3.

5. See generally Munger and Fenno, *National Politics.*

6. The phrase is Bailey's and Mosher's; see *ESEA*, p. 19.

7. See David Braybrooke and Charles Lindblom, *A Strategy for Decision* (New York: Free Press, 1963), chaps. 1–6.

8. Congressional Quarterly, *Federal Role in Education*, p. 22.

9. Impacted areas aid went to 10 percent of all public school districts enrolling 25 percent of the nation's public school children in all 50 states and 317 of 435 House districts. Tiedt, *Role of the Federal Government*, pp. 26–27; and Congressional Quarterly, *Federal Role in Education*, pp. 6–7.

10. Departments of Labor, Health, Education, and Welfare, and Related Agencies Appropriations Act, H.R. 18037, as printed in the *Congressional Record*, daily edition, 11 October 1968, pp. S-12, 670–72. In the face of widespread cuts in the level of domestic spending for 1969, the amount appropriated for the impacted-areas programs was only $10 million less than it had been in fiscal year 1968.

11. Congressional Quarterly, *Federal Role in Education*, p. 4.

12. As quoted in ibid., p. 26.

13. Interview with Senate committee staff member, January 1968. Anonymity guaranteed.

14. Summary based on description in Congressional Quarterly, *Federal Role in Education*, p. 8.

15. Bailey and Mosher, *ESEA*, p. 20.

16. Texts of the reports were later published in *New Frontiers of the Kennedy Administration* (Washington, D.C.: Public Affairs Press, 1961).

17. The text of the report of the education task force appears in ibid., pp. 65–69. Other members of the task force included Benjamin Willis, Chicago superintendent of schools, Francis Keppel, dean of the Harvard Graduate School of Education, John W. Gardner, president of the Carnegie Corporation, Alvin Eurich, a vice-president of the Ford Foundation, and Russell Thackery, executive secretary of the American Land Grant College Association.

18. See Hugh Douglas Price, "Race, Religion, and the Rules Committee," in Alan Westin, ed., *The Uses of Power* (New York: Harcourt, Brace & World, 1962), pp. 1–71. For a discussion of the task force report and Catholic reaction to it, see pp. 21–23.

19. See Milton C. Cummings, Jr., and Robert L. Peabody, "The Decision to Enlarge the Committee on Rules: An Analysis of the 1961 Vote," in Robert L. Peabody and Nelson W. Polsby, eds., *New Perspectives on the House of Representatives* (Chicago: Rand McNally, 1963), chap. 7.

20. See generally, Munger and Fenno, *National Politics*, and Congressional Quarterly, *Federal Role in Education.*

21. Douglas E. Kliever, *Vocational Education Act of 1963: A Case Study in Legislation* (Washington, D.C.: American Vocational Association, 1965), p. 58.

22. Bailey and Mosher, *ESEA*, p. 33.

23. Philip Meranto, *The Politics of Federal Aid to Education in 1965: A Study in Political Innovation* (Syracuse: Syracuse University Press, 1967), pp. 19–20.

24. Bailey and Mosher, *ESEA*, pp. 26–28.

25. See William E. Leuchtenberg, "The Genesis of the Great Society," *The Reporter*, 22 April 1966, pp. 36–39; N. C. Thomas and Harold L. Wolman, "Policy Formulation in the Institutionalized Presidency: The Johnson Task Forces," in Thomas E. Cronin and Sanford Greenberg, eds., *The Presidential Advisory System* (New York: Harper & Row, 1969); and Bailey and Mosher, *ESEA*, pp. 39–40.

26. The task force appears to have been primarily responsible for the idea of

supplementary educational centers authorized in Title III and at least partially responsible for Title IV which authorized the construction of educational research laboratories.

I found considerable difference of opinion among respondents regarding the impact of the Gardner task force on the ESEA. Those individuals who commented from the perspective of HEW and the USOE asserted that aside from Title III, the task force functioned only to crystallize ideas that had been circulating for some time and to legitimize policy planning done elsewhere. On the other hand, observers in the Executive Office of the President claimed that Title IV, and to a considerable extent Title I, under which the bulk of the money was authorized, owed their existence to the task force.

27. Meranto, *Politics of Federal Aid to Education*, p. 40.

28. Bailey and Mosher, *ESEA*, p. 41.

29. Interview with Francis Keppel, 1 April 1968.

30. Meranto, *Politics of Federal Aid to Education*, p. 70.

31. This discussion follows Bailey and Mosher, *ESEA*, pp. 48–58; and Congressional Quarterly, *Federal Role in Education*, pp. 35–37.

32. Meranto, *Politics of Federal Aid to Education*, p. 93.

33. Ibid., p. 81.

34. See Congressional Quarterly, *Federal Role in Education*, pp. 50–53.

35. This discussion is based primarily on an interview with Dwight Ink, assistant secretary of Housing and Urban Development for Administration, 8 November 1967. It also draws from Bailey and Mosher, *ESEA*, Chap. 3.

36. Bailey and Mosher, *ESEA*, p. 90.

37. The loan-program expansion involved a major presidential-congressional conflict. The administration sought to replace the NDEA student loan program with a new program of insured loans from private lenders with interest subsidies for the students. Higher education associations and college and university officials vigorously opposed the proposal and the House defeated it in March. The administration then offered an alternative plan involving loans made with funds obtained through the sale of participation certificates to private investors. The Senate included this proposal in its version of the bill but it was dropped in conference committee. See Basil J. Whiting, Jr., "The Student Loan Controversy," *Public and International Affairs* 5 (Spring 1967): 5–42.

38. Total federal outlays for education, training, and related programs in fiscal year 1967 amounted to $9.2 billion, an increase of approximately $6 billion over fiscal 1963. USOE outlays ($2.8 billion) amounted to almost 30 percent of the total. See "Special Analysis H, Education, Training and Related Programs," in *Special Analyses, Budget of the United States, Fiscal Year 1969* (Washington, D.C.: U.S. Government Printing Office, 1968), pp. 94–114.

39. Interview, 1 April 1968.

3

ISSUES AND PROBLEMS:
THE SUBSTANCE OF EXPECTATIONS
AND DEMANDS

The issues and problems that confronted national educational policy makers during the period of the 90th Congress, 1967–68, reflected many of the same concerns that were prominent prior to the legislative push of the mid-1960s. The new programs, however, generated new expectations and demands with the result that the old issues assumed an altered cast. In addition, problems that had previously been lurking in the background came to the forefront. This chapter examines the continuing issues of federal control, religion, and race relations in the context of an expanded federal role in education and some emerging controversies arising from the claims of special interests, particularly higher education, and educational research.

Federal Control

Perhaps the most comprehensive issue, and the one that touched most of the others, was that of federal control. It contained many dimensions, including religion and race, and appeared to divide most sharply the participants in the educational policy process. Prior to 1965, opponents of federal aid to education legislation regularly raised the prospect of federal control as a major argument against any substantial federal role. Retention of local and state control had a strong emotional and ideological appeal when the alternative was presented as a national educational system. The argument against federal control also reinforced conservative opposition to increased spending generally.

Since 1965, however, the question has not been whether there shall be federal aid to education, but how it shall be administered. Almost all segments of the education community and much of the general public support federal aid—in fact, they demand much more of it—but there has been extensive disagreement over the roles of the federal, state, and local governments in determining the purposes for which the aid is spent. The principal issue is most often stated in terms of the dichotomy between categorical and general aid. The major statutes enacted through 1968 authorized categorical grants-in-aid designed to deal with specific problems. Some of the categories have been rather broad, e.g., aid to educationally disadvantaged children under Title I of ESEA, but they do not, even when taken together, constitute general purpose aid for all educational levels. In contrast, the unsuccessful bills of the 1940s, '50s, and early '60s provided for general aid to education. State and local authorities would have been free to spend the funds provided for a wide variety of purposes and subject to few restrictions.

There were practical political advantages to congressmen in categorical aid bills. Categorical aid permitted them to support specific popular educational goals and to retain a substantial measure of congressional control over the spending, yet it avoided the appearance of a wholesale raid on the treasury. Categorical aid made it possible for many congressional conservatives to support a substantial degree of federal assistance while maintaining steadfast opposition to "federal aid to education." While liberals pushed for general aid bills, they were willing to settle for categorical aid wherever and whenever it could be enacted.

The changes wrought by the substantial categorical programs authorized in the 1965 legislation produced a rise in the salience of the categorical-general aid issue. Schoolmen, and particularly big-city superintendents, welcomed the additional funds, but they were resentful of the application forms, reports, and regulations that are an inherent aspect of categorical aid.[1]

By 1967 substantial opposition to categorical assistance had developed, on the grounds that it was leading to excessive federal control, that it distorted educational goals set by local and state officials, and that it was excessively wasteful of time and money spent on overhead. Officials of the Johnson administration fashioned the case for categorical aid.[2] They argued that federal resources available for education, while substantial, were still too limited to permit much in the way of substantive accomplishments if they were to be distributed on a formula basis to all schools and colleges in the nation.

President Johnson himself denied any desire to dominate educational policy on the part of the federal government. As he defined it, the federal role would be to "point the way . . . offer help [and] contribute in providing the necessary tools." [3] But the fears of possible federal control of education could not be erased through presidential rhetoric. The major programs in the legislation of the mid-1960s were designed to meet needs and deficiencies and to stimulate a reassessment of priorities. State and local officials, in the absence of federal controls, had failed to take such actions. The fact that the federal government's categorical programs enabled it to select some aspects of education for extensive benefits while not aiding others accorded it substantial control, even though it may have been acquired (in the views of many) through default.

The administration's educational policy makers were conscious of the politically sensitive specter of federal control, however, and they argued that it could be avoided. The most effective utilization of limited federal assistance, in their view, would be for the government to promote qualitative improvements in American education by dealing with critical unfilled needs and by promoting innovation, change, and creativity where, in the view of many of the educational "New Guard," it was sorely lacking.[4] The difficulty with general aid, as the New Guard viewed it, was that it offered little inducement for the states to pursue innovative programs and to seek qualitative improvement. Categorical assistance programs permit this to be accomplished, and in areas of primary national concern, without disrupting or destroying the existing pattern of intergovernmental relations in education.[5] Furthermore, contrary to promoting additional central controls over education, categorical programs, such as Title V of ESEA, were actually strengthening the capacity of state and local authorities to fill their responsibilities and to solve their problems. No doubt the truth of the argument lies somewhere between the extreme positions.[6]

During the period of the 90th Congress, the Johnson administration's educational policy makers and its supporters in Congress attempted to protect existing categorical programs by arguing on both sides of the question. That is, they predicted that general aid would inevitably come and advocated it as a long-term goal. At the same time, they sought to build support for the categorical approach "until we can eradicate educational ills . . . and until we have Federal dollars to spare for making good schools even better." [7]

In assessing this issue, it seems manifest that the education establishment's fear of categorical aid had considerable validity. The selection of federal assistance categories, the development of federal guidelines and regulations that must be followed in order to obtain funds, has the unavoidable effect of establishing certain priorities and promoting some values at the expense of others in American education. Yet, federal money with no strings attached was not the solution to the nation's educational problems. President Johnson and his top educational policy makers, Secretary Gardner and Commissioners Keppel and Howe, also sought qualitative improvements. They believed that the solution to the problems of our educational system lay as much with innovations in teaching methods, instructional materials, and educational facilities as with greater infusions of money. Such innovations, they further believed, would occur only under federal stimulation.

This led to the development of an approach to educational policies which resembled the operational pattern of a large philanthropic foundation, such as Gardner's Carnegie Corporation. One education lobbyist described the situation in these not altogether favorable terms:

> Gardner is running HEW like a vast foundation. The use of special panels and task forces is one aspect of this. But more importantly, he only wants to give money to the well-qualified applicants. He doesn't see any benefit in giving it to poor institutions. That is why he is opposed to general institutional grants in higher education and why the Administration is so fond of categorical aid. Because it permits the government, like a foundation, to select its grant holders. He also has succeeded in imparting the foundation philosophy that the purpose of federal grants should be mainly innovative. That is, to start programs and get them going and then to withdraw once other sources of support have been established. The trouble with this thinking is that in many instances the federal government is the only possible source of funds. If programs aren't sustained by it they will die. The government is not a philanthropic organization. It has more fundamental and pressing obligations to society.[8]

These remarks reveal rather clearly the nature of the controversy over categorical aid. The style and assumptions implicit in HEW and USOE operations conflicted sharply with the demands of education lobbies and their constituencies for unrestricted federal funds.

From this type of conflict emerged proposals for revising the pattern of federal assistance in education and other areas. Suggestions for the improvement of existing categorical aids tended to concentrate on the consolidation of highly specialized programs in a broad functional area such as education or health into a single block grant that retained only such general conditions as nondiscrimination and matching funds. The Comprehensive Health Care Planning and Services Act of 1966 (PL 89–749) furnished a model for this type of reform. Efforts to achieve such planning-and-packaging overhaul in education did not progress as far as in the health field. In 1967 an attempt by Republican forces in the House to alter ESEA along block-grant lines failed.[9] By the end of 1968, however, substantial agreement appeared to have developed on the need for consolidation of programs so as to increase their flexibility and render them easier and more convenient to use, but the controversy continued over the extent to which state and local authorities would enjoy decision-making autonomy under consolidated programs.

The federal control issue also played a major role in the conflict surrounding the proposed national assessment of educational progress.[10] The movement for a national assessment of education began during 1963–64 when it became apparent that substantially increased federal aid to education along categorical lines was likely to occur in the near future. It also came to be realized that although the nation was already spending billions on education, there did not exist any basis for a systematic evaluation of the effectiveness of those efforts and of the areas of strength and weakness in the educational system. The fact was that while USOE, the NEA, and educational researchers had accumulated a voluminous amount of data regarding American education —the number of classrooms, teachers, students, etc., as well as evaluational data directed toward the individual student—there was virtually no information that revealed the actual accomplishments of the educational system in terms of what students had learned and how well they learned it.[11] The absence of basic information that would provide answers to questions regarding the effectiveness of American education was perceived as a serious obstacle to maximizing the benefits of the prospective increase in federal funds.

Consequently, in 1963 a group of leading educators and educational officials approached the Carnegie Corporation for funds to finance an exploration of the feasibility of a national assessment of educational progress. Carnegie responded by establishing an Exploratory Committee on Assessing the Progress of Education (ECAPE) headed by Dr. Ralph W. Tyler, director of the Center for Advanced Study in the Behavioral Sciences. ECAPE's task was to confer with teachers, administrators, experts in curriculum and testing, school board members, and others interested in education to obtain advice on how a national assessment could be "structured to provide useful information and avoid possible injuries to our educational efforts" [12] and to develop and test instruments and procedures for the assessment. ECAPE recommended that the instrument be developed in cooperation with teachers and be tried out in the schools, that it cover a wide range of educational objectives, and that it be conducted by a private organization and its development financed by private sources. The goal was to be an educational equivalent of the gross national product.

Almost immediately, extensive opposition to national assessment developed. The essence of the attack was that assessment would force teachers to revise curricula to reflect test content and this would lead to a national curriculum based on standardized test instruments.[13] Individual states and school districts could be coerced into participating in the assessment by threats to withhold federal funds from them—whether or not the federal government administered the program. Eventually, opponents argued, assessment would come under federal administration if only because of its extensive cost. The critics also argued that assessment would lead to vicious competition between schools, school districts, and states resulting in a flight of personnel from the lower-ranking areas to those with higher ranking and in unfair pressures on schools in the lower-ranking areas. Tyler defended the assessment by distinguishing it from testing:

> The assessment will report on the educational attainments of samples of children, youth and adults. It will not provide scores of pupils nor of classrooms but will present examples of what is learned by four different age groups 9, 13, 17, and adult, illustrating what all or almost all have learned, and what is learned by the "average." [14]

But controversy over national assessment was inevitable given the potential it furnished for nationalizing educational achievement standards. As John I. Goodlad, a consultant to the 1965 White House Conference on Education and himself a supporter of assessment, perceptively observed:

> There is little doubt that Congress would use information from such a national assessment of educational performance—whether or not under its sponsorship—for determining the strengths and weaknesses in the American educational system and formulating Federal policy in the field of education. To Congress, such data would be a national indicator. . . . Similarly, it is difficult to imagine State and local school systems not wanting access to results or to the testing procedures in order to determine their weaknesses or to assure themselves that they were, indeed, fulfilling certain selected commitments to a gratifying degree. These near certainties stir up many of the specters so feared by the opponents of national educational assessment. [15]

It was not surprising, then, that the principal opponent of assessment was the AASA. Assessment threatened a loss of local autonomy and possible federal control, it would place roughly half of the nation's practicing school administrators in a position where their districts fell below the national median on the test scores, and assessment was another innovation promoted by the New Guard. The role of Keppel, and later Howe, in backing assessment and of Tyler in developing it with Carnegie and Ford Foundation (through the Fund for the Advancement of Education) support stamped assessment as a threat to the establishment. [16]

Early in 1969, the Committee on Assessing the Progress of Education (CAPE), a private, nonprofit organization headed by Ralph Tyler and with a staff based in Ann Arbor, Michigan, began the actual conduct of the assessment. CAPE received a $1 million grant for fiscal 1969 from USOE to conduct the assessment. The AASA and the NEA, while disclaiming objection to evaluation itself, expressed concern that the assessment as conducted by CAPE would not recognize differences between regions and thus be unfair to many schools and that it would lead to the development of national standards. They expressed their preference for an assessment run by state agencies.[17] Ultimately, control over the assessment project passed to the Education Commission of the States, a "Compact" consisting of most state education agencies. This arrangement apparently proved satisfactory for the issue did not flare up again during the Nixon administration. However, it may do so if the uses made of the findings of assessments appear to be leading to a realization of the fears of its opponents. Certainly the potential for centralized control of education through national standards does exist. Undoubtedly, the benefits claimed for assessment will continue to be assayed in the context of the highly sensitive issue of federal control.

Religion

Although the church-state issue did not prevent the passage of ESEA in 1965, the dispute over aid to nonpublic, primarily parochial, schools remained very much alive. Except for racial segregation it is probably the most controversial unresolved problem affecting national educational policy.

In 1965, the Johnson administration temporarily muted the issue by fashioning a coalition of interest groups—principally the NEA, the National Catholic Welfare Conference (NCWC), and the National Council of Churches (NCC)—each of which pragmatically retreated from positions they previously had held tenaciously.[18] While none of them publicly acknowledged the extent of their withdrawals, they were substantial.

Under the rationale of the child-benefit theory, private school students rather than the institutions they attended would be able to participate in programs authorized in Titles I, II, and III of ESEA, although not nearly as extensively as the Catholic hierarchy desired. The NEA, while troubled by the breach in the absolute wall of separation between church and state, recognized that its opposition might be fatal to a bill that it desperately wanted passed. Furthermore, had the bill passed over the opposition of the NEA, its status in American education and with Congress would have been seriously impaired.[19] The NCC sought some solution to the church-state dilemma and, in keeping with the ecumenical spirit inspired by Pope John XXIII and Vatican II, endorsed ESEA as an instrument of reconciliation. The result was a bill that offered "enough private school assistance to gain the support of Catholics and yet not the kind of aid that would have forced the Protestant groups [and the NEA] into rigorous opposition." [20]

Such a coalition, based as it was on expediency, was bound to be highly unstable. One of its principal architects, former Commissioner Keppel, described it as a "delicate house of cards that can come unglued at any moment." [21] There was little basis for any long-term resolution of the problem; the coalition looked only to the immediate goal of passage of the bill.[22] Nor did all the proponents of rigid church-state separation acquiesce in the compromise with the Catholics.

The American Civil Liberties Union (ACLU) and Protestants and Other Americans United for the Separation of Church and State (Americans United) along with the Council of Chief State School Officers objected to provisions of Titles I, II, and III requiring that local public schools provide certain benefits to private school students as a condition for receiving federal funds under programs authorized by the act. Of particular concern was the provision in Title II that authorized federal administration of programs that violated state laws or constitutions. At least thirty-five states have more rigid church-state separation provisions than does the First Amendment. Although these organizations conceded that ESEA was not unconstitutional per se, they argued that it could easily be administered so as to benefit parochial schools and that it would create expectations of, and demands for, greatly expanded public support of sectarian education. These groups regarded the child-benefit and shared-time rationales as subterfuges that would enable parochial schools to strengthen sectarian programs by shifting resources released by federal funds. They also charged that the act would indirectly undercut existing state constitutions and laws and that it would encourage parochial school supporters to attack them directly.[23] Finally, they regarded the church-state compromise that made ESEA possible a threat to the long-term survival of public education.

Rigid congressional church-state separationists led by Representative Edith Green (D.-Ore.) and Senator Sam Ervin (D.-N.C.) sought to add to ESEA a section that would permit taxpayers to challenge the constitutionality of aid to sectarian schools. They were not convinced that the major Supreme Court decisions cited in support of the type of assistance authorized in the bill clearly disposed of the constitutional issue.[24] The necessity for a judicial review amendment arose from the Supreme Court's 1923 decision[25] refusing to permit taxpayers without vested interests to challenge the constitutionality of federal legislation. The amendment was manifestly objectionable to parochial school supporters, and it also drew the opposition of many liberals with strong sectarian leanings on the ground that it might cause the death of the bill. According to Eidenberg and Morey, in the House, where it lost 154–204, it was "clearly the one amendment which could have split the bill's coalition of supporters asunder" [26] while in the Senate its defeat by a 32–53 margin meant that the bill's backers "had enough support to ward off any amendment." [27]

Developments since 1965 have demonstrated the fragility of the consensus that produced ESEA and the long-term divisiveness of the religious issue. The principal cause of tension has been USOE's administration of the statute. Initial participation of parochial schools in various programs was substantial and relatively free of conflict between federal officials and Catholic educators.[28] In fact, the NCWC played an important part in developing the Title I *Regulations and Guidelines.*[29] Programs approved under Title I at the local level included sending public school teachers into parochial schools during regular hours to provide remedial and enrichment instruction to disadvantaged children (New York), sending parochial school children to public schools for Saturday classes in mathematics and science (Washington, D.C.), inclusion of parochial students in music instruction and job-counseling programs (Pittsburgh), and teacher aides for nonpublic schools (Minneapolis).[30] Under Title II, all states but Oklahoma had filed plans to distribute books to parochial schools under Title II by early 1966.[31] Under Title II books would remain public property and would either be sent to parochial schools on a permanent loan basis or held in a central depository and borrowed for a semester at a time.

Church-state separationists were by no means vanquished, however. They instituted judicial challenges to public aid to sectarian schools in the courts of Maryland and New York. In the former action, the Maryland Court of Appeals held that state grants for the construction of nonreligious facilities to church-related colleges violated the First Amendment to the U.S. Constitution.[32] The Supreme Court refused to review the decision, leaving doubtful the status of the child-benefit theory and the ESEA programs based on it. The New York case involved a statute requiring public school systems to lend textbooks to students in parochial schools. The New York Court of Appeals held that the statute did not violate the First Amendment and the U.S. Supreme Court affirmed the decision on appeal.[33] Recognizing that its actions left unresolved the question of the constitutionality of specific federal aid programs that involved sectarian schools and their pupils, the Court at the same time agreed to permit taxpayer challenges to such programs on grounds of abridgment of the First Amendment.[34] While the Court refused to overrule the *Frothingham* decision's prohibition of general taxpayer suits, it held that the fact that the right invoked was protected by the First Amendment made a significant difference. The *Flast* decision appeared to obviate further congressional efforts to authorize judicial review of the issue.[35] The Court did not rule definitively on the constitutionality of ESEA and other federal aid programs involving sectarian schools and their students, and the issue remained a major factor through the Johnson administration.[36]

Although the Catholic interest in federal educational policy is quite manifest, the position of groups opposed to the church is highly varigated. Morgan has identified three distinct ideological traditions among separationists.[37] The general Protestant position is a desire to keep the state entirely out of the religious realm in order to protect such principles as "denominationalism, voluntarism, and privatism."[38] The Protestant tradition regards the state as a potential threat to religious freedom. The second position is that of secularism. The secularists seek to protect the state from religion. The difference between the two persuasions is significant:

> . . . Protestants expect the state to avoid all involvements with organized religion, but to be "friendly." For some, this even includes a nonsectarian religious element in public education. The secularist expects the state to be indifferent to organized religion, and is especially concerned (as was Jefferson) that religion, with its supposed antirational implications, not pollute education.[39]

The third separationist tradition is that of American Jews. Because of their long history as a persecuted religious minority in Christian nations where the state has supported majority religious activity, Jews in the United States have tended overwhelmingly to oppose any interaction, cooperation, or supportive relationships between religion and the state. With the exception of a few Orthodox groups who maintain their own parochial schools, Jews have adamantly opposed any aid to sectarian schools.

The most active participants in the controversy over public aid to private and parochial schools were three interest groups: the ACLU, a secularist organization; Americans United, a Protestant-oriented group; and the American Jewish Congress (AJC). These organizations and persons associated with them participated in litigation and conducted a public relations campaign against federal and state programs that permit sectarian participation. The activity of Catholic interests was less visible. The hierarchy spoke mainly in restrained tones through the United States Catholic Council (USCC), successor organization to the NCWC, and an ostensibly nonreligious organization, Citizens for Educational Freedom, worked to ensure maximum participation of private schools and their pupils in federal programs. The Catholic strategy was a consciously unobtrusive defense of the benefits won in the legislation since the passage of NDEA in 1958.

The difference in approach was reflected in the tone of separationist and Catholic writings on the subject.[40] The Catholic argument was that the primary effect of the challenged programs is secular, to improve the quality of American education. Furthermore, they contended, since one-seventh of the national educational effort occurs in sectarian schools, it makes little sense nor is it just to deny the children in these schools the opportunity for qualitative improvement on the basis of "brittle legalism." [41]

The separationist position was that the child-benefit theory is essentially fictitious because it is impossible to separate benefits to religion from benefits to children enrolled in church-related schools. Furthermore, the separationists held that programs grounded in the child-benefit theory indirectly violate the Constitution by permitting action that would be patently invalid if done directly.[42] Thus, they viewed any parochial school participation in publicly funded programs as hostile to the very principle of church-state separation. The consequence of existing programs that permit aid to private sectarian schools has been and will continue to be, the separationists argued, efforts to expand such aid. In particular, they feared that state and local decision makers would prove vulnerable to these efforts.[43] The subsequent success of Catholic interests in obtaining favorable responses to requests for additional aid from some state legislatures[44] increased separationist concerns. Whether one regarded the separationist campaign as "a fantastic alliance of secularist liberals and Bible-thumping conservatives," [45] or as a selfless effort to defend a fundamental constitutional principle, the need for judicial clarification of the issue was becoming increasingly manifest. For, as Bailey and Mosher observed, "constitutional law is being affected by political combat and administrative precedent." [46]

The Supreme Court later provided much of the needed clarification in rulings handed down in 1971 and 1973. In response to increased financial pressures on nonpublic schools, several state legislatures had enacted legislation providing for income-tax credits or tuition reimbursements to parents of nonpublic school pupils, direct aid for teachers' salaries and other operating costs, and mandatory cooperation between public and nonpublic schools.[47] President Nixon took a strong stand in support of public assistance to nonpublic schools in an April 1972 speech to the National Catholic Education Association, and in his fiscal 1974 budget he stated his intention to propose legislation authorizing federal income-tax credits to parents of nonpublic school children. In spite of this evidence of strong support for public aid to sectarian private schools, the Supreme Court's recent actions appear to have closed off most avenues of support and sharply restricted those now in use.

In a major 1971 decision, the Court invalidated direct aid for the purchase of "secular educational services" even though reimbursement was limited to teachers' salaries, textbooks, and instructional materials.[48] It found that, despite the secular purpose of such programs, they carried an inherent potential for support of sectarian activities. This, in turn, required careful surveillance by the state to ensure that the constitutional separation under the establishment clause is not breached. Such close supervision, however, leads inescapably to excessive governmental entanglement with religion. Under the *Kurtzman* ruling, direct public efforts to aid sectarian schools are threatened because they may aid religious beliefs, while indirect benefits are in jeopardy because they may place the church and state in an unacceptably close continuing relationship.

The 1973 rulings further strengthened the ban on direct aid [49] and prohibited reimbursement to parents of private school pupils through tax credit or tuition-grant programs.[50] At this writing, the only approach to private school aid that remains untested is a proposed scheme under which parents of all school children would receive a grant in the form of a voucher which could be applied to the cost of a child's education in a public or private school. Constitutionally permissible forms of aid to private elementary/secondary education appear to be limited to providing neutral, nonideological services, e.g., transportation, lunches, health services, and secular tests and instructional materials that do not require entangling interactions arising from necessary surveillance. If voucher plans are tried and fail to withstand judicial scrutiny on First Amendment grounds, then it appears that all further public efforts to aid private schools are doomed. The only recourse of "parochial" supporters at that point will be to seek a constitutional amendment.

Race

Even though the racial issue did not thwart the passage of the major education legislation of the mid-1960s, the politics of education continued to be deeply intertwined with racial questions. In 1967 and 1968 the national educational policy process wrestled with one of the major problems that had perplexed it since 1954: how to implement the Supreme Court's order barring de jure racial segregation in public schools, principally in the South.

The enforcement of Court-ordered desegregation had by 1968 achieved a substantial measure of success in some southern states and cities and at least token acceptance in the most diehard areas of the Deep South. The tactics of massive resistance had slowly given way in the face of judicial persistance and presidential support. The Civil Rights Act of 1964 furnished another weapon in the campaign for desegregation. Title VI of that landmark statute required federal officials to terminate financial assistance to any state or local government practicing discrimination in programs or activities receiving federal funds.[51]

Although neither judicial decrees nor administrative compliance proceedings instituted under Title VI resulted in the end of segregated education in the South (and they had almost no effect in the North where segregation arose primarily from residential patterns), they did result in the abandonment of the "South's fixed-position defenses." [52] In place of dilatory legal and political tactics, however, southern communities developed a mobile defensive strategy designed to meet constitutional requirements while maintaining the essential features of the dual school system. Under "freedom of choice" plans, school attendance areas were abolished and children were permitted to attend any school within their district on a first-come basis. The result was the continuation of two school systems, one predominantly white and the other wholly black, for the choice was largely racial.

Freedom of choice did ensure that no black child would be denied an integrated education (providing his parents were willing to make an extra effort to secure it for him) and it did increase black enrollment in predominantly white schools. It did not, however, erase the fact that most black children in the South (79.7 percent in the fall of 1968) attended all-black schools manned by all-black staffs. Usually, if not invariably, such schools were inferior to predominantly white schools in the same district.

During 1967–68, the NAACP Legal Defense and Education Fund attacked the legality of freedom of choice plans in the federal courts. These efforts were partially successful when, on May 28, 1968, the U.S. Supreme Court ruled that a freedom-of-choice plan could not be "an end in itself." [53] Such plans, while not necessarily invalid, would be acceptable only if they promised "meaningful and immediate progress toward establishing state-imposed segregation." At the same time, HEW officials charged with Title VI enforcement insisted that southern school districts develop alternatives to freedom-of-choice plans that proved ineffective in eliminating the dual school structure.

HEW's Title VI compliance program, administered by its Office of Civil Rights (OCR), made it the focal point of sharply conflicting pressures. The NAACP Legal Defense and Educational Fund and other civil rights organizations criticized OCR for failing to seek total abolition of freedom of choice, failing to apply the guidelines vigorously in districts with a majority of black students, and failure to verify Form 441 certifications of compliance.[54] Southern congressmen attacked OCR as an instrument of tyranny. They retaliated by engineering cuts in HEW's fiscal 1968 civil rights appropriation and by persistent but unsuccessful attempts to enact legislation that would require HEW to recognize freedom-of-choice plans as meeting the Title VI compliance requirement.

The issue of southern school desegregation, although highly volatile, was relatively simple compared with the problem of securing compliance in the North. Northern school segregation was based on residential patterns and not legally sanctioned. School integration efforts outside the South involved fundamentally different circumstances. Dual school systems did not exist in consequence of state laws; rather, racially imbalanced schools tended to develop in cities and suburbs as a result of reliance on neighborhood schools. As housing patterns became increasingly segregated along racial lines, with most blacks living in center-city areas or smaller outlying enclaves, individual schools reflected the racial composition of their neighborhoods. Attempts to eliminate such de facto segregation did not have the support of a Supreme Court ruling. The legal aspects of the school integration situation were quite ambiguous. Clearly, deliberate segregation through gerrymandering and other actions of local officials are invalid. But through 1968, the Supreme Court had never ruled that local authorities were obligated to remedy racial imbalance resulting from causes other than deliberate official actions. Furthermore, Title VI made it clear that racial imbalance was not illegal per se by prohibiting federal action to correct imbalance due solely to housing patterns.

The issue of racial integration in public elementary and secondary schools continued to be highly controversial during the Nixon administration. Substantial progress in school desegregation occurred by the end of President Nixon's first term in office. According to a survey by HEW's Office of Civil Rights, the percentage of black pupils attending all-black schools fell from 39.7 in the fall of 1968 to 10.9 four years later, while the proportions enrolled in majority white schools rose from 23.4 to 36.8 in the same period (see table 3-1). The data show that the most dramatic changes took place in the South between 1968 and 1970.

The eleven southern states were the locus of de jure school systems which were the objectives of HEW enforcement proceedings and court actions. As the federal courts began to order the transportation of pupils (i.e., busing) in nonsouthern cities in which segregation was not required by state law, the controversy became national in scope. In moving against segregation arising from residential patterns and voluntary actions of local school officials, the courts encountered the opposition of nonsoutherners who, although not opposed to racial integration in principle, objected to having their children attend schools of "drastically different racial compositions than the schools they would have attended under the traditional neighborhood social policy." [55] The extent of opposition to busing was reflected in an October 1971 Gallup poll report that 76 percent of the public opposed the practice while only 18 percent supported it.[56]

Important judicial actions appear to have contributed to public concern over busing. The Supreme Court, in a 1971 decision involving the Charlotte, North Carolina, schools, approved of busing as a means of creating a unitary school system.[57] The *Swann* decision also provided some guidelines to be followed in achieving desegregation, but it did not answer the question of whether de facto segregation was unconstitutional. Three U.S. District Court decisions involving busing attracted wide attention: A 1970 decision by Judge William Doyle that unconstitutional de facto segregation existed in Denver's schools; a 1972 order by Judge Robert R. Merhige, Jr., merging the predominantly black schools of Richmond, Virginia, with two primarily white suburban districts; and a 1972 order by Judge Stephen J. Roth requiring two-way busing between schools in Detroit and fifty-three suburban districts.[58] The Supreme Court has not clearly resolved the status of de facto segregation nor the extent to which lower federal courts may go to eliminate it.

President Nixon and many members of Congress responded to rising public opposition to busing. In March 1972 the President proposed to Congress a compensatory approach to the problem of equal educational

Table 3-1
Fall 1972 Estimated Projections of Public School Black Enrollment Compared with Final Fall 1968 and 1970 Data[a]

Geographic Area	Total Pupils	Black Pupils Number	%	BLACK PUPILS ATTENDING SCHOOLS WHICH ARE:						
				0-49.9% Minority Number	%	80-100% Minority Number	%	100% Minority Number	%
Continental U.S.									
1968	43,353,568	6,282,173	14.5	1,467,291	23.4	4,274,461	68.0	2,493,398	39.7
1970	44,877,547	6,707,411	14.9	2,223,506	33.1	3,311,372	49.4	941,111	14.0
1972 (est.)	44,485,568	6,641,343	14.9	2,446,239	36.8	2,953,991	44.5	721,757	10.9
(1) 32 North and West									
1968	28,579,766	2,703,056	9.5	746,030	27.6	1,550,440	37.4	332,408	12.3
1970	29,451,976	2,889,838	9.8	793,979	27.5	1,665,926	57.6	343,629	11.9
1972 (est.)	28,970,304	2,831,080	9.8	822,480	29.1	1,581,871	55.9	284,273	10.0
(2) 11 South									
1968	11,043,485	2,942,960	26.6	540,692	18.4	2,317,850	78.8	2,000,486	68.0
1970	11,570,331	3,150,192	27.2	1,230,868	39.1	1,241,050	39.4	443,073	14.1
1972 (est.)	11,601,027	3,165,229	27.3	1,405,435	44.4	1,001,211	31.6	289,638	9.2
(3) 6 Border and D.C.									
1968	3,730,317	636,137	17.1	180,569	28.4	406,171	63.8	160,504	25.2
1970	3,855,221	667,362	17.3	198,659	29.8	404,396	60.6	134,409	23.1
1972 (est.)	3,914,253	645,034	16.5	218,323	33.8	370,909	57.3	147,844	22.9

(1) Alas., Ariz., Cal., Col., Conn., Ida., Ill., Ind., Iowa, Kan., Maine, Mass., Mich., Minn., Mont., Neb., Nev., N.H., N.J., N.M., N.Y., N.D., Ohio, Ore., Pa., R.I., S.D., Utah, Vt., Wash., Wis., Wy.
(2) Ala., Ark., Fla., Ga., La., Miss., N.C., S.C., Tenn., Texas, Va.
(3) Del., D.C., Ky., Md., Mo., Okla., W.Va.

Source: HEW Office for Civil Rights, *HEW News Release*, 12 April 1973.

[a] 1972 figures are estimations based on latest available data and are subject to change upon final compilation.

opportunity and a moratorium on busing until passage of the equal opportunity bill. Congress did add specific antibusing amendments to the higher education act of 1972 (PL 92-318). The key provision postponed the implementation of court orders requiring busing to achieve racial balance until all appeals had been exhausted.

President Nixon, in signing the bill, criticized the antibusing measures as inadequate. Opposition to busing was stronger in the House than in the Senate. Many members of the House who previously had supported pro-integration measures emerged as opponents to busing. Most notable, perhaps, were five Michigan Democrats from Detroit-area districts. For the most part, Democratic liberals in the Senate held to their traditional position. In January 1973, the Senate Select Subcommittee on Equal Educational Opportunity concluded a three-year study with a report attacking the "misleading" issue of "massive busing" as a threat to the nation's commitment to equality of educational opportunity.[59]

The conflict over busing and integration, along with judicial reluctance to make policy on a general rather than a case-by-case basis, has left the area of race relations in education fertile ground for political exploitation. Candidates for office from the Presidency to local school boards are hard pressed to avoid it, and they have available a considerable range of normative and empirical arguments to support their positions. A quick resolution does not seem likely.

Higher Education Issues

The vast expansion of federal support for higher education—first through research sponsored by NSF, NIH, the AEC, and many other agencies and then through the categorical programs authorized in legislation such as the NDEA, HEFA, and HEA—that had occurred by the mid-1960s was not accompanied by or based upon a general policy. No comprehensive plan of action or set of goals served to integrate federal activities that affected higher education. What did exist was a pattern of support that provided substantial assistance for research, training, construction, and student maintenance. The relationships between higher education and the federal government were regarded as mutually beneficial, but with risks involved for both parties.[60] While welcoming the federal largess, spokesmen for higher education objected to the lack of institutional freedom accorded within the ad hoc structure of categorical federal aid. Yet the diversity of such aid and the absence of effective coordination of federal programs enabled colleges and universities to escape centralized direction and control of their operations.

By 1968, federal expenditures for higher education totaled $4.4 billion, amounting to approximately 25 percent of the total national effort. (In contrast, expenditures of $3.2 billion for elementary-secondary education amounted to less than 10 percent of the nation's effort.) Although some national leaders such as Senator Fulbright warned that the nation's colleges and universities had been corrupted by their dependence on federal funds, the major associations and spokesmen of the higher education community were busy urging and working for new infusions of money. In a widely cited address to the Association of American Colleges in January 1968, Alan Pifer, president of the Carnegie Corporation, observed that "there appears to be a kind of consensus developing that the financial needs of our colleges and universities are now so desperate nothing will save them except major amounts of additional dollars from Uncle Sam." [61] Pifer observed that the higher education community appeared to be agreed that the time had come for the federal government to provide general institutional support.

Indeed, academic spokesmen seemed almost universally to assume the inevitability if not the imminence of a great expansion of federal assistance. They took almost for granted the continued growth of higher education and the necessary assumption of primary responsibility for financing that growth by the federal government. Increased competition for federal funds resulting from Vietnam war spending would, it was recognized, delay the adoption of new programs, but only temporarily. The important issues of federal policy toward higher education were perceived as focusing on the nature of the expanded support when it arrived. The principal question was, assuming full funding of existing categorical aid programs (an eventuality that had not occurred by 1974), how, on what basis, and to whom would additional funds be distributed? The absence of a coherent and clearly articulated federal policy for higher education, a point clearly noted in Pifer's speech, left ample room for discussion and debate.

The most pressing crisis of higher education during 1967–68 appeared to be financial in character. The questions concerning the nature, functions, and purpose of a university that sparked campus confrontations and disruptions were recognized as serious problems, but they had not yet occupied the salient position they were to assume in 1969 and 1970.

In recognition of the emerging problems facing higher education, especially in the financial realm, the Carnegie Corporation in early 1967 appointed a commission to examine those problems and recommend appropriate action. Chaired by Clark Kerr, former president of the University of California, the blue-ribbon panel filed a report in December 1968 that highlighted the dual goals of quality and equality for higher education and recommended federal policies to ensure the achievement of each.[62] The Carnegie report examined and considered five major alternative approaches to furnishing federal assistance: tax credits for parents and donors; grants to the states for general support of higher education; across-the-board grants to institutions on the basis of a formula; loans and grants to students and categorical assistance for purposes determined by the federal government. It rejected outright tax credits and direct subsidies to the states and offered a set of proposals that combined elements of other approaches.

The Carnegie Commission's proposals were also notable for their attempt to develop a cohesive long-range federal policy for higher education. Although the proposals have not subsequently been incorporated into federal policy, they provided a thorough analysis of the various aspects of the financial problem of higher education.[63] Two approaches to that problem that were highlighted in the Carnegie Commission's report, institutional grants and various forms of student aid, were considered extensively during 1967–68 in the education policy system and will receive closer examination here.

Institutional grants that would furnish sustaining noncategorical aid have long received strong support from the higher education associations and from individual college administrators. But while there was substantial, almost unanimous support for the principle of a national program of institutional grants, there was widespread disagreement over the basis of the formula on which such grants would be awarded. The formula would obviously have to take enrollment into account, but pressures also existed to include such factors as the level of instruction (graduate or undergraduate), cost of instruction (science vs. nonscience students), institutional growth rate, and other considerations. Prestigious universities with large graduate and professional schools advocated formulas that would give substantial weight to quality and to the higher costs of specialized instruction and research training. Institutions mainly involved in undergraduate education tended to favor simpler formulas based on enrollment and/or degree production.[64]

In spite of extensive discussion of institutional grants during 1967–68, no legislation providing for general aid based primarily on undergraduate enrollment was drafted or introduced. This may have been due, at least in part, to a pragmatic decision by higher education association leaders not to press the issue prior to the development of consensus regarding the basis of the formula.[65] It is also likely that the widely discussed Miller bill [66] attracted much of the attention devoted to institutional grants.

That legislation, introduced by Representative George Miller (D.-Calif.), had a strong science orientation. It would have furnished aid to all accredited colleges on the basis of a complex formula based upon research grants received in the previous year from USOE, NIH, and NSF, enrollment in science courses, and earned graduate degrees. Although the Miller bill would distribute funds widely, the leading public and private universities that operate large scientific research and training programs would receive a disproportionate share of the benefits. With strong support from such institutions and their associations, mainly the Association of American Universities and the National Association of State Universities and Land Grant Colleges, the Miller bill received serious consideration from the House Committee on Science and Astronautics in 1968, and in 1969 that body approved the bill. The associations representing community colleges, private liberal arts colleges, and smaller state universities, the American Association of Junior Colleges, the Association of American Colleges, and the Association of State Colleges and Universities, expressed varying degrees of opposition to the Miller bill as they stood to obtain more through other formulas. In 1969, at the outset of the Nixon administration, the American Association of Junior Colleges developed and supported a Comprehensive Community College Act.

As of late 1974 neither bill had secured enactment. In fact the condition of higher education was quite different from that which had been anticipated six years earlier. Enrollments had stopped rising and many institutions were losing students. Costs were going up, along with the general price level, at a much faster rate than income. Traditional sources of support—state legislatures, private donors, and income from investments—were unable or unwilling to close the gap. Expectations that the federal government would step in and assume a greater share of responsibility for financing higher education have been largely unrealized. Although the omnibus Education Amendments Act of 1972 (PL 92-318) authorized a new $1 billion program of institutional grants based on the number of federally assisted students, the higher education community regarded the amount as insufficient to meet its growing financial crisis and too restrictive. The American Council on Education expressed a strong preference for aid based on the number of students or graduates and supported the 1972 legislation "reluctantly." [67]

Student aid programs have been operating with federal funds since the World War II GI Bill of Rights. Student aid can take the form of a loan or a grant. Within each of those broad categories, many varieties of support are possible. Student aid programs have been designed according to the criteria of need, level of instruction, method of financing, and method of repayment. Direct assistance to students is justified on the grounds that it recognizes the national interest in maximizing each individual's development, it greatly increases the educational options of the student, and it makes money available to institutions but without compromising their independence because of the federal source of the funds.

In spite of the manifest advantages of direct student aid, the federal government has not been enthusiastic about expanding it. This reluctance appears due to three factors: the high costs of direct grants, the absence of an effectively organized student lobby, and resentment over campus unrest. With limited resources to allocate, policy makers tend to make their decisions on the basis of expressed needs and potential payoffs. Student aid programs have not appeared promising on either count.

In 1967–68 student aid programs included graduate traineeships; fellowships and other grants; National Defense Student Loans (authorized under Title II of NDEA) and Guaranteed Student Loans (authorized under Title IV of HEA) to both graduates and undergraduates; Cold War GI Bill benefits to graduates and undergraduates; work-study grants for undergraduates; and educational-opportunity grants for seriously disadvantaged undergraduates, mainly from low-income, nonwhite families. In fiscal year 1968, student aid program expenditures amounted to $1.45 billion.

The principal issues involving student aid stemmed from the Johnson administration's desire to shift student loans from the NDSL program to the guaranteed-student-loan program. The reasons for this move reflected the budgetary pressures of the Vietnam war. The NDEA loans required a substantial federal appropriation, while the only costs to the government in the guaranteed program were premium payments to insure loans made by private lending institutions and an interest subsidy (half of the 6 percent rate) during the ten-year repayment period after graduation.

Congress, with strong urgings from the higher education associations, insisted that the NDSL program be retained.[68] The educators preferred a relationship between the academic institution and the student to one between a lending institution and the student's parents. Many congressional leaders had serious doubts that in a period of increasingly tight money adequate private capital would be available to fund the guarantee program.

Both the higher education spokesmen and their congressional allies argued that the two programs were designed for different kinds of students. NDEA loans benefited primarily students from low-income families, while the guaranteed loan program was oriented more toward students from middle-income families. It would be contrary to congressional intent to emphasize one program at the expense of the other. These considerations combined to prevent major changes in the structure of student loans through 1968. (Major cutbacks in NDEA loans were to be imposed in 1969 and subsequent years, however, and sharp rises in interest rates greatly reduced the availability of guaranteed private loans.)

The Johnson administration did not request full funding of the Educational Opportunity Grant program, nor was Congress disposed to push it or other forms of aid for disadvantaged students. This was, however, unquestionably an area of great unmet need. The Kerner Commission pointed out that while the Higher Education Act committed the nation to "the goal of equal opportunity for higher education for all Americans" this goal "remains for the disadvantaged student an unfulfilled promise." [69]

In a March 1968 report, the Southern Regional Education Board found in a survey of the 215 colleges and universities considered most likely to have special programs for "high risk" students that 47 percent of them had no involvement whatsoever in such activity. Among the reasons cited for little or no effort were "lack of funds, enrollment pressures, political worries, conflict with the institutional mission, and fear of lowering institutional standards." [70] The SREB report concluded that most of the nation's colleges and universities had not yet decided the nature and degree of their commitment to students whose lack of money, low test scores, spotty high school records, and race and class backgrounds place them at a distinct disadvantage in competition with most college students. Although there was wide recognition of the pressing needs in this area, budgetary constraints and the absence of strongly articulated demands meant that little was done to remove barriers to equal opportunity for higher education.

The administration did propose an Educational Opportunity Act in 1968, but prospects for adequate funding of the legislation if it were enacted (which it was not) were not bright. The report of the Carnegie Commission and an HEW study submitted in early January 1969[71] both directed their major thrust toward a massive increase in scholarship funds for the disadvantaged so as to "attract a great many more students from the lowest income groups and non-white populations to college." [72] However, these reports appeared at the end of the Johnson administration and reflected projected policy developments for the future rather than immediately prospective actions.

Another major development concerning student aid occurred in September 1967 when a presidential advisory panel on educational innovation startled the higher education community with a novel loan plan that would enable a college student to borrow up to the full cost of tuition and subsistence from a Federal Educational Opportunity Bank (EOB).[73] The student would repay the loan by pledging a percentage of his gross annual income for a thirty- to forty-year period following graduation. Those students earning large incomes would repay more than the principal and interest, while those with small incomes would not return the full amount. The bank would be self-sustaining after initial operations under subsidy.

Similar proposals had been advanced and discussed for several years.[74] What made the EOB proposal so notable was its source; it was the report of a panel of the President's Science Advisory Committee. While it did not have the status of an approved presidential document, it was obviously a trial balloon launched under the auspices of PSAC and the Office of Science and Technology. The immediate and sharp criticism that the proposal drew from the two major associations representing public universities, the National Association of State Universities and Land Grant Colleges and the Association of State Colleges and Universities, indicated that they regarded it as a potentially serious threat that should be squelched before it could become incorporated in the administration's legislative program.

Had the EOB proposal not emanated, albeit semi-officially, from the White House science advisory system, it is unlikely that it would have become the focus of an extended debate. The principal arguments for the EOB and other student-loan-bank plans are that they expand the opportunity for college educations, increase student freedom in selecting their institutions while simultaneously easing the financial plight of institutions by enabling them to increase their charges without fear of reducing enrollments. In addition, it was asserted, the greater selectivity accorded students would place institutions under strong pressures to improve themselves and to respond more positively to student needs. Furthermore, these things could be accomplished on the basis of the student's ability to pay in the future, without strapping him or his family, and with only a small drain on the public fisc. The proposal had the "special virtue," as the *New York Times* commented editorally, "of promising aid to the very poor and to hard-pressed middle-income families alike." [75]

The case against the EOB, as expressed by spokesmen for the public institutions, held that it would constitute an abandonment of the principle of societal responsibility for education beyond the high school and a shifting of the full burden to the student. The idea sounded to the *Washington Star* "like a 'Go Now Pay Forever' program that would actually penalize any student who [later] earned too much money." [76] The critics argued that once the plan became operational it would discourage further increases in state and private support for higher education and that it would quickly lead to sharp increases in tuition and other charges at all institutions. Eventually public-private cost differentials would tend to disappear, with most costs falling on the student. Contrary to expectations that the EOB would encourage children of poor families to attend college, its critics claimed that it would have the opposite effect as the poor are disinclined to borrow heavily. Furthermore, it was argued, the plan would be unattractive to students with high income expectations and thus would not likely be self-financing. Nor would the massive amount of loans in its initial years of operation, necessarily financed by appropriations, be without a strong inflationary impact.

Regardless of whether the EOB was, in the words of the panel that proposed it, a "device for enabling students to sell participation shares in their future incomes," or, as the two public university associations characterized it, "a life-indenture in return for the privilege of educational opportunity," it and other loan bank proposals did not acquire a substantial supportive constituency. They appealed to some academicians, particularly economists who found the concept of resource allocation through a competitive market highly attractive, to some federal budget makers seeking effective but inexpensive ways to expand support for higher education, and to certain educational "innovationists" [77] who saw in the idea a means of changing higher education by placing controlled financial power in the hands of students rather than institutions.

The opponents of the loan-bank idea included public university and junior college officials and their associations, some private college officials, groups (e.g., organized labor), and state and local political leaders who are traditionally committed to low-cost, publicly supported higher education.

The intensity of the debate over loan-bank proposals in the absence of strong support for them can be regarded as indicative of the seriousness of the financial crisis in higher education and of the probability that there is considerable merit in them, even though many wrinkles have yet to be ironed out.

The issues raised and considered during 1967–68 did not lead to action until 1972 when the intensity and scope of student unrest had abated substantially and federal budgetary constraints eased slightly. The 1972 education amendments reflected congressional concern over the financial problems of institutions and students. That legislation authorized continuation of the major categorical assistance programs under HEA, HEFA, and NDEA; established a new basic opportunity (BOG) program for low-income students; continued and strengthened existing student aid programs including educational-opportunity grants, work-study, low-interest national defense student loans, and insured student loans; and provided for institutional grants to aid colleges in educating federally assisted students. The student assistance provisions were designed to be flexible and to help students from lower-income families.

The promise of financial assistance which the legislation offered to the hard-pressed higher education community proved to be short lived. The Nixon administration's proposal to fund only the BOG and guaranteed-student-loan programs in fiscal 1974, the subsequent testimony of HEW and USOE officials before the House Appropriations Labor-HEW subcommittee, and an internal USOE long-range planning paper indicate an effort to alter substantially the federal role in higher education. According to John Beckler, the Associated Press congressional correspondent who follows education legislation, the administration clearly intends "to hold the line on educational spending and concentrate what is spent—at the postsecondary level—on students rather than institutions." [78] Beckler notes extensive congressional frustration over this trend and predicts a major battle over the apparent reduction and redirection of the federal role.

Educational Research

One important aspect of the increased federal support for education that had developed by 1967 received little attention outside the education community: the availability of substantial funds for educational research and development. Efforts were made through various categorical programs of USOE and other agencies to replicate in education the dramatic successes of the research and development principle in other social arenas, such as defense, medicine, and agriculture. The expansion of federally funded educational research* did not create major political controversies, but it did result in the

---

* This discussion focuses primarily on federally funded research *about* education as distinguished from federal funding of research at universities.

development of sensitive issues regarding the research roles of the Office of Education, private industry, and universities.

During 1967–68, USOE's Bureau of Research administered the bulk of new federal efforts to improve the quality of education through the production of basic knowledge, the translation of these discoveries into new instructional techniques, and the dissemination of awareness of those practices to the education community. Earlier programs, such as the National Science Foundation's curriculum-improvement projects, continued to operate. The Bureau of Research provided a measure of intra-agency coordination of effort. The Bureau, with the approval of the commissioner, distributed funds among several programs including project research, Research and Development (R&D) Centers, Regional Educational laboratories (authorized under Title IV of ESEA), various research training projects, and an information retrieval and dissemination system (ERIC). The issues arising from the research role of USOE involved primarily the competition for funds between programs and the activities and functions of the regional laboratories. By 1967, it was apparent that sufficient funds were not available to support existing programs. In an attempt to initiate at least some new projects, the Bureau of Research cut back allocations for training and unsolicited research. The Bureau's practice of allocating its scarce resources to special problems provoked the criticism of the American Educational Research Association's newsletter.[79]

The financial squeeze on research was one of the first indications of the impact of Vietnam war spending on federal educational programs. Research was a likely victim for the initial cuts. The results of expenditures for research are not easily demonstrated or perceived. Often they are a long time in materializing, if they do at all, and their ultimate effects even more remote. Consequently, budget makers in the bureaucracy and in Congress tend not to recognize or concede the contributions of research. Nor does research have a large supportive constituency that can quickly and effectively mobilize opposition to threatened cuts. The immediate political costs of curtailing research programs are small relative to those of programs with a broader and more immediate impact.

The regional educational laboratories were the largest element in USOE's expanded research program. Developed with great rapidity following the enactment of ESEA (twenty were in operation by December 1966) the laboratories were regarded as vehicles of applied research. As the Office of Education described them to Representative Edith Green's Special Education Subcommittee:

> The functions of these laboratories are to identify the major educational problems of the region, to choose one or two priority areas in which to mount an effective program, and to devise and administer a coordinated

program to solve those problem areas. . . . This will be done in cooperation with local school districts.[80]

Congresswoman Green criticized the laboratories as being too heavily involved in dissemination and too little in research activities. She argued that their major problem was inadequate staffing stemming from their too-rapid establishment.[81] An educational commentator expressed his concern that the laboratories might usurp the functions of local school authorities. He cautioned that "innovative action tempered by local educational values must be the operating guideline for a regional laboratory."[82] A more acerbic critic regarded the laboratories as "an over-extended concept."[83] Whether because of the budgetary crunch, opposition generated by extensive involvement in local school politics, or thinness of results produced by overextended staffs, the regional laboratories were cut in number from twenty to fifteen in 1969.

In addition to providing for a sizable expansion in federal educational research efforts, ESEA authorized the Office of Education to contract with private corporations for research and development purposes. The opportunities for corporations to profit through sales of education hardware and software seemed manifold in early 1967. Corporate acquisitions reflected the marriage of firms with hardware and software capabilities, for example: RCA–Random House; CBS–Holt, Rinehart & Winston, Inc.; and General Telephone & Electronics–Readers' Digest. New firms such as Westinghouse Learning Corporation or General Learning, Inc., a joint endeavor of General Electric and Silver-Burdett (Time, Inc.'s textbook subsidiary) also appeared on the scene. It seemed as if big business had finally discovered "the education market."

It was not the Office of Education, however, that made the initial efforts to forge a link between the emerging education technology industry and federal agencies having major educational programs to administer. Early in 1966, the Department of Defense invited the National Security Industrial Association (NSIA) to join with it in sponsoring a conference on the subject "The Systematic Application of Technology to Education and Training." It also asked USOE and the Department of Labor to join in sponsoring the conference which was held on June 14 and 15 and attended by over seven hundred representatives of government, industry, and education.[84] NSIA distributed conference proceedings under the title "Engineering Systems for Education and Training." The principal outcome of the conference was the formation of Project ARISTOTLE (Annual Review of Information and Symposium on the Technology of Training and Learning and Education). The purpose of ARISTOTLE was to improve communications in the government-industry-education "interface."

A steering committee manned primarily by NSIA affiliates and chaired by Marvin Kahn, vice-president of Aircraft Armaments, Inc., prepared the first annual ARISTOTLE symposium, held December 6–7, 1967.[85] Participation in ARISTOTLE was predominantly by NSIA members (approximately 80 percent). Over 5 percent had university affiliations and 10 percent came from nonprofit organizations.[86] The most striking thing about ARISTOTLE was that such a manifest example of "interest group liberalism" [87] attracted little attention and virtually no criticism. One administration spokesman, Samuel Halperin, deputy assistant secretary of HEW for Legislation, warned the symposium that the education market was not necessarily a "lush and ready hunting ground for quick profits by enterprising business men." Halperin went on gently to admonish the predominantly business group that "a full and easy role for industry in education has yet to be earned, not enjoyed as a matter of right." [88]

Perhaps more important criticism of the phenomenon represented by Project ARISTOTLE—direct government contracting with industry for educational research purposes—came from the National Education Association in August 1967. In a prepared statement to the Senate Education Subcommittee, Dr. John M. Lumley, director of NEA's Division of Federal Relations, stated that:

> . . . direct contracts between the USOE and profit-making agencies are inherently wrong. . . . This constant effort on the part of the Office of Education to secure authority for the Commissioner to bypass the public and private non-profit education agencies and deal with profitmakers is in our opinion, the most dangerous educational proposal ever to come before the Congress.
> This danger lies in the potentiality for federal control and direction of the entire education effort of this country. . . . [89]

NEA saw direct USOE-industry contracts as leading to a serious erosion of state and local authority over the shape and direction of American education. The prospect of an alliance of well-funded federal agencies and private corporations dependent on federal contracts has not yet been realized. This is no doubt a consequence of budgetary constraints rather than strong opposition within the education community. Certainly if the experience encountered in the formation of the "military-industrial complexes" were to be even partially repeated in education, the locus of control *could* shift radically if federal funding of research were substantial. While federal officials, such as those in USOE, would only do what they considered to be "in the public interest," there is substantial potential for harm inherent in the "working relationship of a relatively small group of planners and thinkers closely coupled with a relatively small group of technicians." [90] This emerging issue, which was no more than recognized in 1967, promises to reassert itself whenever federal educational research is sharply increased. As of late 1974, that development has yet to occur.

The relationship between universities and federally sponsored research that developed during the 1950s and 1960s raised some important issues. These issues have been categorized as reflections of tensions between the "product values" and "process values" of the research and in terms of federal and university perspectives.[91] They involve the determination of the costs and benefits of federally funded university research to the government, the universities, and to society. The product-process value debate focused on the balance to be struck in allocating research funds between the value of the information produced by the research and the value of the research activity itself. The growing recognition of process values in the 1960s led to a demand for research programs administered through institutional grants based on formulas rather than through the project grants based on merit that were characteristic of the earlier emphasis on product values.

The issues concerning the benefits of federally supported university research did not tend to be as acute as those arising from considerations of the costs of such research. The most perplexing questions involved classified research related to national security. Did performance of secret research compromise the professional responsibilities of university-based scholars? Did classified research violate the spirit of free inquiry and wide distribution of findings that is the heart of academic life? Are the social functions of universities compatible with research objectives such as the development of weapons systems? University-centered opposition to the Vietnam war gave these questions a special salience. Other questions involving costs focused on the degree of managerial responsibility universities exercised over research. To what extent should they control federal research activities on their campuses? How can the mutual obligations existing in the triangle comprised of the government, universities, and research faculties be guaranteed? And, by no means least in importance, what is the impact of a substantial university research operation on teaching, especially at the undergraduate level?

These issues surrounding university-based federal research had led to widespread campus disruptions by the end of 1968. They served as a focal point for opposition to the war and for a host of campus grievances against the professionalization and concomitant depersonalization of university life that had taken place since 1945. Except, however, for a few perceptive individuals, e.g., Congressman Brademas and Commissioner Howe, few educational policy makers fully grasped the relationship between federally supported university research and campus unrest. Unfortunately, the war led not to a careful analysis of the issues, but rather to a curtailment of research funds in nonmilitary programs such as education.

Perhaps one of the most critical problems of federal educational research lay in the absence of a general policy to guide the effort. Assuming a federal commitment to support research and development in education, at what level of funding would that support be pegged? What are the specific goals of federal educational research? By whom will the research be performed? What are the implications of research policy for general educational policy? A national educational research and development expenditure in 1968 of $150 million out of a total educational budget of nearly $50 billion suggests that any research policy that could be identified was, at best, "ad hoc and insufficiently considered." [92] This situation continued substantially unchanged in the Nixon administration's early years, and in 1973 sharp curtailments in institutional research grant programs hit hard at leading universities.[93]

The most important contribution of the Nixon administration to educational research and development was the establishment, in 1972, of the National Institute of Education (NIE). This action marked fulfilment of a 1958 proposal of an advisory board set up by the National Academy of Science and the National Research Council. The advisory board had called for a national organization, comparable to the National Institute of Health, to conduct and support research on the educational process.[94] The NIE became one of two principal agencies, along with USOE, in a new Division of Education in HEW. No less than 90 percent of its funds ($500 million were authorized for fiscal years 1973 through 1975) were to be spent through grants and contracts with individuals, universities, and other institutions.[95] It is still too early to tell whether the enhanced organizational status of educational research will, without sizably increased funding, produce results that improve the quality of American education.

Vocational Education

The issues that vocational education presented the policy process in 1967–68 arose mainly from its status, or lack of status, within the education community. The academic orientation of secondary and higher education cast vocational education in the role of a forgotten stepchild. Vocational and technical training have never been fully integrated into the curricula of our colleges and high schools. As a consequence, vocational educators have had difficulty in obtaining adequate funding; they have lacked sufficient innovative capacity to keep their instructional programs consonant with contemporary needs; and they have been charged, accurately but unfairly, with failing to meet the educational needs of the 80 percent of the nation's children who do not go to college.

It was not until the passage of the Vocational Education Act of 1963 that the federal government attempted to utilize the potential of vocational education in meeting the nation's manpower needs. That act represented, however, only the rudimentary beginning of a national manpower policy that recognized fully the importance of the relationship between education and various forms of occupational training.

The weakness of vocational education was also reflected in the fragmentation of federal programs in the manpower–occupational training areas. Major vocational education programs were located in USOE, manpower development and training (MDTA) was lodged in the Labor Department, while the Office of Economic Opportunity ran the Job Corps and a variety of other programs. Competition for funds between these programs and the great variance in the amount of matching state funds required for participation—the range was from 50 percent for USOE's vocational education programs to no state matching in the Job Corps—resulted in an almost total absence of rational coordination in federal efforts. Interagency conflict and duplication of effort were accompanied by distorted state programs that resulted from a "bargain basement" approach, i.e., states sought to receive a maximum amount of federal funds for a minimum commitment of their own moneys.

These conditions provided the background for and were probable causes of two major developments affecting vocational education during the 90th Congress. First, several congressional critics of the administration's educational programs led by Representatives Albert Quie and Edith Green and Senator Jacob Javits pushed unsuccessfully for the establishment of a cabinet-level Department of Education and Manpower. Secondly, the American Vocational Association, the principal professional group in the field, prepared a set of comprehensive amendments to the administration's 1968 vocational education bill. The AVA amendments would have substantially expanded the general authorizations for vocational education programs and for the cooperative work program. They were introduced by two administration supporters, Representatives Roman Pucinski (D.-Ill.) and Lloyd Meeds (D.-Wash.).

Reorganization and demands for more vocational education money were neither highly salient nor successful issues, but they did deal directly with basic problems in this area of federal educational activity. Vocational education made steady but unspectacular progress in its quest for higher priority status in the Nixon administration's educational policies. Enrollments increased from 600,000 to 1,000,000, and the level of federal support rose from $207 million to $379 million between fiscal year 1968 and fiscal 1970.[96]

Observations

Many of the issues and problems that educational policy makers faced during the two years of the 90th Congress have continued to confront the nation and its education community. Several others, however, have passed from the scene. A few of them have been successfully resolved. Many more have been rendered irrelevant by changing conditions, or more importantly, by the continuing domination of federal domestic programs or the budgetary constraints imposed by the war in Indochina and the inflation born of that conflict. Consequently, this chapter sounds a note that combines contemporary relevance with nostalgia; pessimism with optimism. The next several chapters examine the policy process and how it dealt with the demands, conditions, and needs we have just discussed.

Notes

1. A typical criticism of the extensive administrative workload and other complications involved in federal aid appeared in Arleigh McConnel, "Federal Aid: Operation Foul-up," *Journal of Secondary Education* 47 (March 1967): 114–17.

2. For an extended scholarly analysis of the entire system of federal grants-in-aid, see Deil S. Wright, *Federal Grants-in-Aid: Perspectives and Alternatives* (Washington, D.C.: American Enterprise Institute for Public Policy Research, 1968). Wright examines the advantages and disadvantages of categorical grants and explores possible alternatives to the present system.

3. Fred M. Hechinger, "Johnson Bars U.S. Control," *New York Times*, 14 November 1965.

4. See, for example, the valedictory of former U.S. Commissioner of Education Francis Keppel, *The Necessary Revolution in American Education* (New York: Harper & Row, 1966).

5. See Fred M. Hechinger, "The Problem Is to Separate Aid from Control," *New York Times*, 9 July 1967, p. E-9; and Roald F. Campbell and Gerald R. Sroufe, "Toward a Rationale for Federal-State-Local Relations in Education," *Phi Delta Kappan* 47 (September 1965): 2–7.

6. One state education official found the increased use of federal funds as "both a blessing and a problem." See Nicholas P. Georgiady, "The State Department of Education and Federal Funding," *Educational Leadership* 25 (October 1967): 25–27.

7. Harold Howe II, "U.S. School Aid . . . Who Should Run It?" *New York Times*, 12 January 1968, p. 55.

8. Interview, 26 October 1967. Anonymity guaranteed.

9. See chapter 4, below; see also Eugene Eidenberg and Roy D. Morey, *An Act of Congress* (New York: Norton, 1969), pp. 209–13.

10. See Jack Merwin, "National Assessment—A Progress Report" (Paper inserted in the *Congressional Record*, daily edition, 20 June 1967, pp. A-3131–33; editorial, "Who Should Do the Assessing?" *Phi Delta Kappan* 48 (April 1967): p. 377; James Cass "National Assessment," *Saturday Review*, 17 September 1966, pp. 71–72; Ralph W. Tyler, "Let's Clear the Air on Assessing Education," *Nation's Schools* 77 (February 1966): 68–70; Harold C. Hand, "The Camel's Nose," *Phi Delta Kappan* 47 (September 1965): 8–13; and R. W. Tyler, "Assessing the Progress of Education," ibid., pp. 13–16.

11. Nor was the absence of objective measures for the evaluation of governmental programs limited to education. See Daniel P. Moynihan, "A Crisis of Confidence," *The Public Interest* 7 (Spring 1967): 3–10.

12. Merwin, "National Assessment," p. A-3131.

13. See Hand, "Camel's Nose"; and his "Recipe for Control by the Few," *School*

Boards 9 (April 1966): 8–10; see also Elaine Exton, "Wither Federal-Local Relations—Schoolman in Painful Dilemma," *American School Board Journal* 152 (April 1966): 45–48.

14. Tyler, "Assessing the Progress of Education," p. 15.

15. John I. Goodlad, "Assessment of Educational Performance," *Contemporary Issues in American Education:* Consultant Papers prepared for use at the White House Conference on Education, 20–21 July 1965. (Washington, D.C.: U.S. Department of Health, Education, and Welfare, Office of Education Bulletin, 1966, No. 3), p. 49.

16. Cf. Franklin Parker, "Federal Influences on the Future of American Education," *School and Society*, 28 October 1967, pp. 383–87.

17. See William Grant, "Educators Favor U.S. School Study," *Detroit Free Press*, 6 January 1969, p. 1; and Garven Hudgens, "Federal Evaluation of Schools Begins Despite Local Objections," *Michigan Daily*, 24 November 1969, p. 3.

18. Philip Meranto, *The Politics of Federal Aid to Education in 1965: A Study in Political Innovation* (Syracuse: Syracuse University Press, 1967), pp. 66–84; and Eidenberg and Morey, *An Act of Congress*, pp. 59–69.

19. Eidenberg and Morey, *An Act of Congress*, p. 64.

20. Meranto, *Politics of Federal Aid*, p. 81.

21. Interview, 1 April 1968.

22. James W. Guthrie, "A Political Case History: Passage of the ESEA," *Phi Delta Kappan* (February 1968): 302–6.

23. Stephen K. Bailey and Edith K. Mosher, *ESEA: The Office of Education Administers a Law* (Syracuse: Syracuse University Press, 1968), pp. 51–53.

24. The cases were *Cochran* v. *Louisiana State Board of Education*, 281 U.S. 370 (1930) and *Everson* v. *Board of Education*, 310 U.S. 1 (1947). In those cases the Court developed the so-called child-benefit theory which holds that the no-establishment of religion clause of the First Amendment is not violated as long as the primary effect of the aid is for the benefit of the child and the general welfare rather than a religious organization.

25. *Frothingham* v. *Mellon*, 262 U.S. 447 (1923).

26. *An Act of Congress*, p. 101.

27. Ibid., p. 166.

28. Bailey and Mosher, *ESEA*, pp. 201–2.

29. Ibid., p. 202. All was not quite as placid at the local level. See the USOE-commissioned study by Vincent J. Nuccio and John J. Walsh, *A National Level Evaluation Study of the Impact of Title I of the Elementary and Secondary Education Act of 1965 on the Participation of Non-Public School Children: Phase I.* (Chestnut Hill, Mass.: Boston College, 1967). They examined parochial-public school relations in 30 school districts and concluded that while the participation of Catholic schools was "better than nothing," it produced results far short of the full promise of the statute.

30. Leonard Buder, "Church-State Issue in New York," *New York Times*, 10 April 1966; and Gerald Grant, "U.S. Aid Begins to Flow to Parochial Schools," *Washington Post*, 10 May 1966.

31. Gerald Grant, "Oklahoma Only Snag in U.S. Drive to Close Church-State Textbook Gap," *Washington Post*, 21 January 1966.

32. *Horace Mann League, et. al* v. *Board of Public Works of Maryland, et. al*, 220 A 2d 67 (1966).

33. *Board of Education of Central School District No. 1* v. *Allen*, 228 N.E. 2d 791 (1967); affirmed 392 U.S. 20 (1968).

34. *Flast* v. *Cohen*, 392 U.S. 83 (1968).

35. The Senate approved, but the House rejected, judicial review provisions in ESEA amendment legislation in 1966 and 1967. Senator Ervin, the leading congressional spokesman for judicial review legislation, presented a brief before the Supreme Court in the *Flast* case. See "Senator Ervin's Brief As 'Friend of the Court' in Flast Against Gardner," *Congressional Record*, daily edition, 8 February 1968, pp. S-1167–71.

36. For conflicting discussions of the legal and constitutional aspects of issue, see "The Elementary and Secondary Education Act of 1965 and the First Amendment," *Indiana Law Journal* 41 (Winter 1966): 302–27; and "Church-State-Religious Institutions and Values: A Legal Survey—1964–1966," *Notre Dame Lawyer* 41 (June 1966): 713–19.

37. Richard E. Morgan, *The Politics of Religious Conflict: Church and State in America* (New York: Pegasus, 1968), chap. 1.

38. Ibid., p. 22.

39. Ibid., p. 25.

40. For examples of separationists' writings, see: Edgar Fuller, "Government Financing of Public and Private Education," *Phi Delta Kappan* 47 (March 1966): 365–72; George R. La Noue, "The Title II Trap," *Phi Delta Kappan* 47 (June 1966): 558–63; idem, "Church-State Problems in the Elementary and Secondary Education Act of 1965," in American Civil Liberties Union, *The Church State Problem Has Been Handed to You* (New York: ACLU, 1967); Leo Pfeffer, "The Child-Benefit Theory and Church-State Separation," *Church & State* (April 1966): 6–7, 15; idem, "What Price Federal Aid?," *Saturday Review*, 21 January 1967, pp. 59–60, 80. The Catholic position is effectively stated in William B. Ball, "Church and State: The Absolutist Crusade," *Saturday Review*, 21 January 1967, pp. 58–59, 77; and James C. Donohue, "Comments on 'The Title II Trap'," *Phi Delta Kappan* 47 (June 1966): 564–65.

41. Ball, "Church and State," p. 77.

42. See the writings of Leo Pfeffer, note 40.

43. See, especially, La Noue, note 40.

44. For example, following congressional approval of ESEA, Michigan enacted an Auxiliary Services Act similar to Title I; New York adopted a controversial parochial school textbook law that had been under consideration for years, Ohio authorized the use of public funds to pay for equipment, services, and nonreligious instruction in private schools; and New Hampshire authorized sweepstakes receipts to be distributed to parochial as well as public schools although the state Supreme Court later held the law unconstitutional.

45. Ball, "Church and State," p. 58.

46. *ESEA*, p. 204.

47. For an analysis of state efforts to aid nonpublic education, see Comment, "The Sacred Wall Revisited—The Constitutionality of State Aid to Nonpublic Education Following *Lemon* v. *Kurtzman* and *Tilton* v. *Richardson*," *Northwestern University Law Review* 67 (1972): 118–45.

48. *Lemon* v. *Kurtzman*, 403 U.S. 602 (1971). However, in *Tilton* v. *Richardson*, 403 U.S. 673, the Court upheld federal construction grants to sectarian colleges under the HEFA of 1963. In doing so the Court found that the intent of sectarian higher education was, unlike elementary/secondary education, not primarily to inculcate religious beliefs.

49. *Committee for Public Education* v. *Nyquist*, 37 L. Ed. 2d (1973).

50. *Sloan* v. *Lemon*, 37 L. Ed. 2d. 939 (1973).

51. The difficulties encountered by USOE in its initial implementation of Title VI are carefully described and analyzed in Bailey and Mosher, *ESEA*, pp. 142–57; and

in Gary Orfield, *The Reconstruction of Southern Education* (New York: John Wiley & Sons, 1969).

52. Jack Greenberg, "The Tortoise Can Beat the Hare," *Saturday Review*, 17 February 1968, p. 57.

53. *Green* v. *County School Board of New Kent County, Virginia* 391 U.S. 430 (1968).

54. See Greenberg, "Tortoise Can Beat Hare."

55. T. A. Smedley, "The Last Two Years in School Desegregation," *Race Relations Reporter* 4 (May 1973): 14–18, 17.

56. George Gallup, "76% of Public Opposes Busing," *Washington Post*, 1 November 1971.

57. *Swann* v. *Charlotte-Mecklenberg Board of Education*, 402 U.S. 1 (1971).

58. *Keyes* v. *School District No. 1*, Denver, Colo., 303 F. Supp. 279 (1969), affirmed in part and remanded, 37 L. Ed. 2d 37 (1973); *Bradley* v. *School Board of City of Richmond, Va.*, 338 F. Supp. 67 (1972); and *Bradley* v. *Milliken*, 345 F. Supp. 914 (1972).

59. United States Senate, Select Subcommittee on Equal Educational Opportunity, *Toward Equal Educational Opportunity* (Washington, D.C.: U.S. Government Printing Office, 1973).

60. For discussions of the problem, see Homer Babbidge and Robert Rosenzweig, *The Federal Interest in Higher Education* (New York: McGraw-Hill, 1962); John W. Gardner, "Government and Universities," in Logan Wilson, ed., *Emerging Patterns of Higher Education* (Washington, D.C.: American Council on Education, 1965), pp. 286–92; David D. Henry, "The Federal Government and Higher Education," *Journal of Higher Education* 37 (April 1966): 187–92; and John F. Morse, "The Federal Government and Higher Education: General and Specific Concerns in the Years Ahead," *Educational Record* 47 (Fall 1966): 429–38.

61. Alan Pifer, "Toward a Coherent Set of National Policies for Higher Education," *Liberal Education* 54 (March 1968): 1–15, at p. 2. The text of Pifer's address was published in the *Chronicle of Higher Education*, 29 January 1968, pp. 4–5, and inserted in the *Congressional Record*.

62. Commission on Higher Education, *Quality and Equality: New Levels of Federal Responsibility for Higher Education* (Berkeley: Carnegie Corporation, 1968).

63. In 1969 legislation based on the Carnegie Commission's recommendations was introduced in both houses of Congress under the title "Higher Education Bill of Rights." Sponsors of the legislation were Representatives John Brademas (D.-Ind.) and Ogden Reid (R.-N.Y.) and Senators Edward Kennedy (D.-Mass.), Jacob Javits (R.-N.Y.), and Winston Prouty (R.-Vt.). No action occurred during the 91st Congress.

64. For an analysis of five proposed institutional grant formulas, see Robert Farrell and Charles Andersen, *General Federal Support for Higher Education* (Washington, D.C.: American Council on Education, 1968).

65. This suggestion is made by John P. Mallan in an informative and perceptive paper, "Current Proposals for Federal Aid to Higher Education: Some Political Implications" (Washington, D.C.: American Association of Junior Colleges, 1970).

66. H.R. 875, 90th Congress. Reintroduced as H.R. 11542 in the 91st Congress.

67. Congressional Quarterly, *Education for a Nation* (Washington, D.C.: Congressional Quarterly, 1972), p. 18. For a summary of the provisions of PL 92-318, see pp. 90–102.

68. See the account of the 1966–67 student-loan fight by Basil J. Whiting, Jr., "The Student Loan Controversy," *Public and International Affairs* 5 (Spring 1967): 5–42.

69. Kerner Commission Report, p. 452.

70. John Egerton, "High Risk," *Southern Education Report* 10 (March 1968).

71. U.S. Department of Health, Education, and Welfare, *Toward a Long-Range Plan for Federal Financial Support for Higher Education* (Washington, D.C.: U.S. Government Printing Office, 1969).

72. Mallan, "Current Proposals for Federal·Aid," p. 6.

73. Panel on Educational Innovation, President's Science Advisory Committee, *Educational Opportunity Bank* (Washington, D.C.: U.S. Government Printing Office, 1967).

74. See Milton Friedman, "The Role of Government in Education," in Robert A. Solo, ed., *Economics and the Public Interest* (New Brunswick, N.J.: Rutgers University Press, 1955), pp. 123–44, especially p. 140; Charles C. Killingsworth, "How to Pay for Higher Education" (Memorandum submitted in testimony before the Senate Subcommittee on Employment and Manpower of the Committee on Labor and Public Welfare, 87th Cong., 1st sess., Hearings entitled *Nation's Manpower Revolution*, Part 4 [Washington, D.C.: U.S. Government Printing Office, 1963]), pp. 1500–11; Edward Shapiro, "Long-Term Student Loans: A Program for Repayment," *Harvard Educational Review* 33 (1963): pp. 370–78; and William Vickery, "A Proposal for Student Loans," in Selma Mushkin, ed., *Economics of Higher Education*, U.S. Department of Health, Education, and Welfare (Washington, D.C.: U.S. Government Printing Office, 1962), pp. 186–207. Also, Kingman Brewster, president of Yale University, in two widely noted speeches, in 1961 at Yale Law School Alumni Day ceremonies and in May 1967 at Stanford University, advocated long-term student loans financed by an income-tax surcharge.

75. "College Opportunity Bank," *New York Times*, 19 September 1967.

76. "Expensive College Loans," *Washington Star*, 13 September 1967.

77. The term is John Mallan's; "Current Proposals for Federal Aid," p. 14.

78. John Beckler, "The Disemboweling of Aid to Higher Education," *College Management* 8 (May 1973): 14–18, at 18.

79. Jason Millman, "Editorial," *Educational Researcher* 17 (December 1966).

80. U.S. House of Representatives, Committee on Education and Labor, Report of the Special Subcommittee on Education, *Study of the United States Office of Education*, 90th Congress, 1st Session, House Document No. 193 (Washington, D.C.: U.S. Government Printing Office, 1967), p. 227. The study will hereinafter be cited as "The Green Report."

81. "An Interview with Edith Green," *Educational Researcher* 18 (November 1967): 1, 8.

82. Melvyn N. Freed, "The Regional Education Laboratories: Bane or Benefit?" *School & Society* 95 (9 December 1967): 492.

83. J. Myron Atkin, "The Federal Government, Big Business, and College Education," *Educational Forum* 31 (May 1967): 391–402, at 395.

84. This discussion is based on the "Background" section of the program of the 1967 annual symposium of Project ARISTOTLE, 6–7 December 1967.

85. The steering committee was comprised of ten task groups and received assistance in its work from the NSIA staff. The task groups and their chairmen included: *Project 100,000*, Dr. Gilbert E. Teal, Dunlap & Associates, Inc.: *Media*, F. A. Centanni, Sylvania Electric Products, Inc.; *Information Storage, Retrieval and Dissemination*, Dr. Paul Weaver, Xerox Corp.; *Educational Research*, Dr. James E. Gilbert, Northeastern University; *New Developments*, Dr. Harvey J. Brudner, Westinghouse Learning Corp.; *Systems Approach to Education*, Henry Lehmann, General Electric Co.; *Standards, Measurement and Evaluation*, Dr. D. W. Meals,

Raytheon Co.; *Courses, Tasks and Skills,* Walter Stellwagen, Science Research Associates; *Government-Industry-Education Interface,* T. W. St. Clair, North American Aviation, Inc.; and *International Considerations,* T. Jack Heckelman, Philco Corp. This information, is based on Eugene T. Ferraro, "Status Report: Project ARISTOTLE," *Defense Industry Bulletin* (September 1967): 4–6.

86. Ibid.

87. See Theodore J. Lowi, *The End of Liberalism* (New York: Norton, 1969).

88. Samuel Halperin, "Things Don't Just Happen" (Address delivered to the first annual Project ARISTOTLE symposium, December 1967). Inserted in the *Congressional Record,* daily edition, 18 January 1968, pp. E-57–59 by Senator Jacob K. Javits (R.-N.Y.).

89. U.S. Senate, Committee on Labor and Public Welfare, Hearings before the Subcommittee on Education, *Education Legislation,* 1967, Part 4, 7 and 9 August 1967, p. 1372.

90. Fred M. Hechinger, "Will Big Business and Big Government Control R & D?" *Phi Delta Kappan* 48 (January 1967): 215–19.

91. See James D. Carroll, "The Process Values of University Research," *Science* 158 (24 November 1967): 1019–24; and John Brademas, "University Research and the Federal Government: Time for Reassessment" (Address delivered at the annual conference of the National Council of University Research Administrators, Washington, D.C., 29 November 1967). Reprinted in the *Congressional Record,* daily edition, 30 November 1967, pp. H-16127–29.

92. Brademas, "University Research."

93. Beckler, "Disemboweling of Aid," p. 18.

94. Advisory Board on Education, National Academy of Sciences-National Research Council, *Psychological Research in Education* (Washington, D.C.: National Academy of Sciences, 1958).

95. *Education for a Nation,* p. 92.

96. Ibid., p. 21.

4

EDUCATIONAL POLICY AND
THE 90TH CONGRESS

When the 90th Congress convened, it appeared unlikely that education would occupy a substantial amount of its time, at least in the first session. The enactment of major education legislation in the preceding three years—the Elementary and Secondary Education Act of 1965, the Higher Education Act of 1965, the Vocational Education Act of 1963, and the Higher Education Facilities Act of 1963—seemingly left little on the agenda that was of comparable importance. Moreover, authorizations under major education measures were not scheduled to expire until June 30, 1968.

There were strong indications, however, that although new major legislation was not in prospect, education policy makers were due for stormy times. Many of the issues they had previously found so troublesome were being encountered in the administration of the new legislation. In addition, the increased cost of the Vietnam war threatened to curb spending for education and other domestic programs, making inevitable the growth of a disturbing gap between congressional aspirations reflected in authorization figures and budgetary realities.

A harbinger of the conflicts that the 90th Congress would encounter in making educational policies was provided in the closing days of its predecessor. In extending ESEA through fiscal year 1968, the "education 89th Congress" exuberantly boosted grant authorizations above the levels requested in the administration's bill, from $1.75 to $2.35 billion for fiscal 1967, and liberalized the formula for determining the eligibility of disadvantaged children for assistance under Title I. At the same time it demonstrated the sensitiveness of the racial issue by stipulating that the statute did not authorize busing of students to overcome racial balance as a condition of receiving assistance, and it limited the power of the commissioner of education to withhold funds from school districts not in compliance with the Civil Rights Act of 1964.[1] The extension of the Teacher Corps authorization only as far as June 30, 1967, and with no increase in funds, reflected the staying power of the local control issue. The Teacher Corps was unpopular with many members of Congress because it placed federally paid instructors in the public schools.

In spite of the fact that only minor education program authorizations (including the Teacher Corps) were due to expire at the end of fiscal 1967, President Johnson sent to Congress, on February 28, 1967, a broad-gauge education and health message which proposed major amendments to ESEA and HEA.[2] The two bills were developed by a group in the Executive Office of the President composed of representatives from the Bureau of the Budget, the White House staff, and the Office of Science and Technology.[3] This group received suggestions from external task forces commissioned to study various problems and from agency (in this case USOE) proposals submitted through the Bureau of the Budget.[4] Acting on the basis of directives from the President, the group coordinated the development of specific provisions in the legislation with HEW and USOE officials.

Because problems encountered in the administration of ESEA necessitated technical changes in the legislation,[5] and because extension of the legislation was almost certain to involve long struggles over racial integration, state and local as opposed to USOE control of administration, and the Title I allocation formula, it was decided to introduce the bills in 1967 in order to allow sufficient time to work out compromises that would not disturb the fragile coalition that made ESEA possible in 1965. A consideration that worked for early introduction of the higher education amendments bill was the administration's desire to respond to complaints of college officials regarding the disruptive effects of the timing of federal benefits on their planning. The uncertainty created by enacting and funding programs at the end of congressional sessions could be partly alleviated by early renewal of authorizations.

President Johnson's key education proposals were contained in two bills, ESEA Amendments of 1967 and HEA Amendments of 1967.[6] An educational television bill, the proposed Public Television Act of 1967, completed the legislative package, but it will not be examined here as it was referred to the Commerce committees.

The ESEA amendments bill contained provisions to: (1) extend the Teacher Corps for three years; (2) authorize grants under Title V to the states for comprehensive educational planning and evaluation; (3) amend the Vocational Education Act to establish a five-year program of grants to support the development and operation of innovative projects to serve as models for use in vocational education programs; (4) authorize under Title VI the establishment of regional resource centers to determine the special educational needs of handicapped children; and (5) make miscellaneous changes in the impacted-areas laws. The changes proposed in the Higher Education Amendments bill were more substantial: (1) extend, with revisions, HEA, NDEA, and the National Vocational Student Loan Insurance Act, for five years, to June 30, 1973; and (2) consolidate, coordinate, and broaden federal teacher-training programs through passage of an Education Professions Act, which would become Title V of HEA. Ultimately there emerged from congressional consideration of these proposed bills, four statutes: the ESEA Amendments of 1967, the Education Professions Development Act of 1967, the Higher Education Amendments of 1968, and the Vocational Education Amendments of 1968. This chapter examines the process whereby the 90th Congress passed these major education bills and funded the programs of the Office of Education for fiscal years 1968 and 1969.

The Elementary and Secondary Education Amendments of 1967 [7]

The House Committee on Education and Labor conducted hearings on the administration's ESEA amendments bill between March 2 and March 20, 1967. Although the proposed amendments were minor in terms of their effect on the basic objectives of the statute, the committee undertook a comprehensive review of its implementation. It is indicative of the importance attached to the legislation in Congress that Chairman Carl Perkins (D.-Ky.) conducted hearings before the full committee rather than assign the bill to a subcommittee.[8]

The committee took testimony from Commissioner of Education Harold Howe II, several of his subordinates, HEW Secretary John Gardner, representatives of the major elementary and secondary education interest groups, the U.S. Catholic Conference, and from a wide range of public school administrators who provided important feedback information on the operation of ESEA. In the course of the hearings, committee members focused attention on the level of funds for Title I, the administration of ESEA, and the impact of ESEA on federal-state relations in education. They also touched upon the always-present issues of desegregation and church-state relations. Ultimately the committee reported a "clean" bill of its own which substantially expanded the scope of the amendments. During its deliberations, the Republican minority on the committee attempted to replace ESEA's categorical programs under Titles I, II, III, and V with a single general-purpose block grant.

The hearings began rather unobtrusively with a lengthy statement by Commissioner Howe. Much of Howe's verbal testimony involved responses to questions about the Teacher Corps. The administration bill proposed to transfer authorization for the Teacher Corps from the Higher Education Act to Title I of ESEA on the ground that it was essentially an elementary-secondary school program and that corpsmen were to be specially trained to deal with disadvantaged children. Most of the questioning reflected congressional concern that the Teacher Corps might serve as a vehicle to nationalize the educational system. Some congressmen objected to a federally funded "elite corps" of teacher trainees who might conceivably detract from other teacher-training programs. They suggested that a more appropriate way for the federal government to encourage the training of teachers in fields where shortages existed would be through an expanded program of fellowships for college students. The debate over the Teacher Corps demonstrated the continuing sensitivity of the federal control issue.

That issue was broached directly at several points in the hearings with respect to the administration of ESEA. The basic item of contention involved the capability of state education agencies to carry out the objectives of the statute and the degree to which categorical programs should give way to general assistance. Commissioner Howe stated the administration's position succinctly on two occasions:

> MR. DELLENBACK [Rep. John Dellenback (R.-Ore.)]: . . . would we not do better, granted an absence of unlimited funds, to permit a State to concentrate these funds on the problems that it considered most grievous?
>
> MR. HOWE: This is what the Congress attempted to do, to concentrate the funds when it developed the principle of focusing on areas of high concentration of deprived students. This notion of simply turning the money over to the State for any concentration the State wished to make without any congressional direction or policy of any kind would change the total purpose and focus of Title I, which is to get at a broad national problem. . . . If I read correctly what you are suggesting, which is simply giving the State the funds it is eligible for without focus on this particular problem, you would change the whole purpose of the act and the problem would in all likelihood go unattacked.
>
> The States have not tended to attack the problem with funds available to them up until the time this act was placed in being. In all likelihood the pressures in the State would be very great to use these funds for purposes of raising teacher salaries generally, which is the largest financial problem the State has, and you would not be bringing special services to deprived youngsters.[9]

and:

MR. HOWE: Mr. Quie [Rep. Albert H. Quie (R.-Minn.)], it seems
to me that the relationship of the States to local school districts is going to
be different than the relation of the Federal Government to the States,
that the powers and prerogatives which the State has in law for setting
the organization of the schools or certifying teachers, or setting the
curriculum of the schools, these three areas, are powers and prerogatives
which the Federal Government does not have. . . .

But the problem we have in that series of relationships is that State
governments by and large haven't supported their State educational
agencies as strongly as they need to support them in order to bring the
capacities for guidance to local school districts, capacity for planning, the
capacity to do the type of things in Title V.[10]

The case for general aid was most strongly argued by Representative
Quie and supported by Dr. Duane Mattheis, the Minnesota commissioner of
education. According to Mattheis:

Categorical aids tend to treat all districts and States the same, distort
balanced educational programs, develop unnecessary and undesirable
administrative bureaucracies and generally—especially with portions of
ESEA 1965 and some of the 1967 amendments—retain too much control
and direction for local school district and State educational agency
decisions in the U.S. Office of Education.[11]

This position had the support of the Council of Chief State School Officers
(CCSSO), but it was not endorsed by two big-city school superintendents
who testified, Sidney Marland of Pittsburgh and Bernard Donovan of New
York. Marland acknowledged that "more fluidity in the use of funds" would
be desirable, but he stated that retention of existing categorical restraint in
ESEA was necessary to ensure that federal money was "spent where the law
meant it to be." [12] Marland's testimony reflected the belief, which was held
throughout the administration, that state and local education officials could not
be relied upon to spend federal funds wisely without specific guidelines.
Donovan was more explicitly eager for a shift to general aid, but he was
careful to point out that New York's well-qualified state department of
education was perhaps uniquely sensitive to the problems of big-city schools
and the needs of the disadvantaged child.

A particularly salient point in the committee's debate over federal-state
relations involved the administration of Title III of ESEA. That title sought to
encourage innovation and creativity through the establishment of supplementary educational centers. Originally these centers were funded directly by
USOE upon application from local school officials. The CCSSO, through its
executive secretary, Dr. Edgar Fuller, urged that Title III be administered by
state education agencies on the basis of state plans approved by USOE. The

state agencies would evaluate the approved projects proposed by local officials. Fuller told the committee that USOE administration of Title III had favored a few states at the expense of many and that its impact was to help the strong and to deny to the weak the things that would strengthen them.[13] The administration of Title III by USOE received strong support from Dr. Richard Miller, a professor of education at the University of Kentucky.[14] Miller criticized the state education agencies for a lack of innovation and creativity and stated that it would be a "real mistake to turn Title III over" to them "en masse." [15] It would "probably destroy the spirit of Title III," he concluded. Responsibility for administration of Title III was to be a major issue during floor action in both the House and Senate. It symbolized the question of whether the federal role in education would be directive or supportive.

Although Commissioner Howe spoke of Title I in terms of its ostensible purpose of attacking the "broad national problem" of poverty, the issue in the hearings was not how best to do so. For Howe, other members of the administration, the congressmen, and various interest-group spokesmen, the question was how much discretion the state and local education agencies would enjoy in the expenditure of federal funds. The administration believed that unless specific conditions were attached to the money, its objectives of innovation, creativity, and qualitative improvement of elementary education had no chance of being achieved. These goals had the advantage of appearing to be objectively unobjectionable, but they had profound implications for the nation's school system. They constituted an official statement of dissatisfaction with the schools and the professionals who staffed and administered them. Incorporation of the goals in ESEA, and especially Title III, represented an attempt to apply a federal corrective.

The education professions and their supporters reacted predictably. They appealed to the ancient but always popular value of localism, and they denied the substance of the implied charges lodged against them. In seeking to defend their autonomy, they attracted conservative support. In arguing that the educational system was working fairly well, they had the overall affluence of society as evidence. Their position was defensive, but quite strong.

The matter that concerned House committee members only slightly less than federal-state relations was the level and administration of funding under ESEA. Democratic members criticized the failure of the administration to request and obtain appropriations at or close to the amounts authorized. Representative Hugh Carey (D.-N.Y.) conveyed this mood with a somewhat distorted literary allusion when he asserted that "the administration . . . is for all intents and purposes talking like Midas but funding like Oliver Twist." [16] Representative Edith Green (D.-Ore.) also attacked the final fiscal 1968 budget request for ESEA (55 percent of the authorization), but suggested that the fault lay not with HEW or USOE, but with the Bureau of the Budget.[17]

Secretary Gardner responded to similar "friendly" criticism from Representative Ogden Reid (R.-N.Y.) by defining the budget process as a conscientious, reasonable, and fair series of tradeoffs made in face of severe constraints.[18]

In addition to objecting to the underfunding of ESEA, the committee heard feedback testimony from school officials and from elementary and secondary education interest groups calling for forward funding of ESEA programs in order to facilitate more orderly and rational planning by state and local education authorities. The major obstacle to obtaining year-in-advance funding was acknowledged to be coordination of the effort and acceptance by the Appropriations Committees. The concept of forward funding was received sympathetically in the Education and Labor Committee.

A somewhat more contentious point was the formula for allocating Title I funds between the states. Urban state committee members objected to implementation in fiscal 1968 of changes in the formula that had been adopted in 1966. Those changes would have reduced funds available to the 35 most wealthy states and increased funds for the 15 poorest states at the 50 percent level of funding proposed by the administration. Representatives Quie and Sam Gibbons (D.-Fla.) led the attack on a proposed delay in implementation of the formula changes until the achievement of funding at 100 percent of the authorization. The point at issue was whether a state's allocation would be based on the state average expenditure per pupil or the higher of the state or national average.

The hearings also touched on the always sensitive matter of church-state relations when Representative James Scheuer (D.-N.Y.) suggested that the National Advisory Council for the Education of Disadvantaged Children had failed to scrutinize the church-state implications of Title I.[19] Dr. Sidney Marland, a member of the advisory council, replied that it had not detected "any major concerns . . . in this relationship." [20]

The thorny problem of racial integration in the schools received committee attention only when F. Peter Libassi, special assistant to the secretary of HEW for civil rights, testified regarding policies for school desegregation under Title VI of the Civil Rights Act of 1964.[21] Libassi answered numerous questions from committee members concerning the administration of HEW's desegregation guidelines. The major concern of these questions was that school districts involved receive a full measure of administrative due process and that civil rights enforcement not extend to making educational policy.

On April 11 the House Committee reported a "clean" (i.e., its own) bill, H.R. 7819, that substantially expanded the original administration proposals. The committee's markup of the bill witnessed two major partisan controversies. A Republican effort to terminate the Teacher Corps lost, 20–12, with one Republican, Bell of California, voting with the Democrats. Of crucial importance was the defeat, in a 19–13 party-line vote, of a special proposal authored by Quie to concentrate all ESEA funds in a single block grant to the states.

Quie's proposal brought into focus the conflict over federal-state relations that had highlighted the hearings. The committee's bill went beyond the administration's requests by extending the authorization for ESEA through fiscal 1969, delaying the changes in the Title I formula until full funding of authorized amount had been accomplished, deleting the vocational innovation provisions for separate consideration as an amendment to the Vocational Education Act, and splitting the Teacher Corps authorization with program operating funds included in ESEA and funds for the training phase left separate consideration by the Special Education Subcommittee. (That subcommittee, chaired by Representative Edith Green, normally handled higher education legislation.) Although the committee bill expanded and differed technically on many points from the President's original proposals, the administration endorsed it since it retained the basic presidential objectives.

Republican strategy with respect to H.R. 7819 became manifest on April 20 when Quie introduced a sweeping substitute for the relatively uncontroversial committee bill. The precise origins of the "Quie Amendment" are uncertain. It was certainly in keeping with general Republican support for relatively unrestricted block grants in all major domestic policy areas as a means of decreasing centralized federal control and increasing state autonomy. It also had strong support from the Council of Chief State School Officers. An aide to Commissioner Howe claimed that "the amendment came as a result of Quie's relationship with Duane Mattheis, the Chief State School Officer of Minnesota. He wrote the proposal for Quie." [22] Kenneth Young, the AFL–CIO's principal education lobbyist, claimed that Quie and Republican committee staff member Charles Radcliffe drafted the bill. It was unquestionably the product primarily of Quie's thinking with inputs from the other sources.

The Quie Amendment to ESEA (H.R. 8983) would have replaced the categorical grant programs authorized under Titles I, II, III, and V with a set of block grants to the states beginning in fiscal 1969. The states would administer the grants under state plans, drafted in accordance with statutory criteria and approved by the commissioner of education. The criteria were designed to increase the discretion of state education officials in the expenditure of the funds while maintaining an emphasis on the education of economically disadvantaged children. They involved a delicate effort to appeal to conservative states rights advocates while not alienating liberals. Specifically, the state plans under the Quie Amendment would be required to: (1) certify that not less than 50 percent of the funds would have to be spent on programs for educationally deprived children including those in private schools; (2) certify the expenditure of at least 7 percent of the block-grant allocation for the provision of textbooks and other instructional materials for use in public and private schools; and (3) show that highest priority in the allocation of funds for local districts would be given to areas experiencing problems due to high concentrations of poverty, rapid increases in enrollment, and geographic isolation and economic depression.

The Quie Amendment would have altered the formula for allocating funds among the states. The basic factors in the proposed Quie formula would be the school-age population and the relative income per child of school age in each state. Although the states would be subject to some restrictions under the Quie Amendment, they would enjoy far greater freedom in deciding how to spend ESEA funds, and as a result the programs would be encumbered by much less administrative detail and paperwork. Quie concluded his presentation of the amendment to the House with the statement that it "greatly lessens the opportunity for unwarranted Federal interference in our schools" and that it "would significantly reduce the power of the U.S. Commissioner [of Education] in local school decisions." [23]

The Quie Amendment precipitated a major controversy over federal educational assistance. The issue was not over the level of aid—Quie would have authorized $3 billion under ESEA for fiscal 1969, the administration figure contained in H.R. 7819 was only $281 million more—but over the relative power that federal and state authorities would exercise in dealing with local school officials. The Quie Amendment was not, however, a proposal for unrestricted general aid to education. Although it addressed itself directly to the issue of federal control, it had to incorporate some recognition of the racial and religious antagonisms that prevented earlier attempts to enact general aid legislation and that necessitated the poverty-directed categorical approach of ESEA. The intractability of the church-state problem plus the disadvantageous treatment of poorer states under the Quie Amendment's allocation formula ultimately led to its defeat.

The racial issue did not directly affect consideration of the Quie Amendment since Quie made it clear in his initial presentation that Title VI of the Civil Rights Act would apply to it just as it did to ESEA and other federal education programs. But the religious issue immediately arose and remained at the forefront of the thirty-five-day controversy over the amendment. On April 21, Representative Carl Perkins (D.-Ky.), chairman of the House Education and Labor Committee, issued a statement charging that Quie's proposal would "launch a new Holy War, reintroducing the divisiveness of the church-state issue." [24] Three days later, the National Education Association's (NEA) Division of Federal Relations urged support of the committee bill and continuation of ESEA's categorical approach as a "politically feasible" and effective means of "bypassing the emotional and legal issue of church-state separation." [25] The initial version of the Quie Amendment was unacceptable to Monsignor James C. Donohue, head of the

Education Department of the U.S. Catholic Conference. Republican efforts to win Catholic support by revising the bill to guarantee adequate participation by private school students were also unacceptable.[26] Msgr. Donohue issued a statement noting that although "we are satisfied the Republicans made a sincere effort to include us . . . we do not feel we can support their plan." [27]

The principal difficulty facing Quie and the House Republicans was beyond their control; the fact that thirty-five state constitutions contained provisions prohibiting the expenditure of funds for sectarian schools. Catholic school officials feared that block grants that increased the discretion of state officials would be subject to these restrictions and that parochial school children would be excluded. Furthermore, the CCSSO, a supporter of the Quie Amendment, had been a long-time opponent of any public assistance to private schools. As William Consedine, General Counsel of the U.S. Catholic Conference, explained, "the Quie Amendment involved our basic problem—turning the money over to the Chief State School Officers. You can't do that and accomplish much." [28] Even a provision prohibiting commingling of federal and state funds in states where constitutional provisions might jeopardize aid to private school children failed to ease Catholic apprehensions. Whether Quie could have worked out a satisfactory resolution of Catholic fears and objections had he consulted with Donohue and Consedine prior to introducing his bill is questionable. Consedine felt that while Quie "moved in good faith, he acted without realizing what it would mean to us." [29] Quie himself acknowledged that "the Catholics beat my amendment," but he added that "when Viet Nam ends . . . I think I can develop a block grant bill which they can support." [30] Failure to have done so in this instance was a costly, if not fatal, omission.

The defeat of the Quie Amendment also rested on Republican failure to attract crucial support from southerners and from big-city representatives. Big-city school superintendents, such as New York's Donovan, were critical of the bill's failure to guarantee that cities would not suffer from discrimination in the distribution of funds and from the drop in the proportion committed to disadvantaged children. He felt that since the Quie substitute did not authorize sufficient funds for a general aid program, there would be "substantial reductions in the amount of assistance going to the great cities." [31] Nor was it possible to activate the conservative coalition of Republicans and southern Democrats. Quie and his supporters hoped that his amendment, even though it would not affect desegregation enforcement, would attract southerners who would vote their traditional states' rights preferences.

The administration launched a major campaign against the Quie Amendment that included a vigorous statement by President Johnson characterizing the proposal as a "reckless effort" based on "partisan political" considerations that had "stirred up suspicions" and "aroused fears." [32] Additional attacks were made by Commissioner Howe, Representative

Perkins, Secretary Gardner, and House Democratic leaders. High-ranking HEW officials including Under Secretary Wilbur Cohen, Assistant Secretary for Legislation Ralph Huitt, his deputy Samuel Halperin, and the USOE legislative staff marshaled opposition to the Quie Amendment from a wide range of interest groups and supplied the groups and prominent educators with material for letters, statements, and speeches. The organizations joining in opposing the Quie Amendment included the NEA, the National Congress of Parents and Teachers, the American Association of University Women, the National Farmers' Union, the U.S. Catholic Conference, and the NAACP. In addition, the American Council on Education, a major higher education association, voiced objection on the ground that hearings had not been held on the proposal. Support for the Quie Amendment was more limited, but it included the CCSSO and forty-two of its members, the U.S. Chamber of Commerce, and several Republican governors.

In the course of debate on the bill, Quie attempted to reassure its critics with revisions. The ironic consequence of these efforts to meet objections, however, was that they detracted from the flexibility in the administration of ESEA that was its prime objective. As an NEA "flash" to its legislative leaders stated, "each of Mr. Quie's attempts to improve his bill moves it closer to the categorical aids he would abolish." [33] Yet it retained enough of its original purpose of increasing the discretion of state education agencies that it remained highly controversial and its fate was an open question.

As the House moved toward a showdown on the Quie Amendment, Representative Edith Green, on May 19, introduced a series of amendments to H.R. 7819 that were to affect House action significantly. Mrs. Green claimed that her amendments were necessary to ensure passage of the committee bill. The precise role that the Green amendments played is a matter of dispute, but their importance in shaping the final bill cannot be denied. Rejecting the block-grant approach of the Republicans, Mrs. Green was willing to leave Title I untouched, but she proposed to turn Title III over to state education departments for administration under a state plan and to provide for full state administration of Title V, instead of the 85 percent provided for in the committee bill. In addition, she offered an amendment requiring that desegregation guidelines under the Civil Rights Act be "uniformly applied and enforced throughout the 50 states." [34]

Although Mrs. Green's motives were a subject for conjecture and dispute, her strategy was clear. The essence of ESEA, a categorical approach focused on poverty-stricken children, would be preserved, but the authority of USOE vis-à-vis the states would be reduced. Because the bulk of ESEA funds were authorized under Title I and the provision of textbooks and educational materials under Title II was not affected, the delicate religious balance of 1965 would not be disturbed. The uniform enforcement of desegregation guidelines and the diminution of USOE's operational control would cement southern support for the committee bill. The administration and House liberals opposed the Green amendments as a dilution of civil rights enforcement and as destructive of the innovative features of ESEA. Mrs. Green argued, and won chairman Perkins over to her view, that the amendments were necessary to defeat Quie and save the bill.

Kenneth Young, the AFL–CIO education lobbyist, claimed that "Quie was beaten before the Green amendments were offered. She gave a lot of people a chance to get off the hook." [35] A contrary appraisal was offered by Ben Reeves, a key staff aide to Perkins, who asserted that the "Green amendments enabled the bill to pass without the crippling effects of the Quie proposal. The conservative coalition had the votes to kill the committee bill." [36] Unfortunately, the sequence of action on the House floor and the recorded roll-call votes do not provide a conclusive answer to this question, but they do establish Mrs. Green's key role in shaping the end result.

On May 23, the House debated the first Green amendment, requiring uniform application and enforcement of desegregation guidelines throughout the nation, for three hours before passing it by a voice vote. The debate centered on the question of whether the amendment would strengthen or weaken guideline enforcement or, as Mrs. Green claimed, it merely would mean equal enforcement. Democratic leaders Perkins and Carl Albert (D.-Okla.) concluded that it would not weaken the guidelines. HEW civil rights enforcement chief, F. Peter Libassi, stated after hearing the debate that it seemed clear to him that the House wanted to step up enforcement, especially against de facto segregation.[37] Some House liberals were apprehensive about the effect of the amendment. Representative James O'Hara (D.-Mich.), a leader of the Democratic Study Group, called for defeat of the amendment on the ground that it was either "meaningless or mischievous." [38]

The southern forces won a clear-cut victory when the House accepted, on a 116–62 standing vote, an amendment offered by Representative L. H. Fountain (D.-N.C.). The Fountain Amendment, which was adopted after a brief debate, was identical to the one included in the House version of the 1966 ESEA amendments. It required that there be a hearing and a finding of noncompliance with Title VI of the Civil Rights Act before funds could be withheld from school districts.

The House held a thirteen-hour marathon session on May 24, at the conclusion of which it passed H.R. 7819. Although administration forces withstood the challenge mounted in the Quie Amendment, the bill was substantially altered by a coalition of Republicans and conservative Democrats led by Quie and Mrs. Green. Her role was pivotal. She joined with the Democratic leadership—Speaker McCormack, Majority Leader Albert, and committee chairman Perkins—in helping to defeat the Quie Amendment by a teller vote, 168–197. On that vote the administration forces were joined by Mrs. Green, and they received critical support from southern Democrats and a small band of liberal Republicans.[39]

The House then adopted four major amendments over the objection of the administration forces. The first of these was the Gibbons Amendment setting the states' Title I allotments on the basis of one-half the average state expenditure per pupil or one-half the national average, whichever was higher. Adopted by a 123–100 teller vote, and later passed on a roll call, 221–195, the Gibbons Amendment had the effect of giving the fifteen poorest states proportionally more money than the richer states. Gibbons defended this amendment, under which his own state of Florida would receive less money than in the committee bill, on grounds of equity and it also had the advantage of increasing the attractiveness of the bill to other southern Democrats. Mrs. Green, Quie, and most Republicans supported the Gibbons Amendment in spite of the fact that their states stood to lose funds under it. The amendment provided a means of forging a coalition to further alter the bill.

That coalition prevailed on the next three amendments, two of which were offered by Mrs. Green. The Green amendments eliminated direct funding of Title III and V by USOE in favor of administration under state plans. The amendments were a bitter blow to the administration and to House liberals. In their view, the principal innovative component of ESEA, Title III, had been placed under control of state education agencies that were neither inclined toward change nor equipped to handle it, and the Title V amendment merely increased the likelihood that the state agencies would remain in that condition. The Title III amendment passed by a 181–124 teller vote and later a 230–185 roll-call vote, and the Title V amendment carried on a 133–104 teller vote.

Interspersed between the Green amendments was a proposal, offered by Representative John Erlenborn (R.-Ill.), to delete the Teacher Corps authorization from the bill. The amendment, approved on a 186–136 teller vote, had the effect of leaving the future of the Teacher Corps in the hands of Mrs. Green's Special Education Subcommittee.

When the smoke had cleared, only Mrs. Green "could claim victory." [40] Her strategy was multifaceted. By supporting the Democratic leadership in opposing the Quie Amendment she helped maintain the categorical approach of ESEA. Her support was, according to some observers, essential to obtain crucial southern votes. In exchange for those votes, she helped Gibbons to modify the Title I formula to the advantage of most southern states, she led the drive to reduce USOE's control over state education departments, and she supported dropping the Teacher Corps authorization. Her amendments helped the Republicans recoup much of what they had lost in the Quie Amendment defeat. Consigning the fate of the Teacher Corps to her relatively unsympathetic hands won further support from the conservative coalition.

Substantively Mrs. Green maintained a consistent position of strong support for federal aid to education while maximizing state and local control over the funds. She claimed to be motivated by a desire to save the bill and aid American education. Her critics accused her of personal aggrandizement. Whatever the mixture of philosophical commitment and ambition that moved her, she clearly established herself as a major figure shaping federal educational policy.

The Senate Labor and Public Welfare Subcommittee on Education held extensive hearings on H.R. 7819 during July, August, and September. The Senate hearings, which were longer and more detailed than those conducted by the House committee, ranged over the full scope of ESEA.[41] Subcommittee chairman, Senator Wayne Morse (D.-Ore.), brought before the committee representatives of the six major interest groups in the elementary-secondary education area, the AFL–CIO and its affiliate, the American Federation of Teachers, the U.S. Catholic Conference, various groups advocating strict separation of church and state, the NAACP, a broad sampling of state and local education officials, Representatives Quie and Gibbons, the principal officials of HEW and USOE, and a number of other organizations with more than a passing interest in the bill, including the League of Women Voters and the American Library Association.

Although testimony in the Senate hearings covered a panoply of subjects it focused on the general level of funding for education and on three amendments adopted by the House: the Gibbons Amendment altering the Title I allocation formula, the Fountain Amendment relating to enforcement of desegregation guidelines, and the Green Amendment to Title III. During the hearings, Senator Morse made clear his desire to hear all interested parties in order to take to the Senate floor a bill that carried the unanimous support of the committee.[42] The hearings, according to Morse, had a dual purpose: to enlighten the members of the subcommittee and to provide a record that would support the bill on the Senate floor.[43]

The subcommittee faced serious problems with the three major House amendments. It was apparent that a modification of or a substitute for the Fountain Amendment had to be found if the bill was to pass the Senate. Neither the committee members nor a substantial majority of senators would countenance any dilution of civil rights enforcement. Testimony from Clarence Mitchell, Washington lobbyist for the NAACP, and a panel of desegregation workers helped to strengthen opposition to the Fountain Amendment.[44] Secretary Gardner and Commissioner Howe also expressed strong opposition to it. Yet, there was an implicit threat of a filibuster unless southern senators received assurances that desegregation enforcement would not cut funds off from school districts without warning, formal notice, and a hearing.

The problem of the Title I formula became apparent in testimony from state and local education officials. Most state officials, with the exception of New York and California, and the CCSSO defended the Gibbons Amendment, while big-city school superintendents and Johnson administration spokesmen opposed it. The opponents pointed out that although the amendment would tend to equalize funding of Title I *between* states, it would not guarantee the big cities that they would receive equitable treatment when state officials made the allocation of funds *within* their states. The subcommittee members sympathized with the objective of the Gibbons Amendment, but they also were responsive to the needs and apprehensions of the big-city school officials.

The Green Amendment to Title III occupied much of the subcommittee's time. The arguments that had been advanced during the debate in the House were reiterated many times during the Senate hearings. The charge that state education agencies were unprepared to handle the innovative programs in Title III were made by the administration, the big-city school officials, the NAACP, the U.S. Catholic Conference, and the AFL–CIO. It was denied by the CCSSO, the NEA, and Representative Quie.

The Title III changes embodied the question that underlay the House struggle over the Quie Amendment in May—would there be substantial direct distribution of funds and supervision of programs by USOE or would all federal funds be distributed by state education agencies? The extent of direct federal control was at stake. Morse told the subcommittee on July 26 that there was a "legislative advantage" to the House bill with the Green Amendment, that he had not prejudged the matter, and that he would attempt to develop a compromise.[45]

The subcommittee concluded its hearings on September 18, but the full committee did not report H.R. 7819 until November 6. When the bill emerged from committee it contained several amendments, many of which were proposed by Republican members. Morse used the long period of time spent marking up the bill to work out compromises to the Title I formula and the Title III administration problems and to forge unanimous committee support for the bill. The most extensive additions were to authorize ESEA appropriations to be made a year in advance and to extend authorization for three years through fiscal 1971. The advance funding provision was made in response to requests from educators and education interest groups in order to facilitate financial planning. The three-year extension would also contribute to planning effectiveness as well as obviate the need for reconsideration of the legislation until 1970 or 1971. The committee also added a provision automatically continuing authorizations for one fiscal year if Congress did not act to do so by their expiration date.

The formula compromise resolved the city-state and the big state–small state conflicts by providing that no *county* would receive less in 1968 than it got in fiscal 1967. The remainder of the appropriation would be distributed pro rata among the states according to a formula based on the number of children from poverty families (i.e., with incomes below $3,000) multiplied by one-half the higher figure of the average state expenditure per pupil or the national average. This solution had the effect of minimizing the intrastate flow of funds while achieving a measure of interstate equalization but without a loss in funds for any state.

The second major committee compromise embodied a phased shift in the administration of Title III funds, but with USOE retaining substantial direct involvement. The state education departments would control one-third of the money in fiscal 1968, one-half in 1969, and two-thirds in 1970. This approach fell between the administration's strong preference for full federal administration and that of the House bill providing for state agency administration under a state plan beginning in 1969.

Morse solidified committee backing for the bill by accepting in markup sessions amendments proposed by several of its members. For example, the advance funding provision was the special project of Senator Prouty (R.-Vt.); Senator Dominick (R.-Colo.) was responsible for a program of incentive grants under Title I for states that spend a greater percentage of their resources for education than the national average; Senator Murphy (R.-Calif.) sponsored a program for demonstration projects to prevent school dropouts; and a program of demonstration projects to promote school bus safety was added through the efforts of Senator Javits (R.-N.Y.). Morse employed a bipartisan strategy in shaping the legislation:

> I never take a bill to the floor that isn't bipartisan. . . . The Republicans know I will give them a roll call vote on the Senate floor on everything they are defeated on in committee. That way they know they won't be victimized. They vote to report the bill; I protect their rights on the floor. They cooperate fully with us. Often when they offer amendments we accept. I always come out with a compromise bill that is acceptable to both sides.[46]

The Title III compromise that Morse fashioned in the committee reflected this approach. The committee was evenly divided between the administration position and the House-passed Green Amendment. Morse told the Senate in floor debate that he cast the decisive vote against both positions. The compromise embodying a phased transfer of Title III control, an idea he attributed to Javits, was worked out by majority and minority staff members and it received unanimous support as a "fair and sensible adjustment of the differences within the committee."[47]

Floor debate in the Senate lasted ten days. It was primarily taken up by maneuvering over two racial matters, busing and the Fountain Amendment to the House bill, but it also included action on the Title III changes and on the church-state issue.

The church-state matter arose when Senator Sam J. Ervin, Jr. (D.-N.C.) introduced an amendment that would facilitate a judicial test of the constitutionality of federal assistance to sectarian schools. Similar bills had periodically passed the Senate only to die in the House Judiciary Committee. Support for judicial review enabling legislation was traditionally much stronger in the Senate than in the House where Catholic interests had successfully thwarted attempts to pass aid to education bills that did not include aid to parochial schools. The Senate passed the Ervin Amendment on a 71–0 roll-call vote.[48] The formal roll call was taken to demonstrate as emphatically as possible to the House conferees the intensity of Senate feeling on the matter.

The racial issue had both a northern and a southern dimension. The northern aspect arose on December 4, when Senator Everett Dirksen (R.-Ill.) introduced an amendment that would have prohibited the use of federal funds to pay any of the costs of transporting students or pupils to overcome racial imbalance. Dirksen claimed that his amendment would merely implement language in the Civil Rights Act of 1964 which stated that the federal government could not require busing to overcome racial imbalance. Morse claimed that the effect of Dirksen's amendment would be to impose federal control on local officials by prohibiting them from implementing a full desegregation plan. The issue failed to be resolved in three roll-call votes after ten hours of debate.[49] After a second day of debate on his amendment, Dirksen withdrew it "temporarily." His action was not explained formally, but apparently he felt that he lacked sufficient support to have it pass.[50]

The southern dimension of the racial issue arose when Senator Richard B. Russell (D.-Ga.) introduced an amendment similar to the Fountain Amendment. The Russell proposal would have required HEW to inform a school district of the amount of federal funds it was entitled to receive prior to the opening of the school year and prohibited any curtailment of those funds after that time because of noncompliance with the Civil Rights Act. Southern senators threatened a filibuster unless the bill included the Russell Amendment or an equivalent guarantee against arbitrary procedures in desegregation enforcement. Morse and most northerners felt that the amendment would emasculate Title VI of the Civil Rights Act; Russell and most southerners claimed they were merely seeking to avoid the chaos that would result if funds were cut off after the school year had begun.

Morse desperately sought to develop a compromise amendment that would meet southern objections and which civil rights supporters could accept.[51] For a while it appeared that the problem would force delay in passage of the bill until 1968, but a satisfactory solution emerged when Morse secured a letter from Secretary John Gardner outlining in detail the procedures to be followed before funds could be terminated. The letter, which was addressed to Morse, assured the Senate in conciliatory tones that school districts would be informed prior to March 1 of possible civil rights action and that formal notice of noncompliance would be given no later than September 1. This procedure would give school districts at least six months in which to take corrective action.[52] Noting that the letter was part of the "legislative history" of the bill, Russell withdrew his amendment.[53]

The failure of the southerners to press for a roll-call vote on the Russell Amendment should not mask the sensitiveness of the desegregation enforcement issue. They accepted Morse's compromise solution with misgivings as to its effectiveness. That they did so was more a tribute respect for the integrity of Morse and Gardner than any kind of a vote of confidence in HEW or the administration.

The Title III compromise engineered by Morse in committee withstood a surprisingly close test on a roll-call vote, 38–35.[54] An amendment reinstating the House provisions (i.e., the Green Amendment) was introduced by Senator J. Strom Thurmond (R.-S.C.). With statements of support from the NEA, the CCSSO, and many state education officials, Thurmond nearly succeeded in upsetting Morse's carefully constructed bipartisan coalition. The near defeat of Morse's committee compromise on Title III gave indication of the attractiveness of state rather than federal administration of federally funded education programs.

In other action related to the bill, the Senate rejected a proposal by Senator Frank Lausche (D.-Ohio) to limit authorizations for fiscal 1969, 1970, and 1971 to the 1968 figure; an amendment by Senator Vance Hartke (D.-Ind.) increasing adult education authorizations; and another Thurmond amendment deleting the comprehensive planning grants authorized for state agencies under Title V. It accepted Senator Ralph Yarborough's amendment authorizing $18 million for research and demonstration projects for education of the mentally retarded, and an amendment that deleted the committee provision for permanent continuing authorizations. These amendments did not substantially alter the substance of the bill nor affect the solidarity of support for it. The skill with which Morse shepherded it in committee and on the floor was reflected in the 71–7 roll-call vote on final passage.[55] The only opposition came from a small band of southern Democrats. Morse's position as he took the bill to conference was strong on all key issues except the Title III changes.

There were numerous differences between the House and Senate versions of H.R. 7819, but only four issues were of critical importance: the Title I formula, the Ervin judicial review amendment, the Fountain Amendment, and the provisions regarding the administration of Title III. The

Senate conferees were led by Morse who acted on their behalf during most of the conference committee sessions. Morse held proxies from the four other Democratic conferees—Yarborough, Randolph, Robert Kennedy, and Williams—and from two of the four Republicans—Prouty and Javits.[56] The House conferees were a more diverse group. Initially they included Democrats Perkins, Green, Holland, Pucinski, Carey, Daniels, Brademas, and Albert; and Republicans Ayers, Quie, Goodell, Bell, Esch, and Steiger. During the conference sessions, Representative O'Hara replaced Representative Holland and Representatives Gibbons and Ashbrook were added to the Democratic and Republican conferees, respectively. The unusual expansion of the conference membership was not explained on the House floor, but it was apparently done to strengthen Chairman Perkins' position among his colleagues with respect to the Gibbons Amendment.[57] The House conferees were not united and a coalition comprised of the Republicans and Democrats Perkins, Green, and Gibbons "called the shots for the House." [58]

The conference committee solved the problem of the Title I formula, which proved to be its most difficult task, by providing for use of a $2,000 low-income factor until maximum funding on that basis could be achieved. Only then would the formula be based on a $3,000 factor. The concentration of abject poverty in urban areas would continue to accord the cities a substantial advantage over other communities until full funding with the lower income factor. At that point there would be some shifting of intrastate allocations, but not to the absolute disadvantage of any areas. The formula compromise also provided that state and local education agencies would not receive less in subsequent years than they got in fiscal 1967 up to a total appropriation level of $1.5 billion after which no guarantee would be necessary. The formula also retained the option of basing allocations on half the state average or half the national average expenditure per pupil. In this way the concerns of both state and local officials and the wealthy industrial and the poorer, more rural states were safeguarded.

The conference resolved the two other difficult problems with a classic bargain. The Senate conferees receded from insistence on the Ervin judicial review amendment in an implicit exchange for House acceptance of Secretary Gardner's letter in lieu of the Fountain Amendment. As a Senate staff member explained, "we traded them the Ervin Amendment for the Fountain Amendment." [59] The Title III Amendment involved a bargain in which the Senate concept of a phased shift to state plan administration prevailed, but with the House percentages. The states would administer 75 percent of the funds in fiscal 1969 and 100 percent in 1970. Under strong pressure from the NEA, Morse did not push for the Senate percentages which would have retained a sizable role for USOE (one-third of the funds). According to a conference participant, President Johnson was dissuaded from applying pressure on the Democratic conferees by HEW Undersecretary Wilbur

Cohen.[60] The potential benefits of such pressure, Cohen is said to have argued, would be outweighed by the costs including the inevitable publicity attendant on presidential intervention in conference committee deliberations.

The conference also compromised on a two-year extension of authorizations. It deleted the Senate's $20 million program for comprehensive planning grants under Title V, but it approved the Senate's reservation of 5 percent of Title V funds for direct distribution by the commissioner of education. (The House had deleted a 15 percent set aside provision from the administration bill.)

The conference report was in large part a product of compromises between Morse on the one hand and Perkins, Green, and House Republicans on the other. It could easily have faltered on the Title I formula or the Title III administration provisions. It was a satisfactory but not optimal resolution of the differences that existed. The House adopted the report on a 286–73 roll-call vote, and the Senate accorded it an even more favorable margin, 63–3.[61] The bill became PL 90-247 when President Johnson signed it on January 2, 1968.

Congressional action in passing PL 90-247 reflects the importance of feedback in the policy-making process. The concerns of local and state education officials were expressed in the hearings, conveyed indirectly through education interest groups, and directly through communication with individual representatives and senators. The principal items of concern from the field included the problems of adjusting local and state budgeting and financial planning to uncertain amounts and usually late federal funds, difficulties encountered in complying with USOE regulations and guidelines due to their complexity and often their ambiguity, and conflicts over desegregation enforcement in the South. This information contributed to the development of the substance of the legislation and to the strategies employed in its passage.

The Education Professions Development Act

The first piece of education legislation that the 90th Congress enacted was the Education Professions Development Act (EPDA) which became law on June 29, 1967. That statute, which extended the Teacher Corps authorization and an existing teacher-fellowship program and established four new education-personnel training programs, evolved from House consideration of the ESEA amendments and the administration's 1967 proposals for higher education legislation. Although relatively unimportant in terms of the money involved, EPDA provides a good example of the process of legislative development and an illustration of the interplay of issues and procedures in formulating congressional strategy.

In presenting its 1967 proposals for legislation, the Johnson administration recommended that the authorization for the Teacher Corps be transferred from the Higher Education Act to ESEA. Since the initial administration proposals for ESEA amendments were modest and relatively noncontroversial, it was hoped that the legislation would be passed prior to the expiration of the Teacher Corps authorization on June 30, 1967. The unpopularity of the Teacher Corps with many House conservatives and the expanded debate over the ESEA amendments arising from the enlarged committee bill and the Quie Amendment upset the timetable. When the House accepted the Erlenborn Amendment deleting the Teacher Corps from the ESEA bill, its future was placed in jeopardy.

The administration's initial proposals for teacher training and education-personnel development embodied a coordination, rationalization, and expansion of federal efforts in the area. They reflected a serious concern with the problem of recruiting, training, and utilizing a sufficient number of qualified persons from preschool to higher education. The original impetus for the proposals came from a small group of key officials in HEW and from Representative Edith Green and her Special Education Subcommittee. The genesis of the legislation is perhaps best described by one of its prime movers, Dr. Samuel Halperin, deputy assistant secretary of HEW for legislation:

> I guess I had quite a lot to do with the idea behind EPDA. So did Mrs. Green. Back in 1966 her subcommittee held some hearings on the matter of manpower for all of the poverty programs. She was concerned that while we were moving ahead with a whole bunch of new Great Society programs, we were doing little or nothing about developing and training people to run them. Nothing in the way of a proposed bill ever came out of those hearings, however, they set me to thinking about the manpower situation in education. We had no major efforts other than NDEA Title V and Title XI [which authorized guidance and counseling and teacher training institutes, respectively].
>
> I then sent a memorandum to the commissioner [of education] after OE's proposed legislation for '67 came over, asking him why we hadn't included any manpower legislation. He shot back a note suggesting that I get to work drafting something. I turned the matter over to Joe Colemen [deputy assistant secretary of HEW for education] and he sat down and prepared the initial proposal. We then got together—[Assistant Secretary for Legislation Ralph] Huitt, Howe, Colemen, and I—and made some pragmatic decisions about what old laws would be repealed and what new provisions adopted.
>
> We then sent the bill to BOB and they were enthusiastic. Emerson Elliott [assistant division director for education] complained only that we had not gone far enough.
>
> Part E of the act [Training Programs for Higher Education Personnel] did come, I guess, out of discussions in mid-1966 between

Jack Morse of ACE, John Mallan of AAJC, and Huitt and me. But the major authors were myself, Joe Colemen, and Howe with Mrs. Green providing the initial spark.[62]

As Halperin's comments indicate, initiative in the bureaucracy sparked by a congressional leader and supplemented by inputs from interest groups produced the proposal. As proposed by the administration the legislation would, beginning in fiscal 1969: (1) establish a program of grants to institutions of higher education for subdoctoral training of college teachers and administrators; (2) consolidate NDEA institutes for teachers and guidance counselors into a broader, noncategorical program that would include preschool, vocational, and adult education teachers as well as teacher aides and nonteaching professionals; (3) broaden HEA Title V to include fellowships for preschool, adult, and vocational education teachers; and (4) establish a National Advisory Council on Education Professions Development. It was not regarded as a controversial measure and was expected to be considered and pass as part of a broader HEA amendments bill.

Following House passage of the ESEA amendments without any provision for extending the Teacher Corps, Representative Green moved in her subcommittee to link the extension of the Corps to the personnel-training proposals.[63] Her objectives were to amend the Teacher Corps legislation so as to remove operational control of the program from USOE and vest it in the hands of state and local education agencies and to secure passage of the other teacher-training proposals. By removing control of recruitment and training of Teacher Corps interns from USOE and adding guarantees against federal intrusion into local decision making through the program, Mrs. Green obtained the support of committee conservatives.

The urgency of the Teacher Corps extension was made acute by a provision in the 1967 supplemental appropriation bill that $3.8 million allocated to the Corps could not be spent unless its authorization was extended by June 30. This sense of urgency was sufficient to win reluctant administration acceptance of reduced federal control over the corps. Since both education profession proposals and the Teacher Corps were related to meeting the teacher shortage, they could logically be combined in a single bill.

Mrs. Green's strategy of combining a compromised unpopular program, the Teacher Corps, with a set of generally accepted proposals and pushing them through under severe time constraints worked beautifully. The Education and Labor Committee approved the bill by a 26–2 margin with the only dissenters being unrelenting opponents of the Teacher Corps, Representatives Gurney (R.-Fla.) and Scherle (R.-Ia.). In floor action, Gurney's amendment to strike the Teacher Corps authorization failed by a 62–108 teller vote. With strong bipartisan support from the Education and Labor Committee members, the House, on roll-call votes, defeated a recommittal motion, 146–257, and then passed the bill 311–88.

The Senate Subcommittee on Education conducted a hearing on the House bill on June 23, voted favorably on it on the 26th, and the full Labor and Public Welfare Committee voted to report it on the following day. Because of the time factor, the committee refrained from adding amendments that had been tentatively agreed upon. The decision not to add them was made after a late-afternoon conference on June 27 between Senate and House leaders. After being informed of the strong improbability that the House could move to a conference with the Senate in time to save the Teacher Corps, Senator Morse and his colleagues agreed not to press for their amendments. Morse told the Senate on June 28 that all the desired amendments could be considered in subsequent action on the higher education and the ESEA bills. He defended the decision to accept the House bill on the grounds that it was a "fair and equitable compromise" with the House that was acceptable because it was in the "best educational interests of American children." [64]

His Republican colleagues on the committee were not pleased. Senator Prouty, although supporting the bill, remarked that acceptance of the education professions development program was a "price to the House of Representatives in order to save the Teacher Corps." [65] He found the presentation of an either/or proposition which precluded the opportunity to amend the legislation "most distressing." Senator Dominick was even more outspoken: "the Senate is in fact being forced to ransom the Teacher Corps . . . by enacting, without due committee consideration and without amendment, the $775 million of new obligational authority contained in the education professions development program." [66] Without regard to the merits of the Teacher Corps, Dominick opposed the bill on the grounds that the circumstances surrounding it made it a threat to the bicameral character of Congress. Morse responded that it was acceptance of "legislative reality." Regardless of their personal exasperation over having to "ransom" the Teacher Corps from the House, a majority of senators went along with Morse. Two amendments offered by Dominick on the grounds that they were substantively as important as the Teacher Corps were defeated.[67] The Senate then passed EPDA by a voice vote.

Unquestionably EPDA represented a legislative victory for Edith Green and House conservatives. Liberals in both chambers were confronted with strong, potentially fatal opposition to the Teacher Corps on the grounds that it threatened local authority by placing federally paid teachers in the schools. The emasculation of the program as it was originally conceived was the price of its survival.

Through the skillful use of time and careful cultivation of Republican and conservative Democratic support, Mrs. Green secured passage of a greatly modified Teacher Corps authorization and a teacher-training and personnel-development program that bore her imprint. Her subcommittee was the only congressional body that considered the original administration proposals, the development of which she had stimulated. The proposals emerged unchanged except for the addition of a $115 million program, also of her design, for aiding state and local education agencies in recruiting and providing short-term training for teachers and teacher aides in areas with critical shortages.

In an attempt to capitalize on the personnel training and development emphasis on EPDA, Commissioner Howe set in motion a series of events leading to the establishment of a new bureau in USOE. The decision to create a bureau reflected Howe's desire to make education personnel programs innovative and thus recoup some of the impetus lost through the compromise on the Teacher Corps. The attention accorded the Bureau of Education Personnel Development waned after the end of the Johnson administration as its original raison d'être, the critical personnel shortages of 1965–67, vanished. By 1971 the bureau had become one of several operating units in USOE with no special status.

The Higher Education Amendments of 1968

Preoccupation with the expanded ESEA Amendments Act of 1967 delayed consideration of proposed changes in higher and vocational education legislation until the second session of the 90th Congress. Although both House and Senate subcommittees touched on higher education legislation in their 1967 hearings, they did not report any bills for full committee action. Passage of EPDA in June 1967 removed any sense of urgency to consider the higher education bill prior to 1968.

Two task forces reports to President Johnson in the fall of 1967 contributed to the development of his 1968 education proposals. One task force, an interagency group headed by Treasury Undersecretary Joseph W. Barr, analyzed the guaranteed-student-loan program and recommended several changes in it. The most important proposals were for the payment of a processing charge to banks making loans to college students and a program to aid state and private agencies in the expansion of their lending capacities.

The other task force was a group composed of educators and private citizens and chaired by Dr. William C. Friday, president of the Consolidated Universities of North Carolina. The "Friday Task Force" conducted a study of long-range educational problems, but two ideas emanating from it, the Networks for Knowledge and the Partnership for Learning and Earning proposals, appeared in the administration's 1968 education bills. The major features of the 1968 legislation were developed by a high-level interagency task force comprised of departmental officials, agency heads, and key White House and Budget Bureau staff members.[68]

President Johnson's 1968 education message reflected its diverse origins.[69] It was a grab bag containing: a set of proposed new statutes with eye-catching titles, proposals for extending existing legislation, and requests to begin and expand funding of previously authorized programs. The new legislation would include the Partnership for Learning and Earning Act (a strengthening of the Vocational Education Act), Networks for Knowledge (a pilot program to encourage institutional pooling and sharing of facilities, faculties, and resources), and the Educational Opportunity Act (a strengthened program of college student aid). The statutes to be extended were the HEA, HEFA, NDEA, and the National Foundation for Arts and Humanities Act.

The President also proposed to begin funding two new provisions authorized in the 1967 ESEA Amendments, the Bilingual Education Act and the "Stay-in-School" program, the International Education Act of 1966, and the Corporation for Public Broadcasting. He suggested additional funding for two Office of Economic Opportunity programs, Headstart and Upward Bound; Adult Basic Education; EPDA including the Teacher Corps; and the special programs for the handicapped.

The presidential proposals contained a bit of "something for everybody" while adding very little to the full federal effort in education. The rhetoric that encompassed the proposals did not disguise that they were primarily routine requests to extend major legislation with accompanying corrective adjustments and modest pilot programs.

Hearings on the higher education proposals began before Mrs. Green's subcommittee on the day following receipt of the President's message. The substantive provisions of the administration bill, H.R. 15067, received little attention. Mrs. Green and other committee members questioned Commissioner Howe closely on proposals in the fiscal 1969 budget to cut back funds for college construction and on the rationale for adding new legislation before existing programs could be fully funded.[70] The subcommittee devoted much of its attention in the hearings to the effects that changes in draft policy (the elimination of graduate student deferments and the induction of the oldest eligible men first) would have on graduate enrollments and the supply of Ph.D.s.

The Green subcommittee considered the bill during the spring but did not report it until July. Apparently Mrs. Green delayed action in the hope that legislation more to her liking would be obtained in the 91st Congress.[71] Meanwhile, the subcommittee and the full committee approved a "bob-tailed" bill that would extend for two years four college student aid programs that were due to expire on June 30, 1968. That bill passed the House on May 9 on a 349–5 roll-call vote after being amended to deny funds to students participating in riots or campus disruptions.

The antidisruption amendment, which was offered by Representative L. H. Wyman (R.-N.H.) as a substitute for two amendments adopted by voice vote, was adopted on a 306–54 roll-call vote. The Wyman Amendment prohibited payments to any student refusing to obey "a lawful regulation or order" of his college or university when the institution determined that the refusal was "of a serious nature and contributed to the disruption of the university or college administration." [72] The amendment drew criticism from the ACE which issued a statement urging Congress to eliminate the provision on grounds that it might prove inflammatory and that appropriate institutional and legal sanctions were already available.[73] The issue of student disorder was to remain uppermost as Congress considered the 1968 higher education amendments.

On July 2, the House Education and Labor Committee approved an omnibus bill extending HEA, HEFA, and NDEA until June 30, 1970. The committee bill included administration proposals for an increase in the interest rate on academic facilities loans, the Networks for Knowledge program, and a new education for public service program. The latter two, however, were only authorized planning funds for fiscal 1969. The bill did not include the administration's request for a program of grants to "middle-range" graduate schools, it transferred the Upward Bound program from OEO to USOE and merged it with the Talent Search program, and it dropped the so-called forgiveness feature of NDEA student loans except for persons who teach in schools serving disadvantaged children. The bill also incorporated the student-loan extension bill of May 9 which had not yet passed the Senate.

The omnibus higher education bill was a bipartisan measure that secured unanimous committee endorsement. Essentially it was a compromise between the administration's proposals and committee conservatives that Mrs. Green engineered. Rather than continue the partisan strife that proved so costly to them in 1967, liberal Democrats on the committee salvaged what they could during markup sessions and stood behind the bill. When the House considered the bill on July 24, Representatives Brademas (D.-Ind.) and Scheuer (D.-N.Y.) joined with Quie in praising "the gentlewoman from Oregon" for her "fine leadership" and "special interest and direction" in fashioning an absolutely bipartisan bill that "should be supported by every Member of this House." [74]

The only controversy that arose during House consideration of the bill concerned provisions denying funds to students engaging in campus disorders. The House adopted an amendment introduced by Representative Scherle that strengthened the committee provision. The committee had left it to the discretion of colleges or universities to deny aid to students found, after a hearing, to have contributed to disrupting the institution in violation of a lawful regulation. The Scherle Amendment made denial of aid mandatory in such cases. The House passed the bill on July 25 by a lopsided 389–15 margin.

The Senate subcommittee began hearings on the administration's higher education bill on March 25. Its hearings, like those in the House, found Democratic members criticizing the low level of funding in the administration's proposed budget requests for education. Senator Morse, as Mrs. Green had done previously, questioned the priorities that the administration employed in allocating resources. Other than to hear witnesses who also attacked "inadequate" funding levels that the administration proposed, the Senate subcommittee hearings caused little excitement.

The full committee approved an omnibus bill on July 9 that was similar to the administration's proposed legislation. The Senate committee bill was substantially broader than that approved by the House committee. Acting with uncharacteristic speed for education legislation, the Senate unanimously approved the omnibus bill on July 15, a full ten days prior to House action. The only amendment of any consequence that the Senate approved was the addition of a population factor in allocating NDEA fellowships. The Senate bill did not include provisions for withholding funds from students involved in campus disorders.

Although there were almost 100 differences between the Senate and House bills, the two chambers were in agreement on the essential features of the Higher Education Amendments of 1968. The basic statutes, HEA, HEFA, and NDEA would be expanded and extended and several new programs authorized. The House was more conservative in its approach, authorizing funds for two years rather than four, limiting most new programs to planning money for fiscal 1969, sharply curtailing the forgiveness feature of NDEA loans, and adopting strong antistudent disruption provisions. The conferees filed their report resolving the differences on September 25. The major authorizations were extended for three years; most new programs would receive only planning funds in fiscal 1969; the NDEA loan-forgiveness feature was retained for only two years, but with liberalized provisions for designating poverty area schools in which teachers would be eligible for full forgiveness.

The most difficult compromise concerned the antiriot provisions, of student aid programs. Under the compromise, students would lose entitlement to federal aid funds for two years if they were (1) convicted by a court of any crime involving the use of force, disruption of campus activity, or the seizure of college property; or (2) they willfully refused to obey a lawful order or regulation of their institution. The compromise retained the mandatory feature of the House bill, but limited it to serious cases and only then after a hearing and finding by college officials that the offense "was of a serious nature and had contributed to substantial disruption of an institution's administration." [75] With no debate and by a voice vote the House approved the conference report on September 26 and the Senate followed suit on October 1. President Johnson signed the bill (S. 3769) into law on October 16 along with the Vocational Education Amendments of 1968.

Vocational Education Amendments of 1968

The 1968 amendments to the Vocational Education Act of 1963 constituted the final piece of major education legislation produced by the 90th Congress. Introduced as the "Partnership for Earning and Learning Act of 1968," the administration's proposals reflected the influence of the December 1967 report of the Advisory Council on Vocational Education to HEW Secretary Gardner.[76] The administration bill provided for consolidating and improving the operation of existing vocational education programs, broadened eligibility for participation in the Adult Education Program, and it authorized a new program of grants to state and local education agencies. Of particular interest was an innovative program of grants for exemplary projects of a demonstration nature designed to expand occupational aspirations and opportunities.[77] In spite of its attractive packaging, the administration bill contained only $15 million in new authorizations for fiscal 1969, an indication of fiscal stringency resulting from inflation.

Hearings on the bill in both chambers reflected the congressional conviction that the administration, and particularly the Office of Education, had neglected vocational education. The House committee in particular criticized the low priority accorded vocational education in the budget request and also in the organizational structure of USOE. The bills reported unanimously by both committees, the House on July 8 and the Senate three days later, greatly expanded the scope of the proposed legislation. The House committee rewrote the bill with the assistance of the American Vocational Association. The decision to elevate the role of vocational education was a bipartisan action that occurred in spite of White House opposition.[78]

The House bill, as reported and adopted on a unanimous 390–0 roll-call vote, eliminated the categorical approach of the Smith-Hughes and George-Barden acts which earmarked funds for specific occupational training. It concentrated all statutory authority in the Vocational Education Act of 1963 and increased the authorization level to $335 million in fiscal 1969 and $565 million in each successive year. The House added new programs, with authorizations for fiscal 1969 and 1970, for educationally disadvantaged individuals, exemplary projects, and cooperative work-study. The House debate on the bill was notable for its lack of controversy. Members vied in lauding the measure and deploring the lack of sufficient emphasis on vocational education.

The Senate also passed its version of the House bill on a unanimous 88–0 roll-call vote on July 17. The Senate bill contained amendments transferring project Headstart from OEO to USOE and authorizing an additional $50 million a year for the Agriculture Department's school lunch program for disadvantaged children. The Senate measure differed from the House bill primarily in that it authorized the basic vocational education programs through fiscal 1970 rather than indefinitely and authorized new programs for fiscal 1970 instead of 1969.

The conference committee resolved most differences in favor of the House. It dropped the Headstart transfer, eliminated the school lunch provision since its objectives were achieved in the 1969 Department of Agriculture appropriation bill, made the new programs effective in 1969, and accepted the House's higher authorization levels. The Senate's preference for limited extensions prevailed with programs carrying through fiscal 1972. A Senate provision exempting USOE's fiscal 1969 appropriation from the $6 billion expenditure cut required in the Revenue and Expenditure Control Act of 1968 (PL 90-364) was accepted by the House conferees. The House approved the conference report by voice vote on October 3 after the Senate adopted it on a 58–11 roll call the preceding day. Senate opposition was directed at Section 406, the spending-cut exemption for USOE.

As enacted the 1968 Vocational Education Amendments gave notice of a strong congressional commitment to vocational education including post-secondary training of students and teachers. The act consolidated and sought to improve the administration of vocational education programs through establishment of national and state advisory councils and the requirement of state plans for further development. It authorized new or expanded programs for research and curriculum development, exemplary projects, residential vocational schools, cooperative work-study, advanced study for teachers, and institutes for vocational education personnel. The statute authorized $3.1 billion for vocational education programs through fiscal 1972. It was a congressional rather than executive branch product in which the careful initiative of the AVA and pressures from state and local officials and vocational educators played a leading role in generating unanimous bipartisan support in both houses of Congress.

No doubt the popularity of educating for functional occupations was also highly appealing to a Congress that had grown accustomed to open-ended requests for social welfare programs that offered little promise of quick, positive results. Vocational education had the advantage of getting at the roots of poverty through an established, largely decentralized profession rather than through the untried and politically unpopular programs of the war on poverty.

Funding Education Programs: Appropriations for Fiscal 1968 and 1969

The general pattern of appropriations decision making described and analyzed by Fenno and Wildavsky[79] prevailed as the 90th Congress funded the programs of the Office of Education for fiscal 1968 and 1969. The Bureau of the Budget reduced USOE requests, the House further pared the administration's budget, and the Senate restored some of the cuts.

The House subcommittee handling the appropriation for the Departments of Labor and HEW conducted exhaustive hearings that probed deeply into the federal role in education. The subcommittee operated under a new chairman in the 90th Congress, Representative Daniel Flood (D.-Pa.). Since the establishment of HEW in 1953 it had been under the leadership of Representative John E. Fogarty (D.-R.I.), who died on January 10, 1967. Fogarty was known for his friendly attitude toward HEW, especially its health and health-education programs. When the 90th Congress convened, Flood was the only returning Democratic member of the subcommittee. Chairman George H. Mahon (D.-Tex.) appointed "a very conservative committee, with the possible exception of [Representative Neal] Smith" (D.-Ia.).[80] Along with three midwestern Republicans, this gave the subcommittee a definite conservative cast.

Its hearings, especially in 1967, were more on the order of overall program and policy reviews than attempts to determine funding levels through a close examination of justifications. The subcommittee explored the effectiveness of various programs and took up a number of substantive issues, e.g., the proposed national assessment of educational progress and enforcement of desegregation guidelines. The enforcement of Title VI of the Civil Rights Act and busing to achieve racial balance were of particular concern. Commissioner Howe and the chief of OE's Bureau of Elementary and Secondary Education, Dr. Nolan Estes, were sharply questioned with respect to desegregation guidelines and the administration of ESEA. In contrast, the chief of the Bureau of Higher Education, Peter Muirhead, was received in a more sympathetic and understanding manner.[81] The Senate subcommittee conducted more perfunctory hearings that did not delve as deeply into the details of USOE administrative operations.

In the consideration of USOE appropriations by the House and Senate, only three programs were able to withstand the assaults of congressional economizers. These were aid to federally impacted areas, vocational education, and aid to the education of the handicapped (see table 4-1). The staying power of these programs is a function of the support accorded them by small but well-organized clientele groups.[82] The impacted-areas program also enjoys great popularity in Congress by virtue of the fact that one-fourth of the nation's school districts receive funds under it. Members of Congress who do not have some impacted-area funds flowing into their constituencies are a distinct minority. Vocational education and the special programs for the education of the handicapped are also highly popular. They are ideologically appealing to all segments of the political spectrum. Conversely, the Teacher Corps and the International Education Act proved highly unpopular,

Table 4-1
USOE Budget Requests, House and Senate Actions, and Final Appropriations for Fiscal Years 1968 and 1969

(in thousands of dollars)

| | 1968 | | | |
Program	Budget Request	House Bill	Senate Bill	Appro-priation
Elementary/Secondary	$1,680,207	$1,645,707	$1,696,707	$1,677,907
Impacted Areas	439,137	439,137	472,937	439,137
Teacher Corps	33,000	—	18,100	13,500
Higher Education	1,173,194	1,158,194	1,158,194	1,158,194
Vocational Education	252,000	252,000	252,000	252,900
Libraries/Comm. Serv.	165,900	155,500	156,500	156,500
Education for Handicapped	53,400	53,400	58,400	53,400
Research & Training	99,900	90,967	90,967	90,967
Salaries & Expenses	40,253	37,385	37,385	37,385
Participation Sales Insufficiencies	2,625	925	—	925
Total	$3,940,666	$3,833,215	$3,941,190	$3,880,815

Source: *1967 Congressional Quarterly Almanac*, pp. 525–32.

| | 1969 | | | |
Program	Budget Request	House Bill	Senate Bill	Appro-priation
Elementary/Secondary	$1,561,703	$1,434,830	$1,561,830	$1,476,993
Impacted Areas	410,335	520,845	520,845	520,845
Teacher Corps	31,235	15,000	31,200	20,900
Higher Education	708,127	no action[a]	696,307	696,307
Vocational Education	249,995	248,216	248,216	248,216
Libraries/Comm. Serv.	149,199	94,900	143,600	143,144
Education for Handicapped	85,225	78,850	78,850	78,850
Research & Training	142,300	89,417	89,417	89,417
Salaries & Expenses	46,100	42,000	42,000	42,000
Participation Sales Insufficiencies	3,275	3,275	3,275	3,275
Educ. Professions Dev.	215,913	126,900	196,900	171,900
Total	$3,603,402	$2,654,233	$3,612,440	$3,491,847

Source: *1968 Congressional Quarterly Almanac*, pp. 593–603.
[a] The House did not take any action on higher education requests for FY 1969 as no authorization existed at the time that it considered the HEW appropriation. After authorizing legislation was passed, the Senate considered and recommended the figure that was finally adopted.

especially in the House. The House did not like the idea of federally paid teachers in local school systems and was not willing to accord much financial support to the Teacher Corps until the 1967 ESEA Amendments strengthened local control over its operations.

The International Education Act of 1966 was not funded in the 90th Congress. The underlying concept of the act—programs to expand international understanding among American college students—never attracted strong support. According to Representative Melvin Laird (R.-Wis.), the ranking minority member of the House subcommittee, the act failed to win approval because it "did not implement the promised coordination of all international education programs. It was a bad bill. It did not do the job we had requested and the administration had promised so we said no money. If we had funded it we would have been stuck with it. Once you get a program like that underway you can never get rid of it." [83] Without subcommittee approval the act could not be implemented and, in 1967, Flood was the only member who voted to fund it. [84]

In passing the 1968 appropriation bill for USOE, Congress, at the insistence of House conferees, kept all items at or below the administration's request. Its major concerns beyond the level of funding were with desegregation enforcement and the Teacher Corps. Although neither the budget request nor the final appropriation can be regarded as generous, they did not provoke many basic questions about the adequacy of the funding level or force agonizing choices between competing educational programs.

In contrast, the fiscal 1969 appropriation occasioned sharp conflict between the need for economizing and the funding of social programs. The inflationary impact of spending for the Vietnam war was becoming increasingly troublesome. A presidential request for higher income taxation was met by demands from congressional conservatives for economizing in the domestic budget. At the same time, congressional liberals attacked the low funding levels proposed in the President's budget for programs in education and other domestic areas. The question of "guns or butter" was displacing the administration's assurances that the nation could have "guns and butter." Meanwhile, the programs of the Great Society, such as ESEA, were emerging from the development stage and demanding more resources.

Congress responded to this situation in 1968 in a moderately conservative fashion by establishing an income tax surcharge and requiring a $6 billion expenditure cut. It reduced USOE's 1969 budget below the previous year's level but did not dramatically curtail any major programs. In the course of its deliberations it added substantive provisions designed to prevent withholding federal funds as a means to require school districts to act to overcome racial imbalance and to require that colleges and universities cut off federal funds from students engaging in campus disruption in violation of law or of institutional regulations. Both these actions were spillover effects from earlier debates on legislation.

In the appropriations process the claims of federal education programs had to be reconciled with budgetary realities. It was here that hard choices had to be made between the aspirations expressed in authorizing legislation and the necessity to accept much lower funding levels or raise taxes substantially. The impact of appropriations decisions on policy is thus quite direct. No legislation, whatever its merits, is going to accomplish anything without funds. Since funds are limited and demands for them massive, decisions on how to allocate them are of critical importance. Congress faces this task annually and thus maintains a continuing review of policies and programs, but by members other than those who assumed the lead in the enactment of legislation.

Appraisal

This brief survey and analysis of the formulation and enactment of the education legislation of the 90th Congress reveals that the policy process in education had stabilized. A well-established set of federal programs was in operation. The programs were categorical in nature, but they covered much of the broad spectrum of American education. For the most part they avoided direct USOE control of operations in preference for administration under state plans approved by USOE. This was by congressional intent rather than executive design. It marked an obvious compromise between the desire of the Johnson administration to have a more direct impact on education through federal spending and congressional and clientele group fears of determinative federal control of such matters as professional training and certification, curriculum, school design and construction, overall funding and salary levels, desegregation and racial balancing, and programs for the educationally disadvantaged.

The major accomplishments of the 90th Congress were to improve and extend existing legislation. New programs were few in number, modest in scope, and for the most part administered along with existing legislation. Much of what Congress did legislatively involved either coordination and consolidation of statutes on the books or adjustment and reaction to problems arising in the administration of existing programs. As one HEW official commented, "the basic legislation is all on the books. What remains to be done is to make it work." [85]

In spite of its increasingly established status, national educational policy continued to be embroiled in controversy. Old issues such as federal control and desegregation and the new problem of campus unrest frequently entered congressional debates on legislation and appropriations and occupied much of the concern of committee members. With strong budgetary constraints due to inflation quite manifest by 1968, the unlikelihood of fully funding federal education programs in the forseeable future forced reluctant recognition of a more or less permanent gap between aspiration and achievement in the federal educational effort. The demands of education for federal funds are virtually insatiable and most national policy makers had come to a pragmatic appreciation of the limits of support. Even with those limits, considerable optimism remained that the federal government would continue to make a positive contribution to the qualitative improvement and quantitative expansion of American education. Policy makers disagreed sharply, however, over how the federal role should be organized and implemented. Finally, while many individuals and groups contributed substantially to shaping national educational policy, the dominant participants were President Johnson and Commissioner Howe in the administration and Representative Green and Senator Morse in Congress. Power appeared to be concentrated more in the Presidency than any other institution.

Educational Policy in the Nixon Administration, 1969–74

President Nixon did not make education a priority area for domestic policy initiatives, but he did have sharp disagreement with Congress and various clientele groups over funding levels for categorical aid programs. In February 1970 he vetoed the Labor–HEW appropriations bill for fiscal year 1970 as inflationary. Congress sustained the veto and a bill with reduced funds received his approval in March. In April 1970 he signed a bill extending ESEA for three years with the largest authorizations ($24.6 billion) in the history of that statute. In August of that year, however, he vetoed a $4.4 billion appropriation bill for USOE because it exceeded his budget request by $453 million. Congress then overrode the second appropriations bill veto. In August 1972 Congress sustained the President's veto of the $30.5 billion Labor–HEW appropriations bill.

Major presidential initiatives in education occurred, but they were not designed to increase the scope of the federal effort. Rather, they involved the sensitive issue of desegregation, the structure of aid to higher education, and an attempt to move away from categorical aid programs. In meeting the desegregation issue, President Nixon sought to align himself with the large majority of the public which had expressed opposition to busing. In 1970 he proposed a major program to help local school districts meet the costs of desegregation and legislation sharply restricting the busing of pupils. These proposals were repeated in 1971 and 1972. Congress, which was itself divided over the issue, responded by adding antibusing provisions to the Education Amendments Act of 1972. The Senate also created a Select Committee on

Equal Educational Opportunity. Under the chairmanship of a staunch advocate of integration, Senator Walter P. Mondale (D.-Minn.), that committee conducted an extensive study of busing, racial imbalance, school financing, and other problems in securing equal opportunity in education.

In higher education, the Nixon administration sought to concentrate aid more heavily on students and less in categorical programs involving project grants. In addition to its efforts to hold down the level of federal spending on education, the administration attempted through revenue sharing to shift control over the disposition of federal funds from HEW and USOE to state and local officials. The attempts to dismantle the structure of federal aid to education erected as part of President Johnson's Great Society and to redefine the federal role were suspended in the aftermath of the Watergate affair. The issues involved have yet to be decided.

Notes

1. See *Congressional Record*, daily edition, 20 October 1966, pp. H-27059–68; and "Conferees Set Time Limit on School Aid Cutoff," *Washington Post*, 19 October 1966. The final aid cutoff provision was a compromise between the two houses of Congress. It provided that the commissioner could defer funds for 60 days without holding a hearing and for an additional 30 days in which to reach a decision if a hearing had been held. The House had initially voted to prohibit any deferral until after a hearing; the Senate had rejected a similar proposal. Civil rights supporters feared that the House provision, known as the Fountain Amendment, would lead to deliberate noncompliance through an extended hearing process.

2. *Congressional Record*, daily edition, 28 February 1967, pp. S-2677–82.

3. Interview with William Cannon, Bureau of the Budget, 31 October 1967.

4. Cf. N. C. Thomas and H. L. Wolman, "The Presidency and Policy Formulation: The Task Force Device," *Public Administration Review* 29 (September/October 1969): 459–71.

5. See Bailey and Mosher, *ESEA: The Office of Education Administers a Law* (Syracuse: Syracuse University Press, 1968), chaps. 5 and 6.

6. H.R. 6230 and S. 1125 and H.R. 6232 and S. 1126, respectively.

7. This discussion relies heavily upon the excellent description in the *1967 Congressional Quarterly Almanac*, "Two-Year Elementary School Aid Bill Enacted," pp. 611–26.

8. It was suggested by some observers of the committee that Perkins was attempting to establish his position as chairman following the decision of the House not to seat the former chairman, Representative Adam C. Powell (D.-N.Y.). Others remarked that the full committee hearings stemmed from Perkins' desire to avoid turning the bill over to the General Education Subcommittee chaired by Representative Roman Pucinski (D.-Ill.)

9. U.S. Congress, House, Committee on Education and Labor, *Hearings on Elementary and Secondary Education Amendments of 1967*, 90th Cong. 1st sess., 2, 3, 6, 7, and 8 March 1967, p. 307 (hereinafter cited as House Hearings, 1967 ESEA Amendments).

10. Ibid., pp. 594–95.

11. Ibid., Pt. 2, 9, 10, 13, 14, 15, 16, 17, 18, and 20 March 1967, p. 1090.

12. Ibid., p. 352.

13. Ibid., p. 440.

14. Dr. Miller directed a study of Title III for USOE in 1966. See U.S. Senate, Committee on Labor and Public Welfare, Subcommittee on Education, *Notes and Working Papers Concerning the Administration of Programs Authorized under Title III of Public Law 89-10, The Elementary and Secondary Education Act of 1965* (Washington, D.C.: U.S. Government Printing Office, 1967).

15. House Hearings, 1967 ESEA Amendments, p. 970.

16. Ibid., p. 244.

17. See her colloquy with Commissioner Howe on this point, ibid., pp. 289–91.

18. Ibid., p. 536.

19. Ibid., p. 331 and pp. 404–5.

20. Ibid., p. 331.

21. Ibid., pp. 1498–1539.

22. Interview with Louis Hausman, 12 October 1967.

23. *Congressional Record*, daily edition, 20 April 1967, p. H-4431.

24. "What's Wrong With Quie Substitute" (Press release, office of Carl Perkins, 21 April 1967). Inserted in the *Congressional Record*, daily edition, 26 April 1967, pp. H-4714–15.

25. NEA Division of Federal Relations, Memorandum to NEA Legislative Leaders, 24 April 1967.

26. "Catholics Still Oppose School Plan," *Washington Post*, 27 April 1967.

27. "New House G.O.P. Plan Raises Private School Aid," *New York Times*, 27 April 1967.

28. Interview, 28 November 1967.

29. Ibid.

30. Interview, 23 January 1968.

31. Dr. Bernard E. Donovan, 26 April 1967, as reported in USOE press release, "School Superintendents Speak Out on Quie Substitute."

32. "Statement of President Lyndon B. Johnson on the Elementary and Secondary Education Act and the Proposed Quie Substitute," delivered at Crossland Vocational Center, 27 April 1967.

33. Quoted in *Education U.S.A. Washington Monitor*, 8 May 1967.

34. "School Aid Bill Amendments Are Submitted," *Washington Post*, 20 May 1967.

35. Interview, 6 October 1967.

36. Interview, 18 September 1967.

37. The press concluded otherwise. See "South Wins Round on School Bill," *Washington Post*, 24 May 1967.

38. *Congressional Record*, daily edition, 23 May 1967, p. H-5934.

39. "House Blocks G.O.P. Plan on Control of School Aid, *New York Times*, 25 May 1967.

40. "House Revives, Then Clears School Aid," *Washington Star*, 25 May 1967. See also "Battered School Bill Voted in House Fight," *Washington Post*, 25 May 1967.

41. U.S. Congress, Senate, Subcommittee on Education of the Committee on Labor and Public Welfare, *Hearings on Education Legislation, 1967*, 10 parts Washington, D.C.: U.S. Government Printing Office, 1967). (Hereinafter referred to as 1967 Senate Hearings.)

42. Ibid., pp. 236, 1097.

43. Ibid., p. 1101.

44. Ibid., pp. 2238–39, 2337–76.

45. Ibid., p. 1239.

46. Interview, Senator Wayne Morse, 13 June 1968.

47. *Congressional Record*, daily edition, 8 December 1967, p. S-18269.

48. *Congressional Record*, daily edition, 1 December 1967, p. S-17714.

49. The roll calls occurred when Senator Robert Griffin (R.-Mich.) moved to amend the Dirksen amendment so as to leave it up to local school authorities to determine if they would use federal funds for busing. Griffin's amendment lost on a 38–38 tie. Senator Robert Kennedy (D.-N.Y.), who arrived too late to vote, then moved to reconsider the vote. Dirksen then moved to table the motion to reconsider. The motion to table then lost on another tie, 39–39, and the motion to reconsider then carried, 40–38. See *Congressional Record*, daily edition, 4 December 1967, pp. S-17840–42. Also see "School Busing Issue Stirs Debate," *Washington Post*, 5 December 1967; and "Dirksen's School-Bus Defeat Reflects Rise of Griffin," *Washington Post*, 10 December 1967.

50. *Congressional Record*, daily edition, 5 December 1967, p. S-17947. See also "Dirksen Withdraws Anti-Busing Plan," *Washington Post*, 6 December 1967.

51. "Morse Plans School Bill Amendment," *Washington Post*, 7 December 1967.

52. See "14.4 Billion Aid to Schools Voted by Senate," *New York Times*, 12 December 1967. The text of Gardner's letter appears in the *Times* and in the *Congressional Record*, daily edition, 11 December 1967, pp. S-18324–25.

53. *Congressional Record*, daily edition, 11 December 1967, p. S-18326.

54. Ibid., p. S-18316.

55. Ibid., p. S-18357.

56. Interview, Senator Wayne Morse, 13 June 1968.

57. Interview, member of the press corps, 15 December 1967.

58. Interview with a House conferee, 25 March 1968.

59. Interview, 2 January 1968.

60. Interview, House conference committee member, 25 March 1968.

61. *Congressional Record*, daily edition, 15 December 1967, pp. H-17177–78, S-18999.

62. Interview, 23 May 1968.

63. "House Shifts Bill on Teacher Corps," *New York Times*, 16 June 1967.

64. *Congressional Record*, daily edition, 28 June 1967, p. S-9108.

65. Ibid.

66. Ibid., p. S-9109.

67. The first amendment, which lost 28–55, would have extended for two years the school disaster program and temporary provisions for aid to federally impacted areas, and for one year provisions of ESEA relating to children of military personnel overseas and to indian children. *Congressional Record*, daily edition, 28 June 1967, p. S-9114. The second amendment would have extended only the disaster aid and impacted areas programs. It lost 25–56. See ibid., p. S-9117. Morse opposed the amendments on the grounds of their procedural inappropriateness in the situation.

68. See Thomas and Wolman, "Presidency and Policy Formulation."

69. "Education, the Fifth Freedom—Message from the President of the United States," House Document No. 247, 90th Cong. 2nd sess. *Congressional Record*, daily edition, 5 February 1968, pp. H-778–81. This discussion of the Higher Education Amendments of 1968 draws upon the detailed account in the *1968 Congressional Quarterly Almanac*, "Congress Extends Major Education Programs," pp. 491–99.

70. "Johnson Priorities on Education Hit," *Washington Post*, 8 February 1968.

71. Interview, member of House Education and Labor Committee, 25 March 1968.

72. *Congressional Record*, daily edition, 9 May 1968, p. H-3570.

73. "ACE Urges Congress to Eliminate Student Anti-Riot Amendments," *H.E.N.A.* 17 (31 May 1968): 1.

74. *Congressional Record*, daily edition, 24 July 1968, pp. H-7397–400.

75. "Conferees Back School Riot Curb," *New York Times*, 18 September 1968.

76. House hearings held by the General Subcommittee of Education under chairmanship of Representative Roman L. Pucinski (D.-Ill.) gave extensive attention to the report of the advisory council. Several of its members testified and the report received favorable comment. See U.S. House, General Subcommittee on Education of the Committee on Education and Labor, *Hearings on the Partnership for Learning and Earning Act of 1968* (Washington, D.C.: U.S. Government Printing Office, 1968).

77. This discussion draws from the detailed account in the *1968 Congressional Quarterly Almanac*, "Vocational Education," pp. 500–504.

78. See the remarks of Representative Marvin L. Esch (R.-Mich.) during floor debate in the House. *Congressional Record*, daily edition, 15 July 1968, pp. H-6554–55.

79. Richard F. Fenno, Jr., *The Power of the Purse: Appropriations Politics in Congress* (Boston: Little, Brown, 1966) and Aaron Wildavsky, *The Politics of the Budgetary Process* (Boston: Little, Brown, 1964).

80. Interview, Representative Daniel J. Flood, 16 January 1968.

81. See U.S. Congress, House Subcommittee of the Committee on Appropriations, *Hearings on Departments of Labor and Health, Education and Welfare Appropriations for 1968*, pt. 3 (Washington, D.C.: U.S. Government Printing Office, 1967), pp. 89–346 passim.

82. See chapter 5.

83. Interview, Representative Melvin R. Laird, 6 March 1968.

84. Interview, Representative Daniel J. Flood, 16 January 1968.

85. Interview, Dr. Samuel Halperin, September 5, 1968.

III
THE POLICY
PROCESS

5

INSTITUTIONS, INDIVIDUALS, AND THEIR ROLES

The national educational policy process included seventy-seven individuals occupying positions in various institutions: the bureaucracy, the Presidency, Congress, private associations, and organizations outside the federal government. Although the educational policies analyzed are the result of interactions among these individuals and institutions, this should not be regarded as a definitive identification of the participants in a closed system. Rather, it is a working aggregation of persons and groups who manifested much more than a casual involvement in the formulation of the policies implemented in the programs of USOE.

This chapter examines the individuals and institutions comprising the educational policy process. Since, as Emmette Redford has observed, policy is ultimately determined "by interaction among strategic positions within organizations," [1] the analysis focuses on the characteristics and goals of the institutions. Inasmuch as men occupy those "strategic positions," individuals within institutions must also be analyzed if we are to understand the operation of the policy process. Individual behavior in organizations being in large part a function of official positions, the analysis of individuals will concentrate on the official roles of the participants in the policy process.

Using Redford's description, "official roles are patterns of behavior induced by specialized positions, or by the rules and conventions of society for persons occupying positions." [2] Two types of official roles have particular significance for this analysis, purposive and representational. The individuals who were interviewed gave functional descriptions of their policy-related activity, and they indicated to whom they regarded themselves responsible in performing that activity. In order to avoid confusion with the terms purposive and representational as they are commonly employed,[3] and to describe more accurately this data, I will use the terms *policy role* and *accountability perspective*. These are subtypes of official role that describe the individual's perception of his behavior in the policy process and the reference group that he employs to direct and rationalize that behavior.

The interviews strongly suggested that functional policy-role perceptions were primarily institutionally determined. There appeared to be some broader factors influencing accountability perspectives along with institutional considerations arising from the individual's position. The data do not make apparent the extent to which individuals can alter or modify institutional goals and activity, but there are cases in which certain individuals were perceived by others as exerting a determinative influence on specific policy decisions. Since the interviews were open-ended and uniform responses were not obtained from all respondents, the analysis is necessarily qualitative.

The individuals constituting the educational policy process were definitely an elite group as measured by their educational achievement and their occupations. All had baccalaureate degrees, and 85 percent had obtained a graduate or professional degree. Their occupations, as they defined them, were of high status, with professionals in education, law, and public service predominating.

The distribution of the policy makers was strongly skewed with respect to their regional background and their partisan identification. The Northeast and the Midwest were heavily overrepresented while the South and West were underrepresented. The partisan identifications of the policy makers were predominantly Democratic. This condition is not surprising given the fact of a Democratic administration and Democratic majorities in Congress.

Issue Perspectives of Policy Makers

The issue perspectives, policy preferences, and general attitudes toward education of the policy makers were not systematically surveyed. Nevertheless, certain concerns and themes that the respondents expressed with some frequency and often considerable intensity provide a basis for describing the attitudinal climate in the policy process. The policy makers expressed their views indirectly in responding to questions about their roles and their perceptions of the policy process and directly in response to the following questions which were asked randomly as time permitted:

1. What do you think the federal role should be in elementary/secondary education? in higher education?

2. What are your views concerning the question of more general as opposed to categorical aid?
3. How can the federal government most effectively aid in dealing with the problem of unequal educational opportunity?
4. What is the current impact of the church-state issue?

The responses were so varied in frequency, direction, and intensity that the descriptions which follow must be regarded as rough indicators of attitudes rather than a distinctive pattern.

The respondents tended to see two major roles for the federal government in elementary/secondary education: promoter of change and innovation and supporter of existing educational efforts. These roles were not generally perceived as in conflict, although a few respondents raised the question of whether the primary federal role should be additive or innovative. Generally, those persons who commented on the matter appeared to be concerned primarily with either the willingness and capacity of the federal government to continue support of existing efforts or with the capacity of the educational system to develop new techniques and adapt existing ones to the most difficult task that it faced, the education of disadvantaged children. Those who expressed a preference for an additive-supportive federal role tended to be representatives of education associations and members of Congress and their staffs. The principal exponents of an innovative-directive federal role were located mainly in presidential staff offices, including the Bureau of the Budget, and in the university-foundation group of outside experts. Bureaucrats in HEW and USOE seemed to manifest a pragmatic acceptance and appreciation of both roles and the conflict between them.

Much less attention was paid to the federal role in higher education and, indeed, it generated little controversy. Most respondents who expressed an opinion regarded the principal issue as the question of direct unrestricted federal grants to institutions. The prevailing view was that institutional grants were "inevitable" given the "central importance" of higher education in society and the growing gap between institutional resources and expenses. The major difficulty with the concept of institutional grants, noted by both supporters and opponents of the idea, was the basis on which the money would be made available. Representative Sam Gibbons (D.-Fla.), an opponent, argued that it would be "politically impossible" to develop satisfactory criteria for awarding the grants. A supporter of the grants, President William G. Friday of the University of North Carolina, saw the problem in this light:

> The real problem is to provide an instrument or means of federal support which does not destroy institutional quality in the process. Enrollment will obviously have to be a factor, but other variables must be included. If we get head-count federal aid, we will have the same problems with Congress that we now have with our state legislatures.[4]

The alternative to the institutional grants endorsed by Gibbons and a few other critics was direct aid to students. However, the Equal Opportunity Bank proposal of Professor Jerrold Zaccharias (see chapter 3) received only one mention and it was negative.

The question concerning the issue of general as opposed to categorical aid produced the only distinctive pattern of opinion. Of the 30 persons who expressed a definite point of view, 12 were supporters of the existing categorical approach, 8 advocated a move to general aid, and the remaining 10 adopted a mixed position calling for the retention of some specialized categorical programs along with the development of limited and ultimately unrestricted general aid. The proponents of the categorical approach tended to base their case on the argument that only through specific direction and channeling of federal funds could critical problems be solved. They assumed that the existing system of public education was not capable of achieving desired objectives. They were particularly harsh in their criticism of the performance of state education agencies. A prevailing thesis among defenders of categorical programs was that money made available to the states for distribution according to state plans would merely be "poured down a rathole."

Another argument in support of the categorical approach was that it was necessary to prevent a renewed flareup of the church-state issue. Some respondents feared that general aid, even the limited version embodied in the block-grant concept of the Quie Amendment, would result in exclusion of sectarian school children under state constitutional provisions and a conse-quent renewal of Catholic opposition to any federal educational assistance unless it included religious schools and colleges. Defenders of general aid stressed the importance of local and state control and discounted the alleged ineptitude of state education agencies and the threat of renewed church-state controversy. Advocates of a mixed approach tended to agree with the theoretical case for general aid but felt that serious problems would emerge if a precipitous shift were instituted. They also saw great merit in the continuation of a limited number of categorical programs designed to deal with particularly intractable problems.

The disagreement over the structure for administering federal aid did not extend to perceptions of the effectiveness of existing implementation by USOE. Those respondents who took a position stressed the need for more effective evaluation of programs; they deplored the piecemeal, ad hoc, instrumental orientation of federal assistance to education; and they called for a more timely and efficient distribution of funds. Some respondents suggested that machinery for policy coordination that would provide integration and focus for the federal effort in education was urgently needed and that this could be obtained most effectively through the establishment of a cabinet-level Department of Education and Manpower. Most support for an upgrading of the federal education bureaucracy came from education lobby group representatives and from congressional Republicans. The administration opposed such a move.

The question regarding how the federal government could most effectively attack the problem of unequal educational opportunity produced no clear suggestions. Although there was wide recognition of the need to focus federal efforts on underprivileged and handicapped children, there was little indication that anyone felt that a ready solution existed. In fact, there seemed to be substantial agreement that current efforts were largely ineffective. About all that could be cited on a positive note was a general belief in the capacity of further research, federally funded of course, to develop means of improving instruction and making education more effective. Even here, however, a few respondents cautioned that the development and diffusion of innovations requires time as well as money.

The church-state problem was generally regarded as quiescent although all who mentioned it remained acutely sensitive to its potential explosiveness. The response of Ralph N. Huitt, assistant secretary of HEW for legislation, most clearly captured the prevailing position:

> You don't solve these things. You keep moving on them. [The
> church-state issue] will be in a moving balance for the forseeable future.
> Private school kids must be included otherwise there will be no federal
> programs. There will need to be more artful dodges and halfway houses.[5]

There was also a widespread feeling that the Catholics were reasonable and moderate in their demands.

In addition to specific responses to the four questions, there was a pervasive theme that the level at which federal education programs were being funded was grossly inadequate. The ideas were repeatedly expressed that "we need to do more," "we must give the schools money to do what is necessary," "we ought to be funding at the level of authorization," etc. There was also a pragmatic, occasionally wistful, realization that the costs of the Vietnam war and inflation had imposed budgetary constraints that would continue to limit accomplishments and maintain the gap between aspiration and achievement. As William G. Carey, assistant director of the budget, put it:

> Regardless of where our hearts are we may be unable to fully fund the
> authorized programs for education. We may have to cut already
> inadequate appropriations. We may, for fiscal and budgetary reasons,
> have to participate in across the board rollback.[6]

This brief summary of the substantive attitudes and issue perspectives is in no way comprehensive. The attitudinal "profile" sketched here is merely indicative of how educational policy makers tended to view the problems with which they had to deal. It is to the institutional participants in the policy process and the individuals who occupied strategic positions within them that we now turn.

Institutional Participants and Official Roles

The Operating Agency: USOE

At the heart of the policy process is the agency (or group of agencies) with primary responsibility for the operation of the programs that implement the goals of Congress and the President. In the educational policy process, that agency is USOE. It is the primary education unit in HEW and the central federal agency in this policy area.

Established in 1867, USOE is not a newcomer to the federal bureaucracy. For most of its existence, however, it functioned primarily as a vehicle for gathering and disseminating statistics and information on developments in education. With the enactment of the impacted-areas legislation, the Cooperative Research Act, and NDEA in the 1950s, USOE acquired additional tasks that included the administration of formula grants, contracting with parties outside the federal government for the conduct of research, rendition of consultative services, and direct operation of a limited number of special educational programs. This increased activity resulted in an expansion of USOE's staff and budget, but it did not dispel the image of the agency as timorous, unimaginative, hidebound, and unduly responsive to the established education profession and its national associations.[7] As late as 1962, the office "remained suspect of mediocrity if not incompetence."[8] Bailey has characterized the "ancien regime" at USOE as "an 'old-line' bureau" marked by: internal fragmentation with power lodged in "guilds of professional specialists" and no means of policy coordination; "superannuated personnel and personnel systems"; an archaic system of "financial and management accountability"; isolation within the executive branch, particularly with respect to the HEW hierarchy; and a pervasive timidity born of "fear of the charge of Federal control."[9]

The transformation of USOE into a more vigorous agency which would assume a major role in the development and coordination of federal educational policies began in 1962 with the appointment of Francis Keppel, then dean of the Harvard Graduate School of Education, as commissioner. Keppel's initial contributions involved facilitating the enactment of long-delayed education legislation—HEFA and the Vocational Education Act in 1963, ESEA and HEA in 1965—and the appointment of a few key people to positions in USOE's Office of Program and Legislative Planning.[10]

These efforts helped to improve the agency's external relations with the departmental leadership, the White House, and Congress, but they did not correct the internal problems that plagued it. Following the passage of ESEA Keppel moved quickly to gear up the agency for the effective discharge of the multiple responsibilities that the statute imposed on it through a thorough reorganization of both the structure and staff. The story of that reorganization is superbly recounted elsewhere;[11] its major effects were to rationalize the bureau structure of USOE by basing it primarily on educational levels, to provide the agency with a full range of staff offices including a separate unit for planning and evaluation, and to reshuffle a large number of long-time staff members causing many of them to retire or leave for other agencies. There followed a heavy infusion of new officials, most of whom were considerably younger and who came from universities, research institutions, and innovative educational operations.

By mid-1967 the trauma of the reorganization had passed and the changes were institutionalized. The agency had, however, been transformed. Many of the new personnel remained, although there appeared to be a tendency for some of the former types of officials, ex-school administrators and teacher's college faculty members, to be appointed to policy-sensitive positions. The aura of excitement born of innovation and new functions had largely been replaced by a pragmatic determination to implement the new legislation effectively. Change was not dismissed as an objective, but it would be continual and controlled as USOE and the education community adjusted to the agency's new role of distributing substantial funds to state education agencies, local school districts, and institutions of higher education.

Structurally, the Office of Education was organized into five bureaus with responsibility for program operation, seven staff offices whose function was to help the commissioner to coordinate, plan, and evaluate programs, a centralized education statistical service, and the office of the commissioner. Nine regional offices under the direction of an associate commissioner constituted the field service. The bureaus were organized on the basis of three factors, educational levels, educational functions, and special constituencies. The Bureaus of Elementary and Secondary Education and of Higher Education were responsible for programs affecting the two basic educational levels. The Bureau of Adult, Vocational, and Library Programs dealt with major specialized constituencies. The Bureau of Research serviced the other bureaus and was the agency's link with the research community. These four bureaus were established in the 1965 reorganization. In the 1966 ESEA Amendments, Congress "legislated" a Bureau for the Education of the Handicapped, which came into being on July 1, 1967. A Bureau of Education Professions Development was established in February 1968 to consolidate and coordinate education personnel programs.

Since the bureaus are the primary operating units of the agency, their structure is of considerable importance. If statutory policy goals are to be integrated and coordinated by the Office, the structure should facilitate, or at least not impede, the commissioner's capacity to control policy development and program implementation. Internal management considerations dictate that there must be a fairly rational basis for the assignment of responsibilities to the bureaus. However, since the bureaus are the agency's primary links with its environment, their task assignments must also reflect external conditions and constraints. The complexion of political, professional, and other forces in the environment often dictates a bureau structure at variance with that which internal management considerations would suggest. USOE's bureau structure, like that of most agencies, embodied a compromise between internal requirements and external realities. Of course, it should be recognized that administrative structure is dynamic and not static[12] and that there is no one best way of organizing a government agency.

The Bureaus of Elementary and Secondary Education and Higher Education reflected the basic division in the structure of American education which was also recorded in the major education legislation of the 1960s. The Bureau of Adult, Vocational, and Library Programs had responsibility for servicing an amalgam of unrelated and politically less potent education constituencies. The inability of professional vocational education and library interests to secure separate bureau status was regarded as an indication that their programs ranked lower on USOE's priority scale and was a clear reflection of their relative lack of political clout. The administrative efficiency rationale for combining specialized functions in a single bureau was insufficient to prevail against the handicapped children's lobby groups. Although not large or highly visible, those groups enjoyed special access to and support from members and staff of the Senate Education Subcommittee. They were able to convert this asset into congressionally mandated bureau status.[13]

The Bureau of Research represented recognition of the critical importance of research for improving education and promoting change. Commissioner Howe's decision to assign responsibility for implementation of EPDA to a new bureau along with established teacher-training programs and the beleaguered Teacher Corps involved internal and external considerations. It stemmed from a desire to emphasize the high priority accorded education-manpower programs and to give an innovative thrust to USOE's efforts in the area. Howe regarded EPDA as a creative statute and feared that its potential to promote changes in personnel development would be lost if implementation were left fragmented in the hands of established bureaus. The creation of the new bureau also provided a means of affording a measure of protection for the Teacher Corps by grouping it with related programs. Although some fragmentation of areas of responsibility existed, USOE's bureau structure embodied a viable balance between internal requirements of rationality and efficiency and external pressures and program demands.

At least some of the contradictions imposed by USOE's bureau structure were resolved through the internal structures of the bureaus. Within the bureaus were a number of divisions, each responsible for a major program or a group of related programs. Generally, the divisions were arranged to reflect factors not taken into account in establishing the bureau structure. The subdivisions were subdivided in turn into branches which constituted the operating line of the department.[14] The branches dealt with specific programs or sections of major programs. The branch chiefs were the agency's primary contact agents with the field. Initial recommendations were made at the branch level and some staff work originated there. Division chiefs constituted the first level of supervision and management of programs. Bureau chiefs had major coordinating roles to perform and were also the primary policy formulation agents in their respective areas of responsibility. The structure of USOE was hierarchical with three distinct levels below the commissioner: bureau, division, and branch.

The staff offices were designed to assist the commissioner and to centralize performance of administrative functions in the following areas: general administration, which included personnel, budget and financial operations, contracts, and general services; construction services; public information; legislative liaison; program planning and evaluation; and data processing and statistical services. Specialized staff offices existed to coordinate USOE and other agencies' programs for the disadvantaged and to administer desegregation compliance functions. All the staff offices furnished major support functions to the bureaus and the commissioner, but only two of them, Legislation and Program Planning and Evaluation, were extensively involved in the formulation of legislative proposals and general policy development.

The commissioner operated at the "institutional level of the organization." [15] With the direct aid of his deputy, two associate commissioners (for federal-state relations and international education), and two high-level personal assistants, he managed and directed the internal operations and external relations of the agency and functioned as the principal adviser on education policy to the President and the secretary of HEW. The structure of USOE was altered somewhat in the Nixon administration. The most notable changes were the "regrouping" instituted by Commissioner Sidney P. Marland after confirmation of his appointment in December 1970, and the establishment of the National Institute of Education in the Education Amendments of 1972.

Marland placed the major bureaus and offices under five deputy commissioners for management, external relations, school systems, development, and higher education, and designated his principal aide as executive deputy commissioner. He justified the insertion of a new layer of officials between the commissioner and the operating units on the ground that USOE was too complex for a single person to administer. Rather, the commissioner, his executive deputy, and the five deputy commissioners would function as a management team. These changes do not appear to have significantly altered the pattern of USOE's internal operations.

Congress established the NIE as one of the two principal components of a new Education Division of HEW along with USOE. This action lodged responsibility for leadership and support of educational research in a separate agency formally on a par with USOE.

The organizational structure, size, and budget of the Office of Education in 1967 and 1968 were quite different from that of the agency Frank Keppel took over in 1962. No longer was USOE a federal service organization that gathered information and assisted educators in the performance of their roles as they defined them. It had become a major federal operating agency concerned not with "the minutiae of educational operation and administration" but with "providing stimulus and support for programs which will lead to qualitative changes in the nation's education system." [16] That mission, to improve the quality of American education, meant that USOE was inevitably thrust into a maelstrom of political conflict as its proposals and activities had a profound impact on the financing and operation of all segments of American education.

The key strategic positions in USOE were those of the commissioner, the deputy commissioner, the six bureau chiefs, the associate commissioner for federal-state relations, and the assistant commissioners who headed the staff offices for Legislation and Planning and Evaluation. Other officials, although obviously not omitted from the policy-making process, did not appear to have been as centrally involved.

USOE officials filled three primary policy roles which were determined in large part by official position. These can be designated as upper-level policy maker, supportive staff aide, and operating program administrator. The upper-level policy maker represents the agency in its top-echelon relations with Congress, HEW, and the Presidency. The principal policy maker, Commissioner Howe, described his policy role in terms of that involvement:

> I am probably involved more than anyone in [educational] policy development, although my role isn't paramount. . . .
> My role is kind of a middle-level crossroads at the top of the bureaucracy. I know about and can comment on most proposed changes relating to education. . . . My involvement is illustrated by writing the first draft of the President's 1968 education message. Because of his deep interest in education, I am much more involved in policy at the White House level than people connected with programs at this level elsewhere [in the bureaucracy]. There are some programs which I conceive at the start. . . . Increasingly I get a chance to comment and make an input.[17]

The staff aides had varying assignments that facilitated the commissioner's task:

> I am the commissioner's alter ego. My job is to manage the shop in terms
> of personnel, implementation of legislation and budgets.[18]

And:

> I work with the leaders that shape educational policy, the Big Six (i.e.,
> the National Education Association, the American Association of School
> Administrators, the Council of Chief State School Officers, the National
> Congress of Parents and Teachers, the National School Boards
> Association, and the National Association of State Boards of Education).
>   I try to interpret developments out there [in the field] that will have
> an impact on us. I am a feed-in. I am a reporter. I keep the doors open. I
> am paid to know what these organizations are thinking, then I present
> this information to the commissioner. . . . I am the one person who has
> been around, who knows the people in the states, in the field, and in the
> organizations.[19]

Two other principal staff aides described their roles as "a coordinator in the
process of developing legislation," [20] and as "a filter between the parochial
concerns of the bureaus and the broader concerns of the commissioner and the
White House." [21]

The program administrators, who all were the chiefs of the agency's six
bureaus, coordinated and directed USOE's operations. They tended to define
their policy roles within the boundaries of their respective program areas and
to stress the instrumental and implementational rather than the formulative
and developmental aspects of policy:

> We are the OE for elementary and secondary education. Our mission is
> assessing needs, trying to assign priorities to the needs and mapping
> strategies for meeting the needs. Our major role is that of catalyst for
> development. We have to use our [funds] to persuade states and localities
> to use their money in the most efficient way.[22]

Or:

> My role is, hopefully, to carry out the objectives of our bureau's
> twenty-seven programs in such a way as not to intrude on the freedom of
> the educational institutions. I also have a constant concern over whether
> present programs improve higher education and maintain educational
> opportunity. I try to secure the most efficient use of resources.[23]

And:

> I have to assess needs and relate them to available funds. I ask what needs
> to be done, what can be accomplished in terms of the legislation passed

by Congress. I don't sit down and determine policy. But on a pragmatic day-to-day response to problems, concepts emerge that taken together constitute policy. Policy and philosophy come after the fact.[24]

The bureau chiefs contributed to policy formulation largely through recommendations arising in the course of directing program implementation. Their policy roles involved assessment of needs and making choices between alternative expenditures of funds within limits set by higher executive and legislative directives.

All USOE officials recognized their accountability within the bureaucratic hierarchy. Commissioner Howe saw himself as "responsible to the Secretary and the President" while his deputy's accountability was "to the commissioner and beyond him to the administration." Other staff aides also felt that their primary responsibility was to the commissioner. The bureau chiefs manifested similar hierarchical accountability perspectives, but they differed from their colleagues in that they explicitly mentioned responsibility to external reference groups which included "the education community," "higher education as a community," "the professionals in the fields we are involved in," "the four congressional committees," and "the advisory committee" to the bureau.

The recognition of these groups as objects of accountability reflects the political sensitivity of the program administrator's position. The USOE bureau chief operates at a critical juncture in the governmental structure where general policy directives are broken down and transformed into programs designed to translate goals into accomplishments. They must not only give effect to the concerns of the administration, but also must become intermediaries between the field and the higher echelons. It is at this level that the operating problems that arise from the divisions and branches are synthesized and policy changes, in the form of new or modified regulations, guidelines, and basic policy assumptions are suggested. The bureau chief has a perspective that is broad enough to enable him to relate his unit's operations to those of the other bureaus and yet sufficiently close to the field that he can effectively convey an expert assessment of needs, issues, and operating problems to the higher echelons.

Bureau chiefs regularly deal directly with clientele groups, professionals in the field, key congressional committee members and their staffs, and members of the White House staff and the Bureau of the Budget. In this sensitive location, the bureau chiefs often find themselves in conflict with external groups such as professional associations, the upper-echelon planning group within the administration, and with key congressional figures. Although they do not "wheel and deal" at the secretarial and presidential level, they seem to realize that their location at the juncture between the nitty gritty of program administration and general policy determination accords them the opportunity to make a continuous and important contribution. It is a contribution that varies between bureaus, by individual personalities, and with external events and conditions, but it is a substantial one nonetheless.

The HEW Hierarchy

Although USOE is an operating agency of considerable size, it is a part of the Department of Health, Education, and Welfare, and as such its policies are subject to considerable control and direction by the departmental hierarchy. The HEW officials who were centrally involved in educational policy development included the secretary, the undersecretary, the assistant secretaries (for education, legislation, and planning and evaluation), the comptroller, a deputy assistant secretary for legislation, and an assistant general counsel for legislation. While most of them had responsibilities in several policy areas, they all contributed substantially to educational policy. The assigned task of the top HEW executives is to manage, direct, and coordinate a heterogeneous group of agencies that operate a bewildering array of programs. To use an analogy from the business world, the HEW hierarchy is a governmental holding company that has within its empire a diversified group of operating companies held together by their efforts to promote the general welfare. The functional interrelationships of the operating agencies are not strong, while in many cases their independence from departmental control is considerable. In the case of USOE, departmental-agency coopera- tion and agreement on objectives in policy development and implementation were substantial although not without problems. Much of the compatibility that existed appears to have been a function of harmonious interpersonal relations between departmental and agency officials rather than a product of formal structure.

Secretary John W. Gardner, an upper-level policy maker, dominated the HEW participants in the educational policy process. All of them clearly recognized his primacy with concomitant responsibility for policy formulation and implementation. The secretary's concerns extended beyond education, however, and the staff support of his top-level assistants was essential. Their principal policy-role types included manager-planners:

> I'm not just a coordinator. I'm not a eunuch. I get tested about the programs. I become an adviser to the secretary. . . . I am here to help run the Department. I am not shy about making a contribution to the debate over policy alternatives. I have, perhaps, better information [than most other officials].[25]

Substantive experts:

> This is a staff office. My job is to support the secretary on major long-range policy questions. . . . The secretary asks me what HEW

should be doing. It is a long-run task-oriented operation. . . . I also nurture projects—get them off the ground . . . I become involved with various aspects of the legislative and budgetary processes.[26]

And brokers:

We are brokers. We try to put together coalitions on behalf of policies which the secretary and the commissioner want. I try to keep people informed and I send out information. . . . Much of what we do is legwork. There is nothing sophisticated about it. It involves information. It is affected by personalities, tempers, issues, and the time of the year.[27]

All the HEW officials advised the secretary, directly or indirectly, with respect to policy development at various points in the process and all had some degree of responsibility for external relations either within the government or outside. The activities that these officials performed in their policy roles were related to each other in a systematic fashion that helped the secretary to discharge his responsibilities in education. Most of the major difficulties he encountered were the product of constraints outside the HEW hierarchy.

The Presidency

Beyond USOE and HEW in the education policy system were President Johnson and the members of his staff and the Bureau of the Budget officials who had assignments in the area. The institutionalized Presidency is an integral part of all functional policy processes, but with the exception of the Chief Executive himself and a few top aides with broad portfolios, the number of participants in specific policy areas is fairly small. President Johnson's interest in education and other social welfare policy areas made HEW a "presidential department." [28] This meant that ranking departmental and agency executives had ready access to top-level presidential aides and that policy development and implementation in program areas such as education were accorded more careful scrutiny and more time than older established program areas such as agriculture.

One of President Johnson's special assistants, Douglass Cater, was assigned responsibility for liaison within the educational policy process. Cater served as the principal point of access to the White House for Washington representatives of the education associations and members of the education community. He was also one of many points of access to the Presidency for congressional, USOE, and HEW personnel in the educational policy process. Operating with little staff support, Cater saw his policy role as promoting and enhancing the President's interest in education:

It is a nebulous role—not at all systematic. I try to take as much burden as I can off his shoulders. I serve as a liaison with OE, the committees in

Congress and the education constituency. I try to see that there is direction to his thinking. [I am] not an original idea man, but a seeker of ideas. [I] try to get ideas that don't get cranked up through the bureaucracy. I know the President's ideas and try to see to it that they are always considered . . . I keep things moving.[29]

Cater did not, however, play a major role in developing education legislation during the 90th Congress. The President's interests in that task were looked after by the domestic policy staff headed by Special Assistant Joseph Califano and by key Budget Bureau officials. Califano directed an idea-gathering operation that annually tapped governmental officials, leading educators, and private citizens interested in education for policy suggestions and the latest thinking in the area.[30] Each year, the Califano staff developed a set of policy suggestions for the President. These suggestions along with proposals from USOE and HEW were the major sources from which the President's legislative proposals in education emerged.

The Bureau of the Budget was a major institutional participant in the educational policy process. Functioning within the Presidency as the largest and most bureaucratized staff arm of the President, the Bureau provided information and advice to the top-level decision makers and made important substantive contributions to education policy at various stages in the process. Unlike the White House staff, which was small, comprised of presidential appointees, and highly flexible with respect to its structure and the assignment of functional responsibilities, the Bureau was large, its personnel were predominantly governmental careerists, its structure much more permanent, its operating procedures routinized, and it had a well-developed set of institutional perspectives and attitudes regarding its role, the roles of other policy-process participants, and substantive issues of educational policy.

The director of the Budget, economist Charles Schultze, viewed his policy role as directing "a continuous action-reaction situation" between the Bureau and the agencies.[31] His principal functions were to reconcile the fiscal situation and policy objectives. He was more concerned with budgetary allocations than policy development, examining the "tradeoffs" within the "full budget for education." [32] As a presidential appointee who was not a Budget Bureau careerist, Schultze did not express a strong institutional viewpoint. His perspectives were personal and had a presidential orientation.

In contrast, the three Bureau careerists who were participants in the educational policy process spoke explicitly of a collective Budget Bureau role in preference to their individual roles, they had definite substantive policy perspectives, they believed that the Bureau had an important contribution to make to policy, and they expressed a skeptical and somewhat condescending attitude toward HEW and USOE except for the top executives, Gardner and Howe. They saw the Budget Bureau role as extending across the agencies and involving both policy formulation and implementation:

Our role tends to be compensatory in the sense that we as a presidential staff find inadequacies in policy initiative, planning and program development. We try to make up for it by proposing program initiatives and by insistence on rigorous analytic standards to accompany program proposals by action as a hair shirt by pressing for standards of program planning, evaluation and effectiveness that would not otherwise materialize.[33]

The Budget Bureau staff members took their budgetary functions for granted and also saw themselves as playing a major role in policy making. They functioned both "as advocates and critics with respect to the subject." [34] They regarded their participation in developing legislation as "providing a useful and independent source of information" unencumbered by clientele pressures and responsible only to the President.[35] Their responsibility to the President required that they ensure that federal educational policies and programs have the effect of eliminating the educational deficit of the nation, both qualitatively and quantitatively.

Substantively, the Budget Bureau officials admitted a strong bias against the state education agencies, which were seen as an intervening obstacle between the federal government and local authorities, and the established professional education groups, such as the National Education Association (NEA). They strongly preferred categorical assistance programs oriented toward change and innovation. In the Budget Bureau perspective, HEW was "a very loosely structured department distinguished for the weakness of its policy-making apparatus" [36] and USOE was an agency "dominated by state departments of education and schools of education" [37] that had proved insufficiently responsive to presidential leadership in meeting the educational problems of society. To a considerable extent, the Budget Bureau officials believed that money administered by USOE was poured "down a rathole" because it did not provide the desired return on programs. Although the criteria employed in assessing USOE's efficiency were never articulated clearly, these attitudes and perspectives led the Bureau of the Budget to try to correct perceived weaknesses in the policy process in HEW and USOE in order to increase responsiveness to presidential direction and independence from clientele pressures. In the meantime, the Bureau's function with respect to educational policy was "to make things happen that otherwise would not." [38]

It is not surprising, then, that this sharply defined set of policy-role conceptions and policy perspectives was accompanied by substantial tension and occasional open conflict between the Budget Bureau and the bureaucracy, education clientele groups, and their supporters in Congress. The Bureau's role in shaping education policy and in monitoring policy implementation extended well beyond that of mere staff support. Bureau officials functioned as independent experts on public policy who were concentrating on a problem area. They advocated new policies and programs, criticized policy proposals from other sources, and maintained a careful and critical surveillance of existing programs of USOE. They were suspicious of Congress, hostile to education lobbies, and deeply committed to what they regarded as the presidential goal of qualitatively improving American education. They provided the President with sustained staff support in the education area while exerting an important, independent impact on policy.

The policy roles of the participants in the educational policy process located in the institutionalized Presidency included idea brokers, advisers, advocates, and critics. The idea brokers and advisers reflected the obvious need of the President for factual information, analytic studies, and policy advice. The advocates and critics moved with considerable freedom of action to shape policy development and information within limits established by the President's broad policy goals. They were able to function as surrogates for the President because of the limited amount of time and energy that he can devote to any single domestic policy area. The sense of loyalty to the President—or, more precisely, to the presidential interest—was the dominant accountability perspective of these policy makers. They were central figures in the policy process, but their position and influence were dependent on him. While they could often act in his name, they could not have the same effect. Together with him, they were a major institutional participant in the policy process.

Congress: The Education Subcommittees

Legislation affecting USOE and its programs falls within the jurisdiction of the education subcommittees of the House Committee on Education and Labor and the Senate Committee on Labor and Public Welfare. (Education programs administered by other agencies are handled by the committees having jurisdiction over those areas.) The House and Senate education subcommittees presented sharply contrasting patterns of operation with respect to leadership styles, degree of partisanship, and use of staff personnel.

In the House, the Committee on Education and Labor had a long tradition of sharp partisan conflict.[39] The committee also tended to emphasize labor issues and problems in preference to education and its members had a relatively short tenure as they sought to move to positions on more prestigious committees.[40] The education work of the committee was apportioned among General, Special, and Select subcommittees on education which had responsibility for elementary/secondary and vocational education, higher education, and miscellaneous residual areas of education respectively. However, the three subcommittees did not make equally important contributions to education policy. This was due in part to differences in the importance of the subject matter and also to the leadership roles and interpersonal relations of committee members.

The Education and Labor Committee entered a new era with the advent of the 90th Congress. Its flamboyant former chairman, Representative Adam Clayton Powell (D.-N.Y.) was barred from taking his seat in the House and was succeeded by Representative Carl Perkins (D.-Ky.). The contrast between the two chairmen could hardly have been more striking. Powell was a dynamic, aggressive black from an urban ghetto district who ran the committee with a strong hand. He appointed to the committee staff persons with limited expertise in substantive matters and his manner frustrated and angered many of his fellow members. In spite of Powell's undeniable accomplishments and his roguishly attractive personality, the members of the committee had, in 1966, adopted a set of rules that sharply curtailed the powers of the chairman.[41]

Perkins, who became chairman when Powell was denied his seat, was a soft-spoken, modest man from a depressed rural coal-mining district in eastern Kentucky. Although the committee voted to continue the curbs on the chairman's powers in the 90th Congress, Perkins proceeded to dismiss twelve Powell appointees. The altered pattern of operations under the new rules and a different chairman along with decreased Democratic strength (down from 21–10 in the 89th to 19–14 in the 90th Congress) created an unpredictable situation. Fragmentation of leadership was almost inevitable on a committee with a nonassertive chairman with limited powers which had long been marked by a low level of integration and a high degree of interparty conflict.[42] Also, there was a history of an absence of cohesion among committee Democrats.[43] An additional factor contributing to conflict within the committee was its jurisdiction over antipoverty legislation. A major controversy arose in 1967 over extension of the basic authorization for the Office of Economic Opportunity.

In addition to Chairman Perkins, committee Democrats who were major participants in the educational policy process included Representatives Edith Green (D.-Ore.), chairman of the Special Education Subcommittee; Roman L. Pucinski (D.-Ill.), chairman of the General Education Subcommittee; Sam Gibbons (D.-Fla.); John Brademas (D.-Ind.); James O'Hara (D.-Mich.); and Hugh Carey (D.-N.Y.). As major subcommittee chairmen, Green and Pucinski had institutional bases for their participation. Brademas was the unofficial education spokesman of the Democratic Study Group (DSG), an informal organization of liberal House Democrats; O'Hara was one of the DSG leaders; Gibbons was a moderate who enjoyed informal recognition as the southern voice on the Committee; and Carey, an urban liberal, was a vigorous champion of the interests of Catholic education and handicapped children. On the Republican side, the principal policy-process members were Representatives Albert H. Quie (R.-Minn.) and Charles Goodell (R.-N.Y.).

None of the party leaders in the House were participants in the educational policy process although Majority Leader Carl Albert (D.-Okla.) was a member of the full committee.

The policy roles of the House committee members reflected its multiple power centers. Chairman Perkins regarded himself as responsible for securing enactment of the administration's legislative program. He denied that he was a spokesman for the administration, but he spoke of his role in terms of contesting with the Republicans. Mrs. Green also regarded the passage of legislation as her task, but where Perkins saw this in partisan terms, she felt that its objective should be qualitative improvement in education. According to Mrs. Green, the limiting factor in congressional education policy making was its narrow perspective focused on the specific statutes that authorize individual categorical aid programs. As she defined it, her role was to dampen partisan and ideological conflict in the committee by mediating between liberal Democrats and Republicans.[44] The other committee Democrats assumed varying roles based on either a deep interest in education or the special representation of identifiable external constituencies or both.

The two Republican leaders, Albert Quie and Charles Goodell, defined their roles in terms of criticizing the administration's proposals and developing alternatives to them. They expressed a classic legislative opposition leader's role.

The accountability perspectives of the House committee members focused on the educational needs and interests of their constituencies. After constituency needs, they extended to the administration, House Democrats and Republicans, the DSG, special education constituencies, and education generally. Many acknowledged more than one reference group.

The House committee staff members who were participants in the educational policy process included General Counsel H. D. Reed, Associate General Counsel William Gaul, and Minority Counsel Charles Radcliffe. These three staff men viewed themselves in terms of lawyer-client relationship with the committee members in which they performed technical legal services, acted as policy advisers, and performed political chores for the members on the House floor and in reelection contests. They all acknowledged that they had an impact on policy and they regarded themselves as responsible to the chairman or the ranking minority member and to the majority or minority members of the committee.

Other than provision of legal counsel, staff support on the House Committee was weak. According to one observer, the committee had never developed a good professional staff.[45] Instead, it relied heavily on the Office of Education for much of its supportive staff work. The dependence on USOE meant that the committee lacked an independent basis on which to criticize the agency or to develop alternatives to administration proposals. It also had the effect of limiting the influence of the education lobby groups with the committee. Representative Green believed that the committee "desperately needed more staff" both for the oversight of the agency and its programs and to provide technical services to educators in the field.[46] The minority staff, although much smaller, was generally acknowledged to be more effective in support of Republican members than the majority staff was in the performance of its functions.

There appear to be at least two explanations of the House committee's staff situation: first, Powell's extensive use of staff positions for patronage appointments with little or no regard to technical and political expertise provided no tradition of strong staff support; and, secondly, the members of the House, with only one major committee assignment, did a lot of their own legislative work. They did not have to depend extensively on personal or committee staffs.

The House committee participants in the educational policy process operated at two levels, in sub and full committee sessions and on the House floor. Their policy roles were both partisan and interest-oriented. They included majority and minority party leaders, ideological leaders, advocates of the education profession and of special education publics, and supportive staff members. Their policy differences were often sharp, both between and within party groups, and interpersonal relations were frequently acerbic. As a result, floor debate was extensive, amendments representing positions defeated in committee were offered frequently. The final outcomes were usually uncertain.

In the Senate, the Education Subcommittee of the Committee on Labor and Public Welfare presented a striking contrast to the picture of personal and partisan conflict, fragmented centers of power, and weak staff support that characterized the House committee. The full committee, chaired by Senator Lister Hill (D.-Ala.), and the Education Subcommittee, chaired by Senator Wayne Morse (D.-Ore.), had a long record of support for expanded federal aid to education that extended back to the passage of NDEA in 1958. The personal styles and operating methods of the Senate participants in the education policy system were oriented toward compromise and accommodation. The committee operation was, however, more bipartisan than nonpartisan in character. The dominant figure was Senator Morse. The full committee chairman, Senator Hill, concentrated on health policy, leaving education to Morse who interpreted his role as providing "bipartisan educational policy leadership" to the Senate and the Nation.[47] He was a loyal supporter of the administration position on education legislation, but he was willing to compromise, in committee and on the floor, to secure bipartisan agreement.

The major Republican figures were Senators Jacob Javits (R.-N.Y.) and Peter Dominick (R.-Colo.). Javits considered himself "the principal spokesman for the Republican party in the Senate on education legislation." [48] He took "a national perspective," but found that it never "ran at cross purposes" with the "interests of education in New York." Javits and Morse worked closely together in committee and on the floor to secure bipartisan agreements. Their substantive views on education policies were not far apart and they seldom had disagreements. The conservative position on education was expounded and defended by Senator Dominick. He expressed policy views similar to those of Representative Quie and stated that he frequently opposed the position taken by the administration and supported by Morse and Javits. He conceived of his role as "problem solving . . . to try to find new approaches where old ones show defects." [49]

The Senate Education Subcommittee received strong support from its staff. Three staff members were key policy makers: John S. Forsythe, general counsel for the Committee on Labor and Public Welfare; Charles Lee, professional staff member; and Roy Millenson, minority clerk. Lee was the principal staff figure for education. As his title indicated, he was a career congressional staff man. His policy role, as he defined it, was complex and far-reaching:

> The staff performs four or five major functions. The first is pure housekeeping. This involves examining draft legislation from the administration. You raise points concerning the drafts and suggest changes. It also involves scheduling hearings and witnesses, making sure enough senators are present and that they ask the important questions at issue. It involves editing the transcript of the hearings.
> We sit in on the markup sessions. . . . This is an expository function. We give a rationale for the legislation. . . . We try to make sure that all points of view are heard. By the time we get to markup sessions I have a good idea of where the power structure is. We try, however, to operate by consensus. We draw up a list of what is minimal, what can be compromised and what is boiler plate. In markup we use working papers which summarize what the various provisions really amount to. . . . Before this there is a lot of negotiation with the interest groups.
> We try not to make the decisions. We try to set forth alternatives in as careful and rational a manner as possible.[50]

Lee had a "confidential relationship" with Morse that enabled him to act as an alter ego. Repeatedly, I was told that Morse's thinking could be ascertained by talking to Lee and that Lee's acceptance of a point at issue would ensure its approval by Morse and the committee. Undoubtedly Morse depended heavily on Lee for advice and supportive staff work. His responsibilities as a member of the Foreign Relations and the District of Columbia Committees made it imperative that he use staff effectively. His effective leadership performances in conducting hearings, chairing markup sessions, and managing education bills on the floor would have been impossible without the kind of support Lee provided. But Morse was clearly in command of the relationship at all times and Lee pointedly emphasized the limits of the staff man's role and his subordination to his "principal." [51] Morse and Lee were an effective team which gave strong leadership on education to the subcommittee and the Senate.

The two other Senate staff members with a major involvement in education matters defined their roles with reference to Lee. Committee Counsel Forsythe stated that "much of what I do is similar to what Charlie Lee does . . . [but] I'm more concerned with legal problems than he is." [52] Forsythe also spent some of his time on other areas of committee work. Minority Clerk Roy Millenson described himself as "a Charlie Lee for the minority" whose job was "to help the senators . . . to give advice . . . to get the best possible legislation even though imperfect on the books." [53] Millenson regarded himself as responsible to Javits and the Republican members of the subcommittee.

The striking feature of the Senate Education Subcommittee staff, in contrast with the staff situation in the House, was its highly professional character. Senate staff members had strong backgrounds acquired through training or experience in the specialized areas in which they worked. Senators utilize the skills of committee and personal staffs out of necessity. A senator who does not develop reliable staff support cannot hope to be effective across the full range of his committees. This condition, a function of the Senate's smaller size, makes well-qualified staff an operational necessity. It also means that staff members are afforded substantial opportunities to influence policy. The competence of its staff also increased the Senate subcommittee's independence from USOE. Although the senators and the subcommittee staff had frequent interaction with HEW and USOE personnel, they also had close relations with education lobby groups. Their inputs came from a somewhat broader range than those of the House committee, and their perspectives on education issues and legislation were correspondingly less parochial.

Congress: The Appropriations Subcommittees

The subcommittees handling HEW's annual appropriation functioned in the manner described by Fenno's study. [54] The House subcommittee acted as guardian of the treasury with a strong budget-cutting bias and the Senate subcommittee as an appeals court that generally restored part but not all of the cuts. The House subcommittee had a more direct impact on substantive education policies. Its chairman, Representative Daniel J. Flood (D.-Pa.), ranking minority member, Representative Melvin R. Laird (R.-Wis.), and clerk, Robert Moyer, were leading educational policy-process participants.

The subcommittee held extensive hearings on USOE's budget requests for fiscal 1968 and 1969 and closely questioned Commissioner Howe and several of his principal subordinates regarding their operations, the basis for specific USOE policies, future policy intentions and plans, and allocation decisions in their budget requests. In 1966, the House subcommittee was instrumental in affecting a shift in responsibility for enforcing Title VI of the Civil Rights Act of 1964 from USOE to the departmental level under direction of the secretary. The subcommittee also maintained oversight of administrative management practices in the department and its agencies.

The House Appropriations Subcommittee was a tightly integrated bipartisan operation. Its primary decisional norm was "to make the maximum cut and do the least damage." [55] In addition to choosing between alternative uses of limited funds, as in 1968 when it decided not to cut school construction as much as the administration had requested and to make sizable reductions in scholarship and training programs, the subcommittee felt at liberty to require or suggest alternative means for agreed upon ends.

The Senate Appropriations Subcommittee held only perfunctory hearings on USOE's appropriation. Its chairman, Senator Hill, and ranking minority member, Senator Javits, were also members of the legislative committee and tended to support larger funding in this area than the House committee. They did not try to influence education policy through the subcommittee other than to restore some of the House cuts. The clerk of the Senate subcommittee, Herman Downey, disclaimed any policy-making role. "Of course," he remarked, "if I don't like something that is being done, or if I think something ought to be funded more than it is and I tell Senator Hill about it, why something else might happen. But I'm not saying it will." [56] Overall, the Senate Appropriations Subcommittee exerted modest influence on education policy.

Interests and Interest Group Participants

A wide array of interests were represented in the operation of the education policy process, and a number of the more active and forceful groups furnished policy-process participants. Before examining those groups, however, it will be helpful to consider briefly the function of interest groups in American politics. A widely held theory conceives of interest groups as linkages between public opinion and public policy. Generally, they involve a single or a few interests and provide a form of functional representation that supplements geographic representation in legislative bodies. Truman's carefully developed theory of interest groups regards them as the primary units of political behavior.[57] Interests, or shared attitudes, that exist in society are the basis of group membership. The objective of organizing a group is to protect and enhance the interests of its members through associational activities. Interest groups seek to influence public policy by securing access to key political decision makers. The essence of politics is the competitive struggle of groups for access. Interests exist as potential groups which emerge as organized groups when they are threatened or come into conflict with other interests. Government officials and organized groups take the probable effects of activating potential groups into account in making policy decisions. Likewise, to some extent they plan their strategy on the basis of the anticipated reactions of other organized groups and governmental units.

Salisbury, in a provocative discussion, argues that extant conventional theory fails to explain satisfactorily the formation of interest groups, the basis for continued group existence, and group relationship to public policy making.[58] He suggests as an alternative a theory which regards interest groups as benefit exchanges between entrepreneur/leaders and consumer/followers. The leaders "invest" in a set of benefits which they offer to followers at a price: joining the organization. As long as the benefits continue to warrant the cost of membership and as long as the leaders receive sufficient "profit" in return, the organization remains viable. Otherwise it becomes "bankrupt" and collapses.

Interest groups offer three types of benefits: material, solidary, and expressive. Material benefits include tangible rewards of goods and services or the means to obtain them. Solidary benefits are intangible, psychically experienced rewards of group membership. Expressive benefits are the "suprapersonal goals of the organization or group." The entrepreneur/leaders create a mixture of benefits which they offer to a particular market. (The markets in this study consist of particular sets of individuals and groups engaged in or interested in education.) The profits which group entrepreneur/leaders take include salaried positions, opportunities for personal advancement and professional preferment, and psychic avocational or altruistic satisfactions.

It is necessary, according to Salisbury, that the exchange satisfy both parties. It is not only possible for a group to go bankrupt, but also for it to acquire a "surplus." Group leaders may distribute this surplus in varying ways: securing increased benefits for the members, building elaborate headquarters facilities, raising their own salaries, or lobbying for public policies that they favor independently of the views of their members.

Lobbying, a term which applies to all interest-group efforts to influence public policy and thus encompasses most group political activity, is explained in part as the expenditure of "surplus profits" in accord with the personal values of the leaders. Recognition of this fact, says Salisbury, may help to account for the uneven response of policy makers to group pressures. But lobbying is also a logical imperative for group leaders. It is instrumental for initiating and maintaining the "benefit flow and exchange of the group." [59]

In the educational policy process, governmental benefits, e.g., categorical aid programs, must be reauthorized periodically and their level renegotiated annually. This, along with pressure from group members for the expansion of benefits and the desire of the leaders to make their enterprises more "profitable," results in a continual flow of lobbying activity.

This digression into interest-group theory should provide a basis for examining the interests participating in the educational policy process. Many aspects of interest-group activity that cannot be accounted for in terms of the extant theory are clarified if viewed in terms of Salisbury's exchange theory.

Elementary/Secondary Education Groups

The principal groups attempting to influence federal policies affecting elementary and secondary education included the National Education Association (NEA) and five affiliates (commonly known as "the Big Six"): the U.S. Catholic Conference and its related professional organization, the National Catholic Education Association; the American Federation of Teachers and its parent, the AFL–CIO; the American Library Association; the National Audio-Visual Association; and the U.S. Chamber of Commerce. The NEA, an organization of 1.1 million education professionals, dominated the Washington lobbying scene. It acted as an "umbrella" association by coordinating the policy influencing efforts of the American Association of School Administrators, an independent division of NEA, the Council of Chief State School Officers, the National Association of School Boards, the National Association of State Boards of Education, and the National Congress of Parents and Teachers. These organizations, the Big Six, frequently issued joint position statements and attempted to work together on legislative matters. The other groups, although not formally tied to the Big Six, maintained close liaison with them through the NEA's federal relations office. These groups took care to avoid open conflict with the NEA on policy issues.

The NEA was a large organization with an elaborate structure of state and local affiliates, a sizable staff which performed information, research, and service functions as well as the lobbying operation, and it owned an attractive headquarters building in Washington's fashionable Northwest business district. Although its officials were school administrators, most of the NEA's members were classroom teachers. They joined through 56 state and over 8,000 local education associations, membership in which brought automatic NEA affiliation. To attract members, the NEA had long emphasized its position as *the* professional education association and stressed the professional status of teachers and school administrators.

Its informational and statistical activities were used to support both the research and lobbying operations. Research activity designed to assist teachers and administrators in the performance of their tasks, and lobbying had the manifest goal of securing governmental benefits for education, especially the members of the NEA. Services included such benefits as insurance and retirement plans and travel opportunities. The NEA also acquired members through vigorous recruitment, particularly by its administrator members.[60] According to Carl Megel, president of the rival American Federation of Teachers, many school systems coerced teachers into joining the NEA by making membership in the state association a condition of employment or retention.[61] In any case, the selective benefits that the NEA offered to its members were substantial. Its leaders (entrepreneurs) were turning a sizable "profit."

The association was not without competition, however. The AFT, a union of classroom teachers affiliated with the AFL–CIO, had acquired 150,000 members by 1968. It had won representation election contests with local NEA affiliates in a number of large cities by promising better salaries and other benefits through the use of militant collective-bargaining tactics culminating with the strike if necessary. In response to the threat to its preeminence posed by the AFT, the NEA had dropped its traditional opposition to collective bargaining and had urged a militant stance on its local units in their salary negotiations. It made the improvement of teacher welfare its primary policy goal.

As the 1970s progressed, hostility between the NEA and the AFT lessened. In large part this development reflected the spread of collective bargaining among all categories of public employees. NEA's teachers recognized increasingly that the AFT's militant approach to negotiations with local school boards was proving highly productive. The belief that collective bargaining was unprofessional was yielding to considerations of economic self-interest. Indeed, by 1972 the question of merger between the two organizations was openly debated at the NEA's annual convention and a formal separation of the organization's teacher and administrator members was a distinct possibility.

The NEA–AFT competition for members had only limited impact on the educational policy process. Modest tension arose between the NEA and the NASB, but since federal policies did not encompass the realm of salary negotiations, the solidarity of the Big Six was not appreciably weakened. Nor did the NEA and AFT compete in lobbying. AFT depended on the parent AFL–CIO for its lobbying activity.

The NEA had an especially close relationship with the AASA. Until December 1967, the two organizations issued joint policy statements through the Educational Policies Commission. Over the thirty-three years of its existence, the EPC had examined a wide range of critical issues and problems and had spoken with a strong voice supported by the prestige of its members (which had included Conant, Eisenhower, and Killian) and the influence of its participating organizations.[62] Its statements were carefully reasoned and moderate in tone, but they were accorded considerable persuasive power. The abolition of the EPC reflected a growing divergence of interest between the NEA and the AASA which had its roots in their need to speak out separately for teachers and administrators in the growing conflict over negotiations. The need of the organizations for greater independence was also manifested when AASA established its own federal relations office in February 1968.

The NEA's ties with the other members of the Big Six were never as close as those with the AASA. The CCSSO was a small but potent organization that spoke for state education agencies. Its members usually had friendly senators and congressmen who were eager to protect the interests of the states. The NASB was a younger but active group that sought to obtain recognition for the special concerns of local school boards as distinct from those of teachers and administrators. The national PTA was a cumbersome volunteer organization that tried to give voice to parents of schoolchildren. A legislative committee of national officers formulated policy proposals which required approval by thirty-one state organizations. An information committee of six Washington area members and the national legislative chairman, all volunteers, comprised its lobbying force. Most of its efforts to influence federal policy were in concert with the Big Six. The NASBE, a relatively inactive group, supported the goals of the Big Six mainly by lending its name.

These organizations constituted the "establishment" in elementary/secondary education. They were strongly supportive of USOE, and their major goal was increased federal aid without accompanying additional controls. The establishment contributed five participants to the policy process: Dr. Sam M. Lambert, executive secretary of the NEA; Dr. John Lumley, executive officer of the NEA's Legislative Commission; Forrest Conner, executive secretary of the AASA; Dr. Edgar Fuller, executive secretary of the CCSSO; and Paul Carlin, director of federal and congressional relations for the NASB.

The establishment associations shared their interest in elementary/secondary education policies with a number of other groups. The American Vocational Association represented professional vocational educators. The AVA cannot appropriately be classified as having a major interest in either elementary/secondary or higher education as "voc-ed" has an identity and status of its own. Yet it is concerned with federal policies for each level as the allocations affect the amount available for voc-ed. The AVA enjoyed considerable congressional support, but its executive director, Lowell A. Burkett, believed that USOE had been structured to exclude voc-ed from top-level policy making.[63] This perspective affected Burkett's operating style, for although the AVA's major concerns were program-oriented it was necessary to work indirectly through Congress. While he would have preferred more direct relations with USOE, he lacked adequate access to and representation in the agency. Consequently he had to try to get Congress to act independently of the administration.

Not all officials of professional education associations operating outside the Big Six felt the sense of exclusion from the policy process that the AVA's Burkett expressed. Although Miss Germaine Krettek, associate executive director of the American Library Association, also felt that there should be a bureau-level unit for library programs, she did not think her organization could presume to dictate the structure of USOE. Rather than attempt to build support independently of USOE, she worked diligently on behalf of any education legislation that had some relationship to libraries. In this way she increased the effectiveness of her policy role as the Washington representative of the organized library profession.

Catholic interests in federal education policy were the primary concern of the U.S. Catholic Conference, the secretariat for the bishops of the church. Its principal participants in the policy process were Monsignor James Donohue, education director, and William Consedine, general counsel. The bishops accorded Donohue and Consedine considerable discretion in their operations. This flexibility enabled them to obtain access to and develop a cooperative relationship with government officials and to come to terms with the education establishment regarding Catholic participation in federal education programs.

Two other educationally related groups that played a role in the policy process merit mention. The National Committee for Public Schools (NCPS) was a citizen's organization which maintained a small Washington staff and ran an annual conference of laymen and educators on topics of current interest. It was primarily an informational rather than a lobbying organization. The American Association of University Women closely monitored all education policy developments with a special concern for the interests of women, particularly education professionals. Its Washington representatives enjoyed access to many key policy makers (in particular to Edith Green) but they directed any efforts to influence policy through individual members and local chapters.

The non-education groups seeking to influence federal education policy furnish additional examples of Salisbury's exchange theory. The AFL–CIO can be regarded as a group spending some of its profits. It did not initiate policy proposals, but it evaluated and took stands on all major education issues as an essential component of its overall domestic program. Its perspective was "primarily from the viewpoint of labor education." [64] Internally, the Executive Council of the union set its education policy on the basis of resolutions prepared by the Education Department. The Legislative Department then assumed responsibility for implementation of that policy in Congress. Even the AFT worked through the Legislative Department, whose representative for education, Kenneth Young, was an active participant in the educational policy process. He dealt solely with Congress and devoted most of his time to education legislation.

The policies that the AFL–CIO espoused were liberal and supportive of the administration. However, they went beyond the administration's program in pushing for higher expenditures in elementary/secondary education and for direct aid to college students. The AFL–CIO's strong pro-integration stand was at odds with the position of a majority of the membership.[65] The union leaders were, because of their success in providing direct material benefits to the membership, able to play a major role in the educational policy process in spite of the member's lack of support (or even hostility) to their goals. This was a clear case of the expenditure of profits in terms of exchange theory.

Two business groups also maintained an active interest in federal education policy. One, the U.S. Chamber of Commerce, was a major national organization. It had an educational program that emphasized business perspectives and it had developed an explicit policy toward the federal role in education. Its education program manager, John Miles, did little direct lobbying. His "most effective contacts with the government" occurred when officials requested information regarding the position of the Chamber and the business community.[66] In spite of the Chamber's low lobbying profile it was explicitly referred to by an official of a Big Six organization as "the only effective opposition to us." [67]

The other business group, the National Audio-Visual Association (NAVA), was a trade association comprised of manufacturers, dealers, and sales representatives. NAVA worked actively to encourage the expansion of the federal role in education. The motivation was to obtain passage of legislation authorizing programs that would create markets for audio-visual equipment. NAVA's leaders maintained a federal relations effort out of proportion to the organization's small membership (750, of which 225 were manufacturers) as an economic imperative. As long as programs authorizing equipment purchase were continued and funded, the benefit exchange was satisfactory.

The roles of the policy makers concerned primarily with elementary/secondary education fell into two broad categories: associate executives and lobbyists. The association executives were divided, in turn, into those who did a substantial amount of lobbying or otherwise interacted with federal officials and those who engaged comparatively little in such activity. The lobbyists regarded the effort to influence policy as their major function. Those roles were mutually supportive of each other and collectively the individuals performing them provided elementary/secondary education with diverse and effective representation in the policy process. Not surprisingly, they all tended to have accountability perspectives that focused primarily and somewhat narrowly on the interests represented in their associations and only secondarily on the general public interest in education.

Higher Education Groups

The groups attempting to influence federal higher education policies manifested some similarities to and sharp differences from the groups concerned with elementary/secondary education. There was a comprehensive umbrella group, the American Council on Education, that worked in concert with a number of more specialized organizations which constituted an unofficial "establishment." [68] In addition, a number of other organizations operated outside the establishment or as adjuncts to it. The principal establishment groups included the American Council on Education (ACE), the National Association of State Universities and Land Grant Colleges (NASULGC), the Association of American Universities (AAU), the Association of State Colleges and Universities (ASCU), the Association of American Colleges (AAC), and the American Association of Junior Colleges (AAJC). Membership in all these organizations was institutional. They encompassed the full range of institutions in American higher education. Also associated with the ACE were six other organizations: the Council of Graduate Schools, the National Association of College and University Business Officers, the National Commission on Accreditation, the higher education division of the National Catholic Education Association, the American Association of University Professors (AAUP), and the American Association for Higher Education. These last three were individual-membership organizations. The National Commission on Accreditation was a creation of the regional accrediting agencies and the institutional associations, and the Council of Graduate Schools and the Business Officers' Association represented specialized functions performed within academic institutions.

The six latter groups had an appreciably lower level of interest in and impact on federal policies affecting higher education than did the "establishment" groups. The formal mechanism for coordination of the twelve organizations was the ACE's Secretariat, a monthly meeting chaired by its president, Logan Wilson, and attended by the chief Washington officials of the groups. (No deputies or emissaries were permitted to attend.)

In addition to these organizations, some universities maintained Washington offices and various professional societies representing academic disciplines had some interest in shaping federal policies. Neither labor nor business took an active interest in higher education policy. Perhaps one of the sharpest contrasts between higher education groups and those operative in elementary/secondary education was the absence of formal associational representation for state or local governments or of governing boards of colleges and universities. Closely related to this difference was the much greater reliance of higher education associations upon institutional heads for direct contact and lobbying efforts with governmental officials. Unlike the Big Six and other elementary/secondary groups, higher education associations were reluctant to attempt to wield influence openly and directly.

The ACE, as the umbrella group, had the task of representing the totality of interests in higher education to the federal government and presenting governmental concerns to colleges and universities. By 1967 it had divested itself of operating programs and devoted its efforts principally to federal relations and to research on problems and developments in higher education. The ACE's approach to influencing federal policies was to develop a consensus within higher education. This it accomplished through the Secretariat and its Commission on Federal Relations. Both the ACE's president, Logan Wilson, and the director of the Commission on Federal Relations, John F. Morse, stressed the importance of consensus. This meant, however, that the ACE avoided taking positions on issues, e.g., tax-credit plans and the Educational Opportunity Bank, which could lead to membership showdowns. If conflict over issues could not be suppressed, the ACE left advocacy to the various member organizations. The ACE attempted to speak with one voice, even if equivocal, for higher education, and most member groups willingly left it to the ACE to pursue their interests on matters of common concern.

Although Wilson was clearly the ACE's chief executive officer, its principal participant in the educational policy process was Morse, who did "almost no lobbying on the Hill." [69] His activities mainly involved participation with USOE officials in developing guidelines and regulations and with the HEW legislative staff in shaping legislation.

The other five groups constituting the higher education establishment varied greatly with respect to the scope and nature of their federal relations activities. In part this variance reflected their different membership basis and in part it stemmed from differing operating styles of their chief executive officers. Two of the associations, NASULGC and the AAJC, wielded substantial independent influence in the policy process. Two others, the AAC and ASCU, had a much lower profile. The fifth, the AAU, was taking initial steps in 1968 to assert itself more forcefully.

The most prestigious and visible public universities were members of NASULGC. It included both land-grant colleges and large complex institutions with extensive involvement in graduate and professional education. The importance of these institutions in their respective states generally provided them with access to and support from influential members of their congressional delegations. Often a university president had a close relationship with at least one of his state's senators and one or more congressmen. The NASULGC institutions also held a large proportion of federal research and development grants, and their students received substantial amounts of financial aid through the programs of USOE and other agencies.

NASULGC's potential for advancing its own interests, at least in the short run, was considerable. Its staff and its federal relations operation were rather modest, however. Its long-time executive secretary, Russell Thackrey, acknowledged that there were increasing pressures to assume new functions and that expansion would occur. But this would not happen until after his retirement in 1969. Thackrey explicitly avoided initiating contact with

Congress. That task was performed by the presidents of member schools. His role was to act as "a lightning rod for anyone who wants to know about state universities." [70] Information would be provided willingly when requested. Although Thackrey's own activity was largely confined to the other associations and agency officials, the power base of his association and his effectiveness in presenting and advocating its policy preferences combined to accord him a highly influential status.

The AAJC has a sharply different but also very powerful membership base. With a large and growing number of institutions located in every state and most congressional districts, it was in a position to pursue an independent course of action if it chose to do so. The rapid growth and popularity of community and junior colleges as a means of expanding postsecondary educational opportunities in nonacademic as well as academic fields contributed to the AAJC's favorable situation. The organization chose, however, to work in collaboration with ACE in its federal relations efforts. According to the AAJC's director of governmental relations, Dr. John Mallan, the probable short-run benefits of an independent stance would be substantially overbalanced by the long term costs. [71]

The AAJC maintained a sizable staff operation in Washington. Its budget amounted to $2 million, most of which came from foundation grants. [72] It provided its members with a broader range of services than any higher education group except the ACE. Perhaps the most notable difference between the AAJC and the other higher education groups was its greater degree of contact with congressional personnel. AAJC officials made no mention of a conscious desire to "stay off the Hill." The directness of their dealings with Congress, even though coordinated with ACE's activities, and the willingness of AAJC officials to speculate openly about "going it alone" no doubt contributed to some of the apprehension that other higher education lobbyists expressed about the association's potential for independent influence.

The AAU presented a sharp contrast to the AAJC. An establishment association composed of forty-four of the most prestigious public and private universities, the AAU had never been an activist group in terms of efforts to influence federal policies. It was beginning in 1968, under prodding from presidents Goheen of Princeton and Pusey of Harvard, to try to take a more active role but in 1967 and 1968, it was still a "club of presidents." [73] The principal interests of the AAU were in graduate and professional education and research. It was the only organization providing explicit representation for these concerns. It also served as the major vehicle for interchange between public and private universities. That the major proponents of a more active AAU federal relations effort were heads of private universities reflected the absence of any other organization to perform this function for them and the fact that NASULGC performed it for the public institutions.

The two remaining establishment associations represented smaller or less prestigious institutions. ASCU was a new organization, formed in 1967, of public colleges and universities not belonging to NASULGC. Its first executive director, Allan Ostar, described his group's role as "helping the institutions develop their own identity in higher education—to see if they are a distinctive type of institution." [74] A former staff member of NASULGC, Ostar patterned his organization after the older group. It had a smaller staff, relied heavily on member presidents to do its work, and Ostar adopted an approach to federal relations that emphasized involvement with HEW and USOE and minimal contacts "on the Hill." Ostar acknowledged that ASCU's identity was "still unclear," that it had not developed its own legislative program, and that it did not "have any votes." But a large number of rapidly growing multipurpose state institutions and the effectiveness with which many of them pursued their goals in state political systems made the new organization a participant of considerable importance in the educational policy process.

The AAC's function was to represent the interests of undergraduate education. Its officials emphasized that they acted on behalf of undergraduate liberal arts education rather than specific types of institutions. Private liberal arts colleges comprised the bulk of AAC members, 80 percent, but public four-year colleges and arts and sciences units from major universities contributed most of its income. Although the AAC rejected any public-private distinction, its independent private college members were demanding in 1967 and 1968 that the organization speak more explicitly and forcefully for their interests. The AAC's emphasis on undergraduate education rather than institutional interests affected its operations. Federal relations involved very little lobbying, participation with HEW and USOE in developing legislation and guidelines, and advising and assisting member colleges in approaching federal agencies. This function was especially critical to colleges without a research–graduate training operation.

The AAC worked through the ACE in most of its efforts to shape federal policies. It was in many respects a service organization for its members and federal relations was one of many services. Its internal conflict over its role, as spokesman for undergraduate liberal arts education rather than for independent liberal arts colleges, made a low profile necessary and limited its influence potential. It had a difficult task in that it had to represent a crucial, but not faddishly popular, component of higher education in competition with some more potent associates. Its leaders were pressed to offer its members a set of benefits that they would find attractive and work-maintaining. Private colleges wanted explicit recognition and representation of their special character. Public members had such representation through other associations and sought only effective presentation and advancement of the claims of undergraduate education against graduate education, research, and community colleges. The threat of a new organization, to represent private colleges, would seriously weaken if not destroy the AAC. The realization of the small independent colleges that an independent association would lack political clout forced a continuation of the uneasy alliance within the AAC. The tension eased in 1971 when the National Council of Independent Colleges and Universities was established to speak for private higher education as an affiliate of the AAC.

The higher education association participants in the policy process fell into two basic policy role categories: executives and federal relations officials. The executives had broad responsibilities that principally involved directing the operations of their associations. They became active in the policy process whenever it appeared necessary formally to inject the association's presence. Personal prestige and organizational positions were the bases of their influence which were most frequently and effectively exerted through presidents of their member institutions. When they did involve themselves, their contacts were mostly with HEW and USOE officials.

The federal relations officials devoted most of their efforts to the tasks of monitoring governmental activities and attempting to influence administrative and congressional policy making. They derived their influence mainly from the information they possessed and their knowledge of the policy system. Like the executives, they also maintained a low profile in their contacts with governmental officials. The accountability perspectives of the higher education policy process participants were directed toward specific types of institutions, e.g., land-grant colleges, or toward specific concerns, e.g., undergraduate education.

Higher education's efforts to influence federal policy centered around the ACE and its secretariat and were based on a belief in the necessity and the efficacy of presenting a united front. All the higher education participants in the policy process expressed a commitment to the consensus approach. Its obvious limitation, of substantially restricting the scope of higher education's policy goals and potential accomplishments because of the de facto veto possessed by each major group, was regarded as an inevitable cost if any significant benefits were to be obtained.

Outside Experts and Other Participants

In addition to the individuals affiliated with Washington lobby groups, the educational policy process contained a number of participants located outside the nation's capital. These individuals included scholars, public school officials, university presidents, foundation executives, and private citizens. They were located throughout the nation but tended to be concentrated in the East. Their activity in the policy process took the form of serving on various advisory bodies, testifying in congressional hearings, formally consulting with federal officials, and informally conveying their ideas to other participants in the process. From a group of 40 such outside experts and influentials I selected a broadly representative sample of 12 of the most visibly active, 10 of whom were interviewed.*

These outsiders were representative (in terms of my criteria) of specific types of participants in the policy process. All but two of them had a definite organizational position. They tended not to regard themselves as involved in shaping federal education policies, but they were all vitally interested in contributing to the improvement of education through their activities. Their accountability perspectives tended to be formulated broadly in terms of the public interest rather than specific interests.

Two of these outsiders were based in universities, William G. Friday, president of the Consolidated Universities of North Carolina, and John H. Fischer, president of Teachers College, Columbia University. Friday served as chairman of President Johnson's 1967–68 task force on education, had been a member of the ACE's executive board for five years, and was a member of a special five-man AAU policy group. His activities typify the policy involvement of leading university presidents. Fischer had been a member of three presidential task forces on education.

The other active educational official interviewed was Sidney P. Marland, superintendent of schools in Pittsburgh, Pennsylvania.† Marland was a member of an informal group for six big-city school superintendents which met periodically with Commissioner Howe for a mutual exchange of concerns and ideas. He had served on the 1964 White House task force chaired by John Gardner and the 1967 group headed by William Friday and several other advisory bodies. He had attracted national attention through the innovative implementation of the "educational park" concept in Pittsburgh.

A considerably different type of outside expert with major policy process involvement was the foundation executive. Two foundations, Ford and Carnegie, had made outstanding efforts to improve American education. In doing so, they acquired a great amount of practical knowledge and theoretical understanding of education problems and developed ideas regarding appropriate solutions. Consequently, they were drawn into the policy process as advisers and consultants to Congress, the bureaucracy, and the Presidency. The foundation participants in the policy process included F. Champion Ward and Edward J. Meade, Jr., of Ford, Alan Pifer and Lloyd N. Morrissett of the Carnegie Corporation, and Harold Gores of the Education Facilities Laboratory, a "spinoff" of the Ford Foundation.

Some members of the education establishment associations spoke dispar-

* Ideally, all 40 should have been interviewed, but limited funds made it necessary to restrict my efforts.

† I attempted unsuccessfully to interview the late James Allen, the New York state commissioner of education. Allen was the most visible and prestigious chief state school officer and was widely regarded as an innovator. Significantly, both Allen and Marland were to serve as commissioners of education in the Nixon administration.

agingly of the foundations, prestigious private universities, intellectuals, and journalists as constituting a "new establishment." Located mainly in the Northeast and with ready access to the Presidency, especially through the Bureau of the Budget, with two of its members, Gardner and Howe, in key positions, this new establishment was considered by many old-line education lobby group members to have usurped the old establishment's position of paramount influence in the policy process. This, it was implied, was not quite legitimate, since the members of the new establishment did not "really represent anyone."

The critics of the foundations and the people linked with them attributed far too much influence to the new establishment. Although federal officials did turn largely to sources other than the traditional education associations for new ideas and approaches, they remained acutely sensitive to the residual strength of the established clientele groups. White House and Budget Bureau staff members may have distrusted and resented groups such as the NEA, AAAS, ACE, and NASULGC as supporters of the status quo, but these organizations wielded influence in congressional decision making and administrative implementation that no foundation executive, university professor, or journalist ever dreamed of, let alone sought. If the concept of an education establishment is of questionable validity, that of a "new establishment" stands on much less solid ground.

The two private citizens who were active in the education policy system were Ralph W. Tyler, a distinguished psychologist who has served from 1953 to 1967 as director of the Center for Advanced Study in the Behavioral Sciences and who in 1968 was president of the Academy of Education, and Terry Sanford, who as governor of North Carolina from 1961 to 1965 attracted nationwide attention through his efforts to improve the state's public schools. Both men had served on a number of federal advisory bodies. If Tyler can be taken as representative of scholars who become involved in the policy process either on the basis of their expertise, a sense of duty, or other factors, Terry Sanford was perhaps typical of distinguished laymen who, because of a deep personal interest and commitment to education, were willing to devote time and energy to advisory service and other activities that enhanced education.

It is difficult to gauge, even crudely, the impact of outside experts in the educational policy process. Their participation was based on two factors: expertise and status within the education community. Through formal roles as advisory body members and informal contacts with federal officials they provided a set of inputs to Congress and the bureaucracy that stretched well beyond those generated by the national associations comprising the education establishment and by other Washington lobby groups. While both kinds of nongovernmental participants made demands upon and furnished support for the official policy makers, the experts also provided new ideas and critical analyses of existing problems and programs that were not so closely tied to specific interests in education and were more objectively framed from the perspective of a general public interest in education as they defined it.*

There was, however, no clear line of demarcation between the two categories of nonofficial participants as some persons, e.g., Friday and Marland, did overlap and both sets of individuals were a part of the educational elite. The principal distinction to be made is that the Washington-based association personnel constituted USOE's clientele groups in the usual sense in which that term is used, while the outside experts were a less formalized element in the policy process drawn from a broader, but still elite base. They provided for substantial, but not complete, representation of interests in the policy process.

Summary

The educational policy process during the period of the 90th Congress consisted of seventy-seven elite individuals occupying strategic positions in a set of specialized institutions. These individuals were linked together by their policy roles which were normative descriptions of their behavior and, in some cases, the expected behavior of others. These policy roles were in large part institutionally determined; the individuals formulated their role perceptions and behavioral expectations in terms of the functions formally assigned and informally attached to the positions they occupied.

The integration of the various policy roles in an interaction process that produced policy decisions was accomplished through the accountability perspectives of the individual policy-process participants. A sense of loyalty, responsibility, and obligation to one or more of four general reference groups provided the motivation for obedience, coordination, reciprocity, and compromise required to reach agreement on complex policy matters.

The policy role types and the accountability perspectives identified in the educational policy process are summarized in table 5-1.

The operation of the policy process described in this chapter is the subject of the next two chapters. Redford has referred to it as the interaction of minorities of men in key positions, while Herring and Bailey have depicted it in shorthand fashion as the interaction of the "four is": ideas, issues, individuals, and institutions.

---

* I have no intention of entering the morass that comprises scholarly efforts to operationalize or rationalize the concept of the public interest. I use the term advisedly and with great reservation and only because it seems to be the most appropriate way of distinguishing between the accountability perspectives of the Washington-based lobbyists and the outside experts and influentials. Of course, everyone claims to be dedicated to and working in behalf of the public interest. But the outsiders appeared, in my interviews at least, to have a broader, more general perspective and were less inclined to appraise and evaluate federal policies and programs in terms related to their current positions and the sector of education with which they were concerned.

Table 5-1
Policy Roles and Accountability Perspectives in the Educational Policy Process

A. Policy Roles by Institution

Operating Agency—USOE
Policy manager
Staff expert
Program administrator

Department—HEW
Policy manager
Staff expert
Power broker

Presidency
Power broker
Adviser-advocate
Adviser-critic

Congress
Administration spokesman
Opposition spokesman
Ideological spokesman
Special-interest spokesman
Legal counsel
Professional staff man

Interest Group–Washington Based
Association executive
Legislative lobbyist
Federal relations official

Outside Experts
Education administrator
Foundation official
Citizen influential

B. Accountability Perspectives

1. Hierarchical
2. Organizational
3. Special interest
4. Public interest

Notes

1. Emmett S. Redford, *Democracy in the Administrative State* (New York: Oxford University Press, 1969), p. 44.
2. Ibid., p. 46.
3. See John C. Wahlke, Heinz Eulau, William Buchanan, and LeRoy C.

Ferguson, *The Legislative System: Explorations in Legislative Behavior* (New York: John Wiley & Sons, 1962).

4. Interview, William G. Friday, 15 February 1968.

5. Interview, Ralph K. Huitt, 9 January 1968.

6. Interview, William G. Carey, 24 January 1968.

7. See Harry Kursh, *The United States Office of Education* (Philadelphia: Chilton, 1965), pp. 40–42 and 132–38.

8. Jonathan Spivak, "Education's Muddled Bureaucracy," *The Reporter*, 8 April 1965, pp. 33–36.

9. Stephen K. Bailey, "The Office of Education and the Education Act of 1965," Inter-University Case Program, No. 100 (Indianapolis: Bobbs-Merrill, 1966), pp. 10–11.

10. Stephen K. Bailey and Edith K. Mosher, *ESEA: The Office of Education Administers a Law* (Syracuse: Syracuse University Press, 1968), p. 73.

11. Bailey, "Office of Education"; and Bailey and Mosher, *ESEA*, chap. 2.

12. Cf. Herbert Kaufman, "Emerging Conflicts in the Doctrines of Public Administration," *American Political Science Review* 50 (December 1956): 1057–73; and his "Administrative Decentralization and Political Power," *Public Administration Review* 29 (January/February 1969): 3–15.

13. Interview, Charles Lee, professional staff member, Senate Labor and Public Welfare Committee, 18 September 1967.

14. See the discussion in Keith Goldhammer, John E. Suttle, William D. Aldridge, and Gerald L. Becker, *Issues and Problems in Contemporary Educational Administration* (Eugene, Ore.: Center for the Advanced Study of Educational Administration, 1967), chap. 3.

15. Ibid., p. 62.

16. William G. Land, "Washington Report: The Machine at Bay," *Phi Delta Kappan* 49 (February 1968): 319–20.

17. Interview, Harold Howe II, 9 January 1968.

18. Interview, Graham Sullivan, 5 January 1968.

19. Interview, Wayne Reed, 21 December 1967.

20. Interview, Albert Alford, 19 December 1967.

21. Interview, Joseph Froomkin, 12 December 1967.

22. Interview, Associate Commissioner for Elementary and Secondary Education Nolan Estes, 27 December 1967.

23. Interview, Associate Commissioner for Higher Education Peter Muirhead, 27 December 1967.

24. Interview, Associate Commissioner for Adult, Vocational, and Library Programs Grant Venn, 19 December 1967.

25. Interview, William Gorham, 4 January 1968.

26. Interview, Dr. Paul Miller, 10 January 1968.

27. Interview, Samuel Halperin, 12 December 1967.

28. The distinction between presidential and nonpresidential departments was made by former Director of the Budget Charles L. Schultze, in an interview, 29 February 1968.

29. Interview, Douglass Cater, 23 February 1968.

30. See Norman C. Thomas and Harold L. Wolman, "The Presidency and Policy Formulation: The Task Force Device," *Public Administration Review* 29 (September/October 1969): 459–71; and Patrick Anderson, "Deputy President for Public Affairs," *New York Times Magazine*, 3 March 1968.

31. Interview, Charles L. Schultze, 29 February 1968.

32. Ibid.

33. Interview, William D. Carey, assistant director, Bureau of the Budget, 24 January 1968.

34. Interview, Herbert Jasper, assistant director, Office of Legislative Reference, Bureau of the Budget, 26 February 1968.

35. Interview, Emerson Elliott, assistant division director for education, Bureau of the Budget, 24 January 1968.

36. Carey interview.

37. Elliott interview.

38. Jasper interview.

39. See Frank J. Munger and Richard F. Fenno, Jr., *National Politics and Federal Aid to Education* (Syracuse: Syracuse University Press, 1962).

40. See Julius Menacker, "The Organizational Behavior of Congress and the Formulation of Educational Support Policy," *Phi Delta Kappan* 48 (October 1966): 78–83; and James W. Dyson and John W. Soule, "Congressional Committee Behavior on Roll Call Votes: The U.S. House of Representatives, 1955–64," *Midwest Journal of Political Science* 14 (1970): 626–47. According to Dyson and Soule, mean seniority per term was lower (3.8 years) for Education and Labor Committee members than that of all but one other House committee and the Committee ranked 17th among 20 committees on a combined index of attractiveness in the period studied.

41. "House Panel Strips Power of Powers by a 27–1 vote, and He Hails Decision," *New York Times*, 23 September 1966.

42. Dyson and Soule, "Congressional Committee Behavior," pp. 636 and 640.

43. Ibid., p. 642.

44. Interview, Representative Edith Green, 24 February 1968.

45. Confidential interview.

46. Interview, Representative Edith Green, 23 February 1968.

47. Interview, Senator Wayne Morse, 13 June 1968.

48. Interview, Senator Jacob Javits, 5 March 1968.

49. Interview, Senator Peter Dominick, 11 January 1968.

50. Interview, Charles Lee, 2 January 1968.

51. Ibid.

52. Interview, John S. Forsythe, 16 January 1968.

53. Interview, Roy Millenson, 16 January 1968.

54. Richard F. Fenno, *The Power of the Purse: Appropriations Politics in Congress* (Boston: Little, Brown, 1966).

55. Interview, Robert Moyer, 8 January 1968.

56. Interview, Herman Downey, 23 January 1968.

57. David B. Truman, *The Governmental Process* (New York: Alfred A. Knopf, 1951).

58. Robert H. Salisbury, "An Exchange Theory of Interest Groups," *Midwest Journal of Political Science* 13 (February 1969): 1–32.

59. Ibid., p. 28.

60. See Carl J. Megel, "Teacher Conscription—Basis of Association Membership?" *Teachers College Record* 66 (October 1964): pp. 7–17.

61. Ibid.

62. Leonard Buder, "The Silencing of a Vigorous Voice," *New York Times*, 10 December 1967.

63. Interview, Lowell A. Burkett, 6 February 1968.

64. Interview, Walter Davis, director, Department of Education, AFL–CIO, 2 October 1967.

65. Emanuel Gutman, "Social Attitudes of Trade Unionists," *Dissent* 15 (January/February 1968): 12.

66. Interview, John Miles, 27 March 1968.

67. Confidential interview.

68. The term "establishment" issued with some trepidation in describing the higher education associations. Russell Thackrey, former executive director of the National Association of State Universities and Land Grant Colleges, wrote in 1968 that the use of the term to "describe the 'established' major national non-governmental organizations, no longer makes sense—if it ever did." See "National Educational Organizations and the Changing Politics of Education," *Phi Delta Kappan* 49 (February 1968): 312. Although there is considerable merit to Thackrey's objection, it was my experience that most individuals involved in the education policy process had a clear understanding of the term and used it as a convenient shorthand referent, albeit with a somewhat negative connotation, to the major established clientele groups. Accordingly, I have determined to employ it.

69. Interview, John F. Morse, 12 March 1968.

70. Interview, Russell Thackrey, 1 February 1968.

71. Interview, Dr. John Mallan, 3 June 1968.

72. Interview, Edmund Glaeser, Jr., 24 June 1968.

73. Comment by a higher education official; confidentiality requested.

74. Interview, Allan Ostar, 5 February 1968.

6

COMMUNICATION PATTERNS AND
INFORMATION SOURCES*

Analytically, the policy process is the decision-making activity of individuals occupying strategic positions in institutions. In chapter 5 I identified the institutions and the individuals involved in the educational policy process and examined their official roles as they perceived them. Their role perceptions and their behavior in those roles are, at least in part, a function of their interactions with one other. An understanding of the educational policy process, then, necessitates (among other things) an analysis of interaction patterns.

Interaction is a many-faceted concept, but "almost invariably [it] refers to communications between persons." [1] As Thibaut and Kelly define it:

> By interaction, it is meant that they [two individuals] emit behavior in each other's presence, they create products for each other, or they communicate with each other. In every case we would identify as a case of interaction, there is at least the possibility that the actions of each person affect the other. [2]

Here, I am defining interaction as communication (unilateral or bilateral) between the participants in the educational policy process that involved the transmission of information related to education and/or educational policy.

* Portions of this chapter are adapted from "Bureaucratic-Congressional Interaction and the Politics of Education" by Norman C. Thomas, *Journal of Comparative Administration*, Volume 2, Number 1 (May 1970), pp. 52–80, by permission of the Publisher, Sage Publications, Inc.

The fact that communication occurred does not, however, imply that an influence relationship existed, although there is always the possibility that it did. Thus, the greater the frequency of communication between two individuals, the greater the probability that an influence relationship can develop.* Although the measurement and analysis of communication frequencies within the education policy process will not reveal the structure of power and influence, it should suggest where influence relationships are likely to develop.

The major portion of this analysis of communication patterns in the educational policy process is based on perceived frequencies of communication during the first eighteen months of the 90th Congress between the policy makers. The respondents received instructions to include all personal contacts, telephone conversations, and direct written communications that involved federal educational programs and/or policies with each of the other participants in the policy process. Indirect communications, e.g., magazine articles on public speeches, were not included. They reported the communications on a check list at three frequency levels: none, 1–10, and over 10. These data were obtained from 66 of the 71 policy makers with whom it was possible to obtain interviews.

An additional data set provides a partial check on the communications data as well as an indication of the principal cue-giving institutions and individuals employing the policy makers. The respondents were asked to designate their main sources of information and their major external contracts. Their responses included both individuals and groups in the policy process and outside it as well as publications.

Communication Frequencies

Analysis

The objective of the analysis of the communication-frequency data is to identify communication patterns between individuals and groups in the educational policy process, suggest some explanations of those patterns, and examine the influence relationships that the patterns suggest. The number of potential explanatory variables that might lend order and understanding to the analysis of the patterns observed are many: the institutional affiliations of the respondents; their policy roles; the level of education with which they are primarily concerned; individual characteristics such as party identification,

---

* Repeated interaction between two individuals will often lead to the development of perceptions and expectations based not only on positionally determined roles, but also of personal characteristics. For example, over time Bureaucrat B and Congressman C may come to regard each other and to react to each other in terms of their attitudes, socioeconomic backgrounds, common acquaintances, shared experiences, etc. Unfortunately, I lack extensive data regarding such interpersonal expectations and behavior.

education background, length of service in position, length of participation in the process, security of tenure in their positions; common acquaintances; shared experiences; attitudes on policy issues; and many others. The analytical problem involves the difficulty of demonstrating the relationship of the potential independent variables to the communication frequencies and the patterns that they contain.

Social psychologists and sociologists frequently use sociometric methods to gather and analyze data on the interaction patterns of members of groups.[3] Sociometric techniques are particularly appropriate for the identification and description of clusters, subgroups, and discriminatory patterns within a group. The number $(N-66)$ of educational policy makers made the use of conventional sociometric techniques impractical,[4] however, it proved possible to overcome the limitations through the use of the smallest space analysis, a technique that combines multidimensional scaling with nonmetric factor analysis.[5] Without going into an extended explanation of the logic underlying SSA,[6] it takes as input the nonsymmetric matrix of data, in this case the three categories of communication frequency, O, 1–10, and over 10, preserves order relations in all possible pairs between participants in the policy process, and using a minimum number of dimensions (thus, smallest-space analysis) produces two solutions, one for rows (or senders) and one for columns (or receivers). In this analysis, a three-dimensional solution proved to be most appropriate.

The data should be interpreted as a configuration of points, each representing a member of the educational policy process, in three-dimensional space.[7] The configurations for the row and column solutions are similar, but they differ in the perceptual set of the respondents, the row solution revealing how the configuration appears to senders of communications and the column solution how it appears to receivers. Because of the difficulty of representing a three-dimensional configuration in a two-dimensional space, the configurations are presented here in the form of two-dimensional plots, or maps (see figures 6-1 through 6-4). While there are three possible mappings for each solution, I have only shown the first two maps (dimensions 1×2 and 1×3) in order to avoid unnecessary confusion. The location of an individual in the configuration can be visualized by projecting him upward or downward from his location on the plane of the mapping of the first two dimensions by the value of his coordinates on the third dimension.

Because SSA employs a principal-axis rotation, the first dimension explains more of the variance in distance than the second dimension which in turn has greater explanatory value than the third dimension. However, the focus of the analysis is the configuration since it reveals the structure of the communication network. An individual's location in the network is determined by his vector coordinates. The closer he is to the point of origin of the configuration (i.e., the smaller his coordinates), the more central his position

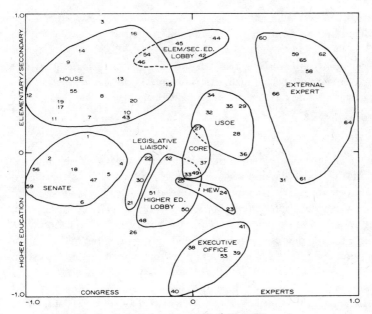

FIGURE 6-1. *Sender Solution for the First Two Dimensions*

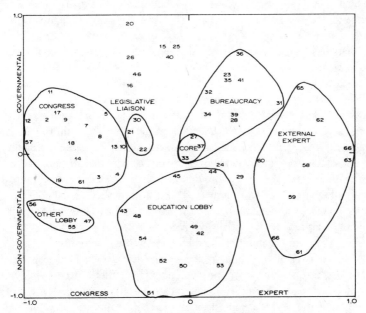

FIGURE 6-2. *Sender Solution for the First and Third Dimensions*

in the network. The configuration also reveals the distance between any pair of individuals and the existence and location of groupings and clusters in the network. (I have defined groupings as sets of individuals for whom it is possible to identify a common characteristic; clusters are groupings whose members are close together.) Finally, the configuration suggests relationships between groupings and identifies the key individual participants.

Interpretation

The first step in interpreting the configurations was to determine the meaning of the three dimensions and thus the identity of the principal independent variables. The meaning of the first dimension was quite clear for both the row (sender) and column (receiver) solutions. The participants in the policy process were distributed according to institutional affiliation from external experts to Congress. Bureaucrats tended to occupy the midsection of the dimension, suggesting their central position in the communication network.

The meaning of the second dimension was the same for both sender and receiver solutions, although it was somewhat less manifest than that of the first dimension. The participants appeared to be distributed according to the level of education toward which they were oriented. High positive scores reflected a strong elementary/secondary education orientation while high negative scores indicated an orientation toward higher education. The distribution was more concentrated in the midsection for the receiver solution than for the sender solution which revealed greater distribution at the extremes. This indicates that individuals more sharply defined their own educational level orientations than did their fellow participants. The positioning of HEW–USOE bureaucrats near the midpoint of this dimension reflects their concern with all levels of education.

It was considerably more difficult to determine the meaning of the third dimension. Several interpretations appeared to be possible with the most plausible being that the participants were distributed according to the exclusiveness of their contacts with governmental as opposed to nongovernmental personnel. A high positive score denoted almost no external communications, and a high negative score indicated almost no governmental contacts. The sender solution appears to reflect the governmental-nongovernmental ordering somewhat more clearly than the receiver solution.

In interpreting the meaning of the three dimensions, I found that none of several alternative explanatory variables for which I had data had any apparent relationship to the distribution of the respondents on the dimensions. The variables included party identification, educational background, length of service and security of tenure in position, length of participation in the process, and age (there was only one woman and one black so sex and race

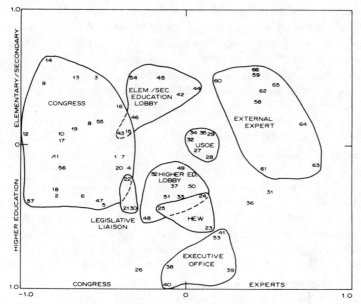

FIGURE 6-3. *Receiver Solution for the First Two Dimensions*

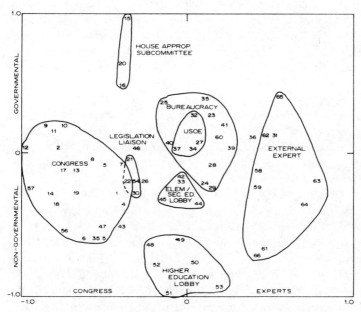

FIGURE 6-4. *Receiver Solution for the First and Third Dimensions*

were obviously not relevant). While this cannot be interpreted as demonstrating the insignificance of such factors in an explanation of the complete operation of the policy process, it does mean that they were not significantly related to the structural patterns revealed in this data set.

The most striking aspect of the communication network as represented in the configurations is the central location of most USOE officials. They formed a distinct bureaucratic core in the receiver solution and were not a great distance removed from any other groupings. The members of this agency-based core included the commissioner of education (respondent no. 27), his deputy (28), the associate commissioner for federal-state relations (29), and the associate commissioners serving as chiefs of the Bureaus of Elementary and Secondary Education (32), Adult and Vocational Education (34), and Research (35), respectively. A similar core existed in the sender solution, but with some changes in personnel. In addition to the commissioner, the core for the sender solution included the associate commissioner for higher education (33) and the presidential assistant with special responsibility for education (37). The other USOE officials formed a cluster close to the core with an orientation more toward elementary and secondary education and contacts that tended to be more governmental than nongovernmental.

The difference between the two solutions indicates that other policy makers viewed the USOE officials as more centrally involved in the communication network than they themselves did. The particular location of the chief of the Bureau of Higher Education (33) reflects the special orientation of his bureau and its clientele. The Bureau of Higher Education is the only bureau in USOE without a substantial involvement in elementary and secondary education. The bureau chief's apparent location in the higher education grouping on the plot of the first two dimensions (for both solutions) disappeared with the introduction of the third dimension. The higher education lobbyists moved down toward the nongovernmental end of that dimension while he remained close to the point of origin and the bureaucratic core. This suggests that he functioned as a link between the agency and its higher education clientele—a normal role for a bureau chief. The other bureau chiefs were located much closer to the elementary and secondary education lobbyists.

Both the sender and receiver solutions revealed the presence of a higher education grouping and an elementary and secondary education grouping, each composed of lobbyists. The higher education lobbyists were located near the nongovernmental extremity of the third dimension, reflecting their strong inclination to "stay off the Hill." The elementary/secondary lobbyists were somewhat less likely to have primarily nongovernmental contacts. Both groups were approximately the same distance from the USOE bureaucrats and the experts. However, the higher education group was closer to the Executive Office and the elementary/secondary group is closer to Congress.

In both solutions there was a definite but loose grouping of diverse external experts who tended to be oriented more toward elementary/secondary educaion (their backgrounds were predominantly in that area) and to have primarily nongovernmental contacts. There was also an Executive Office grouping with a strong higher education orientation and somewhat more governmental than nongovernmental contacts. Congressional personnel also constituted a definite grouping in each solution. They tended to have more nongovernmental contacts than the bureaucrats and they divided regarding the level of education with which they were concerned. The Senate personnel appeared to have a stronger orientation toward higher education while the House seemed more oriented toward elementary/secondary education.

The two solutions also revealed small groupings of HEW officials (23, 24, 25) and legislative liaison agents (21, 22, 30). The former, all assistant secretaries, were located between the higher education group, the Executive Office personnel, and the USOE. The distances between these assistant secretaries suggest that too much significance should not be attached to this particular grouping. The location of each official seems to depend more on his particular function and background than on any institutional basis. For example, the two officials closest to the higher education grouping were the assistant secretary for education (24) and the HEW comptroller (25). The former was an ex-college president and the latter had responsibility for supervising the administration of HEW grants. The assistant secretary for program coordination (23) was responsible for developing PPB in HEW, an assignment which involved him with the White House staff and the Bureau of the Budget. Of these three officials, only the assistant secretary for education, as the principal policy adviser to the secretary, had extensive nongovernmental contacts.

The legislative liaison cluster was positioned between the lobby groupings and Congress. In terms of educational level, the liaison officials (all former political science professors) were somewhat more oriented toward higher education; however, they were fairly close to the elementary/secondary lobbyists on the governmental/nongovernmental dimension. Their distance from the bureaucratic core was somewhat greater than might be expected given their institutional base. This suggests that while they functioned as brokers between Congress, the lobby groups and the bureaucracy, they were not as centrally involved in the communication network as the commissioner of education and his principal subordinates. Since two of the liaison officials were members of the HEW hierarchy and the other was affiliated with USOE, it appears that their functional activity more than their institutional affiliations determined their location in the communication network.

The configurations revealed additional findings based on distances between groupings and clusters. USOE, and to a lesser degree HEW, officials were, from their central location in the communication network fairly close to all other participants. Bureaucrats in the Executive Office, with the exception of the presidential assistant for education, were quite distant from all participants outside of the administration. Congressional participants in the education policy system tended to be closer to lobbyists than to the bureaucracy, except for legislative liaison personnel. The external experts were far distant from Congress, substantially removed from the lobbies and only moderately close to the bureaucracy, especially to USOE.

This analysis of the configurations confirmed the initial expectation that communication patterns in the policy process, as reflected in the groupings and clusters were, in large part, institutionally determined. The only functionally identifiable groups were lobbyists and legislative liaison bureaucrats. The level of education toward which the participants were oriented and the extent to which their contacts tended to be exclusively governmental or nongovernmental were reflected in the communication network much more than policy roles or other factors.

Perhaps the most important finding is the identification of a bureaucratic core, based on the USOE, and positioned near the center of the communication network. Although this is neither serendipitous nor unanticipated, it does confirm the centrality of the operating agency in the national policy process that has been taken for granted since the days of the New Deal.

Information Sources

One important aspect of the communication process in the educational policy process is not fully revealed in the frequency data just analyzed. The frequency check lists did not indicate which sources of information provided the most useful cues to the respondents. There is no means of distinguishing, other than speculatively, between the quantity and quality of the communications.

Although it is obviously not possible to measure accurately the substantive importance of communications sent to and received by each participant in the policy process, some enlightment can be obtained from the policy makers' perceptions of their most useful sources of information. In order to ascertain what the respondents considered their most important sources to be, they were asked: "Where would you say that you usually obtain the information which enables you to act knowledgeably and rationally with respect to educational policy?" A variety of sources received citations including individuals, groups, institutions, and publications. The most meaningful classification of the sources incorporated individuals and institutions in the following categories: Congress—members; Congress—staff; bureaucracy —HEW–USOE; bureaucracy—Executive Office of the President; Washington-based lobbies; state and local education officials; universities; foundations; and others. The miscellaneous category included professional journals, education-oriented newsletters, the news media, education critics, federal officials not included above, state and local public officials not involved in education, and noneducation political action groups.

The most frequently cited sources were HEW–USOE, the lobbies, state and local education officials, and universities (see table 6-1). The operating bureaucracy was of prime importance as an information source, a reiteration of its centrality in the communication network revealed in the three-dimensional configurations produced by the smallest-space analysis of the frequency data. However, the nongovernmental sources, i.e., lobbies, state and local officials, and universities, were more salient for the policy makers than the frequency of contacts with them indicated. This suggests a qualitative difference in the communications that cautions against attaching definitive significance to the configurations. Without discrediting the value of the communication patterns mapped through the use of smallest-space analysis, it must be recognized that information obtained from or cues given by a highly respected and valued source is going to weigh more heavily with a policy maker than that which comes, even with great frequency, from less highly regarded sources.

Of particular significance is the importance attached to state and local officials and universities. These information sources are located outside the Washington community and yet each is almost as useful to policy makers as the national education associations and other lobbies. Apparently policy makers recognize the need for new and feedback information from the field if they are to act effectively. Furthermore, it seems safe to assume that a substantial proportion of the information obtained from the lobbies and from the HEW–USOE bureaucracy originates with state and local officials and university personnel. They are the final recipients of federal funds and the ultimate outcome of all programs depends on them. Hence, the Washington-centered insularity of the configurations, which was to a considerable extent unavoidable given the manner in which the policy process was defined and the participants in it identified, can be regarded as somewhat more apparent than real.

The respondents' information sources varied according to their institutional affiliation, policy role, and party identification (see table 6-1). The bivariate cross tabulations produced no surprises and appear to have logical explanations. The small number of entries in several cells calls for caution in analyzing the table. Also, citations of sources located outside of the respondents' immediate institutional context, e.g., Congress or the bureaucracy, are of more interest than those within it. The former reveal inputs to policy makers and are suggestive of potential for exerting influence. The latter are indicative of the extent of reliance on withinputs and do not suggest influence potential.

Table 6-1
Information Sources by Institutional Affiliation, Policy Role, and Party Identification

Source:	N	Congress Member	Staff	HEW–USOE	Executive Office	Lobbies	State/Local	Universities	Foundations	Other
Institutional Affiliation										
Senate	6	17%	67%	83%	0%	83%	50%	33%	0%	33%
House	14	29	50	79	0	50	64	50	14	36
HEW	6	50	50	100	67	50	17	33	0	0
USOE	10	10	30	80	20	60	60	60	20	30
Executive Office	5	40	20	100	40	20	60	60	20	20
Lobby	16	38	38	75	0	75	56	44	0	38
Expert	9	22	0	67	11	44	22	78	56	56
Total	66	29	36	80	14	58	50	52	15	33
Policy Role										
Legislator	13	31	62	69	0	46	77	62	15	39
Legislative staff	7	14	43	100	0	86	29	14	0	29
Policy manager	6	17	17	83	33	50	50	67	33	50
Broker	3	33	67	100	33	100	33	33	0	0
Bureaucrat	12	33	33	92	42	33	50	50	8	8
Lobbyist	16	38	38	75	0	75	56	56	00	38
Expert	9	22	0	67	11	44	22	78	56	56
Total	66	29	36	80	14	58	50	52	14	33
Party Identification										
Republican	11	27	46	82	0	73	73	64	9	27
Democrat	46	30	35	78	17	57	44	54	15	35
Independent	3	0	33	100	00	33	67	0	0	67
Total	60	28	37	80	13	58	50	53	13	35

Since the policy process was largely defined in terms of institutions, the institutional affiliations of the participants could be expected to manifest a definite relationship to the information sources. Policy makers located in the Senate cited the HEW–USOE bureaucracy and Washington lobbies as their major sources. They placed modest reliance on external sources other than foundations. The importance of staff personnel in the Senate is also reflected in the data. House policy makers differed from their Senate counterparts in that they placed less reliance on lobbies and congressional staff and a proportionally greater amount on outside sources, including modest reliance on foundations. No congressionally affiliated participants in the policy process considered the Executive Office of the President to be an important information source. The greater reliance of House than Senate personnel on non-Washington sources may be due, at least in part, to the closer contact that House members maintain with their smaller constituencies.

HEW policy makers differed substantially from those located in USOE in their citation of sources outside the department. The HEW officials, who were located closer to the top of the hierarchy, found the Executive Office and Congress to be of most value, while USOE personnel relied more extensively on lobbies and non-Washington sources. This reflects USOE's status and concerns as the operating agency. Its personnel quite naturally tended to find information originating at the grass roots more useful than that trickling down from above and they undoubtedly received more of it. Executive Office policy makers found the bureaucracy the most useful source, and they depended fairly heavily on state and local officials and universities. This pattern reflected the policy leadership position of the presidency and President Johnson's quest for ideas from outside the government.

The policy makers affiliated with Washington-based lobby groups regarded the HEW–USOE bureaucracy as their main information source and evidenced no reliance on the Executive Office or the foundations. They also found external sources to be slightly more useful than those located in Congress. The value accorded congressional sources is somewhat less than might have been expected. It undoubtedly reflects the superior information resources of the bureaucracy as compared to Congress and the fact that Congress depends more on the lobbies for information than vice versa. The lobbyists' exclusion of the Executive Office confirms the lack of interaction revealed in the configurations generated by the analysis of communication frequencies as well as the reciprocal hostility and disdain that the two groups expressed for each other in interviews with the author. The lobby groups' hostility to the foundations is also apparent in the data. Not unexpectedly, policy makers located outside Washington relied more heavily on universities and foundations than did any of the Washingtonians. Even they, however, found the HEW–USOE bureaucracy a highly useful information source.

The utilization of information sources by persons performing different policy roles differs somewhat from the institutional usage pattern. Legislators, as compared with legislative staff members, rely much more on outside sources and correspondingly less on lobbies and the HEW–USOE bureaucracy. This probably reflects the broader scope of the legislators' activities. They have fairly extensive constituency contacts while their staff members tend to be Washington-bound. Among the respondents with bureaucratic policy roles, the policy managers (Commissioner Howe and five bureau chiefs) relied more on external sources than on Congress or the Executive Office, a pattern stemming from their line function. The brokers, whose assigned task was legislative liaison, found lobbies and congressional staff most useful. The bureaucrats, who performed various staff functions in HEW, USOE, and the Executive Office, employed all information sources, placing slightly more reliance on state and local officials and universities and considerably less on foundations than they did on Congress and the lobbies.

The partisan affiliations of the respondents also had some relationship to the kinds of information sources they found most useful. As the party out of power, Republicans relied more on congressional staff, lobbies, state and local officials, and universities. The Democrats, members of the in-party, found the Executive Office of some value as a source, while Republicans, naturally, did not. Democrats also placed a slightly higher value on the foundations, possibly a reflection of their stronger commitment to innovation. Members of both parties placed equally heavy reliance on the HEW–USOE bureaucracy.

To summarize these data, the HEW–USOE bureaucracy was by far the most useful information source in the policy process. Its value ranked high for policy makers in all types of institutions, members of both political parties, and in all kinds of policy roles. Lobbies, state and local officials, and universities were, in the aggregate, more useful than congressional sources. The Executive Office was utilized very little as an information source, a manifestation of its intelligence processing function for the President and other top policy makers. Congress also appeared as more a consumer than a producer of information. The foundations merit special comment. Their low standing as an information source was a mild surprise. On the basis of background interviews, I had expected them to show up more strongly. Their failure to do so suggests that either they were not as potent or pervasive an influence as their critics asserted, or that their impact on policy was indirect, being filtered through people in the field and various publications.

In addition to the tabulated data just analyzed, the respondents' comments attest to the paramount importance of USOE, the operating agency, as an information source for the policy process. Commissioner Howe cited as his main information sources, "Froomkin's [program planning and evaluation] shop and the bureaus." [8] A Bureau of the Budget official stated that "the agency is the major source of our information." [9] And Representative Green commented that although she did "obtain some information from people in OE," she knew that "they are limited by what the Budget Bureau and the Administration will permit them to say." [10] Mrs. Green's skepticism about the quality of information furnished by USOE highlighted a strong sense of dissatisfaction with both the quality and quantity of the information available to policy makers generally. Assistant HEW Secretary William Gorham, whose departmental planning operation depended on information stated the problem pithily:

> The information we have to work with is lousy. I use whatever shreds that come in through the normal data system. My staff gets information from the journals, OE, and the universities. [But] this is soft information. Hard information is hard to get.[11]

Nolan Estes, chief of USOE's largest bureau, regarded information inadequacies as critical:

> A critical problem is information. We have a poor system for gathering it. . . . Our procedures for receiving input are inadequate and informal. We lack the basis for a solid statement of needs. . . . We depend too much on word of mouth, informal visits, and ad hoc inputs to the staff. The people in the field simply report what they think we want to hear.[12]

The inadequacies of the formal information system may partly explain the use of informal sources mentioned by a number of policy makers. Commissioner Howe felt that informal contacts with "self-selected" educational experts such as members of the National Academy of Education were "terribly important." [13] James Gallagher, the psychologist who came from academia to be the first chief of the Bureau for the Education of the Handicapped, depended primarily on "informal and formal contacts with outside people" and consultants from "the profession." [14] Gorham and his staff resorted to direct contact with "school superintendents and their research directors." [15] Representative Laird encountered a different problem as a member of the House Appropriations Subcommittee that dealt with HEW and USOE. Not finding the hearings to be too helpful, he employed other means of eliciting information:

> I get a lot of information informally from the agency heads. They tell me things off the record that are of immense value. I get them in here [in the subcommittee office] after the hearings and they open up. They are much more guarded in the hearings.[16]

Dissatisfaction with the formal information gathering process and the employment of informal means of obtaining data as well as the inherent difficulties of all aspects of the task make it difficult to determine the relative

importance of the various information sources. Beyond the obvious significance of USOE, the operating agency, and its dependence on the field for its
information, the data are inconclusive.

Summary and Conclusions

In almost every respect, this analysis of communication interaction in the
educational policy process substantiates the observation of a leading member
of the House Committee on Education and Labor, that "the executive
(agency) is central to the policy process, it tends to dominate." [17] The analysis
confirms the central position of the bureaucracy, and especially the principal
operating agency, in a network that includes interest groups, congressional
committees and outside experts. This provides support for Freeman's
conclusion that bureaus have a more influential role than departments in their
relationships with Congress. [18] The principal agency participants in the
communication network, the commissioner, his deputy, and the bureau chiefs,
are political executives with responsibility for program implementation and
development of new legislative proposals. They, along with congressional
committees, were a key point of access for interest groups. They were also
centrally involved in the communication process within the administration.

The key function of legislative liaison officials as major channels of access
to political executives and as internal communication linkages between
governmental institutions furnishes evidence of the importance of brokerage
in the policy-making process. In the educational policy process the communication patterns of the liaison agents indicated that they helped to coordinate
agency-departmental action and that they were in a position to mobilize
interest group support behind the administration's legislative program and to
help secure its passage.

To the extent that communication is related to influence, the Washington-based education associations appear to be almost as potent as those who
speak of the "education establishment" imply. Yet, a number of the
respondents made such assertions as "the education lobbies are not as
important as some people think" or "the education community is highly
influential, but not necessarily through the associations." The lobbies' value as
a source of information also increases their influence potential, however.

The substantial distance, in the configurations and in the physical world,
of presitgious outside experts from other members of the policy process and
from the center of the communication network as well as the low level of
activity of most experts as communicators suggests that the extensive influence
attributed to foundations and university-based persons may be somewhat
overstated. An alternative suggestion emerges from the outsiders' standing as

information sources. It appears that although innovators and experts in the field are not heavily involved in the communication patterns of the policy process, their ideas and advice are of substantial value. They exercise influence through other means than the communication network examined here. The information source data indicate that at some point their ideas are embraced and moved by brokers and decision makers in the policy process.

The relationship between the bureaucracy and Congress is, of course, vital, and this analysis reflects this. As one would expect, the data reveal frequent communication between key congressional figures such as committee and subcommittee chairmen and staff directors and bureaucrats having legislative liaison and program control functions. Although Congress does not appear to be as effectively integrated with the operating agency as major interest groups, it does serve along with the agency as a major point of access for the lobbies. Since the policy makers were not in a major innovating period during the 90th Congress, as was the case with the 89th, it is quite natural that the lobbies were more attentive to the bureaucracy than to the legislature.

Institutional affiliation appears to have been the most important determinant of communication patterns in the educational policy process. The level of education toward which the participants were oriented seems also to have had a fairly strong impact on the structure of the communication network, indicating that the substantive focus of legislation and programs are reflected in communication patterns in the policy process. The third factor which appeared related to the observed structure of communications was the exclusiveness of governmental or nongovernmental contacts. The relationship here, however, was much less pronounced.

Institutional affiliation also appeared related to the importance of various sources of information employed by members of the policy process. A similar relationship prevailed between policy roles and institutional affiliation. Party affiliation was related to information-source utility insofar as the party out of power made somewhat more use of sources outside the federal government.

Regrettably, individual factors that were not systematically measured, such as background, previous experiences, and attitudes, appeared to have had some impact on communication patterns and information source usage in the policy process. Undoubtedly certain positions with specific responsibilities involve an individual more extensively in the communication network and lead him to obtain information from different sources than other positions and functions. But there does appear to be room for extensive variation between individuals. To a large degree it is difficult, if not impossible, to know how much communication, interaction, and ultimately influence depend on "the luck of the draw." [19] The effects of individuals, interest groups, institutional forces, and external pressures are difficult to define analytically let alone measure operationally. Indeed, it may never be possible to determine if the fact that certain individuals occupied critical positions at a particularly propitious time produced the policy choices made or whether those decisions would have happened regardless.

In addition, external factors such as the political context of the policy-making process, the constraints on spending for domestic programs, the popular appeal of education as a claimant on scarce resources, and the goals of the President are not incorporated in this chapter's analysis. Nor does the data permit an assessment of the importance of the President from a communications perspective or, most importantly, a determination of who influences whom. Before attemtping to speculate upon this and other crucial questions such as the determinants of education policy, an exploration of the operation of the national policy process in education is required.

This chapter has been a descriptive analytical exercise that has not attempted to explain why the educational policy process operates as it does. Ultimately, I will extrapolate beyond the data. This analysis is intended to provide a better basis for that speculation by identifying patterns of communication and sources of information in the policy process.

Notes

1. Harmon Zeigler and Michael Baer, *Lobbying: Interaction and Influence in American State Legislatures* (Belmont, Calif.: Wadsworth, 1969), p. 8.
2. John W. Thibaut and Harold H. Kelly, *The Social Psychology of Groups* (New York: John Wiley & Sons, 1961), p. 10.
3. For explanatory discussions of sociometric analysis, see: E. F. Borgotta, "Sociometry," in *International Encyclopedia of the Social Sciences* (New York: Macmillan and Free Press, 1968), 15: 53–56; Fred N. Kerlinger, *Foundations of Behavioral Research* (New York: Holt, Rinehart & Winston, 1964), chap. 31; Gardner Lindzey and E. Borgotta, "Sociometric Measurement, in G. Lindzey, ed., *Handbook of Social Psychology*, vol. 1 (Cambridge, Mass.: Addison-Wesley, 1954), chap. 11; and Charles H. Proctor and Charles P. Loomis, "Analysis of Sociometric Data," in Marie Jahoda, Morton Deutsch, and Stuart W. Cook, eds., *Research Methods in Social Relations*, pt. 2 (New York: Dryden Press, 1951), chap. 17. This discussion follows that in Proctor and Loomis.
4. See Proctor and Loomis, "Analysis of Sociometric Data," pp. 563–69.
5. The program employed in the analysis was SSA-II of the Guttman-Lingoes nonmetric series. See James C. Lingoes, "An IBM 7090 Program for Guttman-Lingoes Smallest Space Analysis," *Behavioral Science*" (1965): 487.
6. SSA derives its basic logic from multidimensional scaling. See the explanation by J. B. Kruskal, "Multidimensional Scaling by Optimizing Goodness of Fit to a Nonmetric Hypothesis," *Psychometrika* 29 (1964): 1–27. A more extended description of the methodology employed in this can be found in my "Bureaucratic-Congressional Interaction and the Politics of Education."
7. For the interpretation of data generated by the use of SSA in another area of political inquiry, see John P. Robinson and Robert Hefner, "Perceptual Maps of the World," *Public Opinion Quarterly* 32 (1968): 273–80.

8. Interview, 9 January 1968.

9. Interview, Emerson Elliott, 24 January 1968.

10. Interview, Edith Green, 23 February 1968.

11. Interview, William Gorham, 4 January 1968.

12. Interview, Nolan Estes, 27 December 1967.

13. Howe interview note 8.

14. Interview, James Gallagher, 21 December 1967.

15. Gorham interview, note 11.

16. Interview, Melvin R. Laird, 6 March 1968.

17. Interview, John Brademas, 20 February 1968.

18. J. Lieper Freeman, *The Political Process: Executive Bureau–Legislative Committee Relations* (New York: Random House, 1955), pp. 62–65.

19. The former director of the Budget, Charles Schultze, emphasized the importance of chance as a determinant of policy decisions and he used this phrase to make his point. Interview, 29 February 1968.

7

POLICY-MAKING STAGES

The national policy process in education is more or less continuous, but for analytical purposes it is helpful to divide it into three sequential stages: formulation, adoption, and implementation. This chapter examines the operations of the policy process in terms of these three stages.

Formulation*

The analysis of the formulative stage of the policy process raises a host of intriguing questions for which there are comparatively few definitive answers. What the interviews and other information generate in abundance, however, are tentative interpretations and suggestive explanations. The principal questions that will guide this inquiry into educational policy formulation focus on the origination of ideas and their movement onto the agenda for action. For example:

Where do ideas originate?
How are they moved forward?
What means are employed to establish an agenda for action?

* Portions of this section are adapted from Norman C. Thomas and Harold L. Wolman, "The Presidency and Policy Formulation: The Task Force Device," *Public Administration Review* 29 (September/October 1969): 459–71, by permission of the American Society for Public Administration and Harold L. Wolman.

What and who determine which ideas are not included on the agenda?
Or, alternatively, who determines priorities?
Who does not contribute to setting the agenda and determining priorities?
What roles do individual actors and institutions play?

The question of where ideas come from is almost impossible to answer with precision. The task of tracing the exact origin of significant new policy proposals may be fruitless, but it does seem that Yarmolinsky's suggestion of a "theory of simultaneous and seemingly spontaneous invention" [1] applies to education. For instance, seven people including Abraham Ribicoff, Francis Keppel, Wilbur Cohen, Senator Morse, Charles Lee, and Representatives Pucinski and Dent are credited with or claimed credit for tying aid to elementary and secondary education to the war on poverty in a manner that facilitated circumvention of the church-state issue. A major source of new ideas in education is, naturally, the academic community. Academia was the origin of such suggestions as the Educational Opportunity Bank, the voucher system, and open schools. Proposals for institutional grants in higher education originated with several unknown university and college presidents and were advanced by most national associations in higher education.

In addition, the NEA maintained its own sizable research staff and, until 1968, supported jointly with the AASA the highly respected elite group of educators and laymen known as the Educational Policies Commission. The philanthropic foundations have devoted much of their energy and resources to generating and demonstrating new approaches and techniques for solving a wide range of problems in education. Professionals in the field and line administrators in government agencies continually make suggestions that filter up through professional associations, educational institutions, and public bureaucracies to the point where one or more participants in the policy process adopt and advocate them.

Economic and political conditions outside the policy process have a substantial impact on the speed with which an idea moves ahead. General aid to elementary and secondary education provides a case in point. A familiar proposal of the NEA since the 1940s, it has been advocated in turn by congressional liberals and conservatives but never adopted. The threat it presented to other values, first local control of the schools and later a presidential commitment to educational change, made adoption too costly. Meanwhile, numerous other proposals have appeared, been adopted, and in some cases terminated.

The factors that account for the success or failure of an idea or that explain the duration of its gestation are too complex to describe in detail. Some of the more prominent influences seem quite manifest, however. They include cost, in absolute terms and in relation to competitive programs; the threat that they present to established interests and values; the level of presidential interest and the President's policy objectives; the individual policy makers who endorse and oppose the idea; and the political climate. Generally, but not always, ideas that carry a high price tag will have a more difficult time than those that do not, especially if there is intense competition for funds. Ideas that sharply challenge the status quo, and many innovative proposals do just that, tend to be resisted more actively than those which make incremental changes. Ideas that can be subjected to bargaining will probably move more rapidly toward adoption, albeit in amended form, than those which are not negotiable. Presidential support and approval is virtually a necessary but not a sufficient condition for the successful embodiment of an idea in policy. Key individuals who possess great prestige or are highly skilled in manipulating the policy process can contribute to the progress or blocking of an idea. And, if the political climate is receptive or hostile to new policies an idea's chances will be affected accordingly.

There was no shortage of ideas in the education policy process during the 90th Congress (see chapters 3 and 4). A major problem confronting the policy makers, however, was that of discriminating between viable proposals and suggestions which, regardless of their merit, had little or no chance of adoption. As knowledgeable and expert as they were, the policy makers still required some means of analyzing a vast amount of information and synthesizing it into an ordered agenda for action. In education, as in other national policy areas, the Presidency performed this function through the preparation of the President's legislative program and the budget. These documents, i.e., presidential messages and the annual budget, and specific authorization and appropriation bills, serve as the basis of congressional action. They establish a set of definite, but not inflexible, boundaries within which most serious policy deliberation occurs.

The policy formulation stage is crucial for it is where major innovations are spawned and matured. In all but the most exceptional circumstances, new policy departures and significant changes in existing policy must survive the process of agenda setting in order to receive consideration in Congress. This does not mean that modest, incremental changes are not possible without formal incorporation in the presidential policy agenda. They occur routinely through legislative and bureaucratic initiative. Nor does it deny the probability that presidentially supported proposals may be defeated or substantially modified by subsequent action elsewhere in the policy process. But it is manifest that unless and until major policy innovations, e.g., educational vouchers, federally funded open schools, institutional grants to colleges and universities, unrestricted block grants to the states, full-expense loans to college students with long-term repayment, and similar proposals are accorded a high presidential priority, the chances of their adoption and implementation are very small.

In establishing priorities, or in setting his policy agenda, the President necessarily employs the resources of his staff, the Bureau of the Budget (now the Office of Management and Budget), and other units of the Executive Office. In this respect, it is more accurate to speak of policy formulation by the Presidency, with the President as the principal individual participant in that institution. The general pattern of presidential policy formulation was developed under Presidents Roosevelt and Truman and had become a systematic routine by the early years of the Eisenhower administration.[2]

The legislative program emerged from proposals prepared by departments and agencies who based them on administrative experience and suggestions and ideas from their clientele groups. The Presidency was dependent on the bureaucracy for information, ideas, and new policy proposals. While the bureaucracy had vast information resources and no end of proposals, its perspective was limited and it tended over time to offer suggestions that were remedial and incremental rather than innovative and imaginative. The limits of bureaucratic initiative are almost an article of faith in the presidency. White House staff members and Budget Bureau officials during the Johnson administration were particularly skeptical of the capacity of HEW and USOE to be an effective agent of change in American education. A high-ranking Bureau of the Budget official, Philip S. Hughes, summed up this presidential staff perspective:

> . . . The routine way to develop a legislative program has been to ask
> the departments to generate proposals. Each agency sends its ideas
> through channels, which means that the ideas are limited by the
> imagination of the old-line agencies. They tend to be repetitive—the
> same proposals year after year. When the ideas of the different agencies
> reach the departmental level, all kinds of objections are raised, especially
> objections that new notions may somehow infringe on the rights of some
> other agency in the department. By the time a legislative proposal from a
> department reaches the President, it's a pretty well comprised product.[3]

The last three Presidents have sought to overcome some of the liabilities of their dependence on the bureaucracy in program development through the use of task forces of experts, knowledgeable laymen, and public officials. President Kennedy commissioned 29 and President Nixon 18 task forces to report on a wide range of policy problems prior to their inaugurations. The reports of these pre-inauguration task forces provided a reservoir of proposals which policy makers used during the ensuing presidential administrations. Neither President continued to use task forces systematically, although each appointed similar groups on an ad hoc basis to deal with a variety of domestic and foreign policy problems.

Shortly after taking office, President Johnson appointed a series of task forces to study specific policy areas.[4] Acting at the suggestion of advisers who were familiar with the Kennedy task forces, President Johnson sought to obtain ideas and suggestions from outside the federal government which would serve as the basis of a legislative program that was distinctively his own. In order to avoid having to defend the proposals before they became the basis for action, Johnson directed that the task forces operate under a cloak of secrecy. Their members, the content of their hearings, their deliberations, and their reports were not made public during his incumbency.

The 1964 experience with task-force operations was so successful that it was refined and expanded in the following years. Under the direction of Special Assistant Joseph A. Califano, the White House staff assumed the paramount role in setting the framework for legislative and administrative policy making. President Johnson brought the function of policy planning more effectively under his control through the integration of the task-force operation with legislative submissions and budget review and the creation of a small policy staff under one of his key assistants.[5] The impact of the departments and agencies in the development of the presidential legislative program may still have been considerable, but it tended to come more through the participation of their policy-level personnel in White House meetings where task-force reports were evaluated. Commissioner Howe acknowledged that in the past few years "much policy development in education has moved from here (USOE) to the White House." [6] Similarly, a career official in the Bureau of the Budget observed that "at the stage of developing the presidential legislative program, the task-force reports play a more significant role than any documents or proposals emanating from the agencies." [7]

The agencies proposed a substantial amount of technical legislation which corrected defects and filled gaps in existing statutes, but the most important substantive contributions came from elsewhere. "The task forces presented us with meaty propositions to which we could react," recalled a former Budget Bureau official, "not the nuts and bolts stuff which we usually got from the agencies." [8] The agencies also made major contributions to public policy by refining and making workable the general ideas of the task forces in the course of drafting bills and implementing programs, but their participation in the formulative stages was somewhat reduced during the Johnson administration.[9]

The processes of policy formulation in the Presidency varied widely in the period from 1964 through 1968, but a general pattern appears to have emerged in the cycle of the task-force operation as it developed under Califano and his staff.[10] Each year in late spring, Califano and his assistants visited a number of major university centers throughout the country in order to glean ideas for new programs. At the same time, the White House canvassed the administration for new ideas. Various officials who were regarded as "idea men" were invited to submit proposals on any subject directly to the White House. This permitted them to bypass normal bureaucratic channels and departmental and agency hierarchies.

After receiving them, Califano's assistants prepared written one-page descriptions of all the ideas. These "write-ups" included a "proposal" section which briefly explained the idea, a description of the problem, and its relationship to ongoing programs and a recommendation for action. Next, these papers were categorized and a high-level group within the Presidency reviewed them. This group also reviewed the reports of previous task forces, presidential commissions, and other advisory bodies which were filed during the course of the previous year. In 1967 this group included Califano, Budget Director Charles Schultze, his deputy Phillip S. Hughes, Chairman Gardner Ackley of the Council of Economic Advisers, Special Counsel to the President Harry McPherson, and Califano's staff. Following the review, Califano and his assistants compiled the remaining ideas which were grouped by substantive policy areas. The screening group then reconvened for a second examination after which it sent the book to the President with a cover letter indicating the areas that it felt required further study. The President and Califano then reviewed the proposals deciding either to abandon them, study them further, or mark them for additional study if time and staff were available.

Further development of the ideas that were not abandoned occurred through referral to individual consultants or formal advisory councils, study by departments and agencies, or examination by task forces. Reports of individual consultants were not often made public and their impact is difficult to assess. Advisory council reports usually are public documents. Their influence appears to vary with the reputations of their members, the quality of their content, and the current political significance of the subject matter. Agency studies also vary greatly in impact, but generally they can be regarded as contributing to internal bureaucratic thinking and policy development.

The assignment of a task force to examine an idea or a set of related ideas signified that the President and his top advisers regarded the problem as one of considerable significance. Although task forces did not routinely operate in all the Great Society areas, they did function fairly frequently. In 1967 a total of fifty separate task forces were operating in various domestic policy areas. Task-force assignments, which varied in scope and purpose, determined whether their members would be drawn from people outside or inside the government or from both groups.

Outside task forces were the primary means of securing new ideas for the development of policy. According to participants on various task forces in education, they received broad directives which accorded them maximum freedom to come forth with ideas.

There was some adjustment in the functions of outside task forces after

1964. In the words of one participant, the 1964 task forces were "happenings." President Johnson used the 1964 task forces as ad hoc devices to develop proposals which almost immediately became part of his legislative program. By 1966 the task forces were a normal and rather elaborate aspect of the operations of the Presidency. The President began to use them to take a long-range view of major policy areas and problems as well as to develop immediate legislative proposals. He and his staff took steps to institutionalize the task-force operation by integrating it with the highly structured and formal budget review process.

As compared to outside task forces, inside, or interagency task forces functioned more to coordinate agency approaches, to obtain some measure of interagency agreement in areas of dispute, and to review, in broad terms, the recommendations of outside task forces. While interagency groups may have generated some new proposals, their major purpose was to provide the President with a coordinated overview of functional problems that cut across departmental and agency lines and to suggest alternative solutions to them. An important aspect of this coordinating function of the interagency task forces was to conduct a "detailed pricing out of all proposals."

Members of the inside task forces usually included representatives of the Bureau of the Budget, Califano's staff, and agency heads or departmental assistant secretaries. Interestingly, legislative liaison personnel, who as brokers were well aware of the limits of political feasibility imposed by congressional and lobby group attitudes, did not usually participate. Apparently, the potential attenuation of the innovative thrust of the outside task-force reports that would accompany the involvement of such power brokers was considered too steep a price to pay for increased viability of the final proposals of the interagency bodies.

Once the task forces had written their reports, they submitted them to the President and deposited them with the Bureau of the Budget. Usually, outside task forces reported in the fall. (It is necessary to say "usually" because the entire process of policy formulation is flexible and somewhat unstructured. What happens in any given case often is dependent on idiosyncratic personal and situational variables. There is a great temptation for the analyst to impose a more rational order on the patterns of the governmental process than may be empirically justified.[11]) Then the Bureau and the relevant departments and agencies forwarded their comments directly to the White House.

Following the initial evaluation, the White House staff, under Califano's direction, took the lead in winnowing down task-force proposals. If it appeared that an outside task-force report should be followed by an interagency task force, that decision was made by Califano, the Budget director, the chairman of the Council of Economic Advisers, and the appropriate department and agency heads. Otherwise, in a series of White House meetings, the department and agency heads and their top assistants, representatives of the Bureau of the Budget's examining divisions, representatives of the Council of Economic Advisers, and members of Califano's staff examined the reports. The participants received continuous direction from the President as to his priorities. After much discussion and some bargaining, they developed a proposed legislative program which was presented to the President for final decisions.

The major task forces concerned with education during the Johnson administration included: (1) the Gardner* Task Force (1964), (2) the International Education Task Force chaired by Secretary of State Dean Rusk (1965), (3) the Ink Task Force (1965), (4) the 1966 Interagency Task Force, (5) the Task Force on Early Childhood Development (1966), (6) the Friday Task Force (1966–67); (7) the 1967 Interagency Task Force, (8) the Interagency Task Force on Child Development (1967), (9) the Task Force on the Education of Gifted Persons (1967–68), (10) the Task Force on Urban Educational Opportunities (1967–68), (11) the Interagency Task Force on Administration of Academic Science (1967–68), and (12) the Cohen Task Force (1968).

The reports of these task forces were made public in January 1972. The remarks of former HEW Secretary Wilbur Cohen at ceremonies marking the release of President Johnson's education papers provide a brief summary of the consequences of this activity.[12] The Gardner Task Force of 1964 was responsible for Title III and contributed to Title IV of ESEA. The International Education Task Force developed the proposal for the International Education Act, which Congress passed in 1966 but refused to fund. The Ink Task Force developed the plan for the 1965 reorganization of USOE. The Interagency Task Forces of 1966 and 1967 proposed amendments to existing legislation which were embodied in presidential messages in the following years, some of them were eventually adopted. The Early Childhood Development Task Force recommendations were the basis for the "Follow Through" program and Parent and Child Centers in the Johnson administration and for the establishment, during the Nixon administration, of HEW's Office of Child Development. The Interagency Task Force on Child Development was involved in implementing the outside group's report and in reviewing all HEW programs for children. The Friday Task Force contributed recommendations that appeared in President Johnson's 1968 education message. The four remaining task forces produced substantial reports which are chocked full of recommendations that comprised a lengthy agenda for future action.

Although I have not had the opportunity to examine these reports and

---

* Often, outside task forces were referred to by the name of the chairman. The chairmen who lent their names to education task forces were John W. Gardner, then president of the Carnegie Corporation; President William G. Friday of the University of North Carolina; and Dwight Ink, a career civil servant then with the Bureau of the Budget.

consequently have not traced the fate of the myriad of recommendations and proposals they generated, it is apparent that the early task forces had greater impact on legislation. As the task forces proliferated and the scope of their inquiry broadened, their uniqueness declined and their proposals became increasingly commonplace. In the last two years of the Johnson administration, interagency task forces were centrally involved in policy formulation and played a more important role than outside groups.

Membership on the two task forces on which I have data was neither carefully balanced nor broadly representative (see table 7-1). The Gardner Task Force contained a wider range of individuals than the Friday group, which was dominated by academicians, but neither included representatives of national associations in education or other prominent lobby groups, e.g., the NAACP, the AFL–CIO, or the U.S. Chamber of Commerce. Because the composition of the task forces was kept secret, the administration could avoid striving for balanced representation in favor of imaginativeness. To the extent, however, that quickly salable proposals were desired, task-force membership tended to be more representative. In 1964, President Johnson sought a report from the Gardner Task Force that would serve as the basis for an immediate legislative triumph, hence it included businessmen and as many state and local officials as any other category. The Friday Task Force of 1967 had as its mission the development of solutions to problems in urban education and the financing of higher education. It was instructed to come up with approaches at four different funding levels and not to worry about questions of political feasibility. Its membership reflected the more theoretical character of its task.

Table 7-1
Membership on Outside Task Forces in Education

	State and Local Officials	College Administrators	College Professors	Business	Foundation Officials	Other
1964	3	3	2	2	2	1
1967	2	6	3	0	1	1

Usually the President and his top policy advisers selected the members of outside task forces. The selection process operated quite informally. The White House staff, the Bureau of the Budget, the Office of Science and Technology, and in some cases the department and the agency suggested prospective members. The White House staff screened the initial nominations with the President making the final choices. As indicated above, the criteria for selection tended to vary with the mission of the task force. Many respondents emphasized the importance of independence of viewpoint;

however, it was acknowledged that persons holding "radical" * views were not likely to be included. Occasionally federal officials served on outside task forces, e.g., Commissioner Keppel and the Gardner Task Force, or they sat with them on a fairly regular basis, as did Secretary Gardner and Commissioner Howe with the Friday group.

In selecting task forces a conscious effort was made to avoid formal representation of established clientele groups such as the NEA and the ACE which customarily worked closely with HEW and USOE in developing policy. As USOE's role in policy initiation began to decline as a consequence of the task-force operation, the access of the lobby groups to policy makers who set the agenda for action also began to fall. These groups responded with hostility toward the task forces. A typical reaction was that of a higher education association official who stated, "The task forces represent the worst form of intellectual and educational elitism. They are based on the implicit assumption that the education associations are incapable of any sort of creative or innovative thought." [13] Input from the education establishment groups to the task forces was limited to brief presentations by a few leading figures such as former NEA Executive Secretary William Carr.

Generally, the task forces began their work with one or two day-long meetings at which the members, in the course of reacting to a broad position paper, ranged over the entire subject. During these sessions they identified areas for future study and commissioned additional position papers which served as the basis for discussions at subsequent sessions. After a few more meetings, either the staff or a task-force member, usually the chairman, prepared drafts of various sections of a proposed report. Further discussions focused on the drafts and the task forces moved toward consensus on recommendations and reports.

The task forces do not appear to have used formal votes to reach decisions. The usual mode of decision was bargaining until a consensus developed. When members raised strong objections, efforts were made to satisfy them. Although the task forces were not broadly representative, their members apparently did not represent institutional and professional interests to a considerable degree during deliberations.

The secrecy of the task forces was one of their most important operational characteristics. In the eyes of President Johnson and his staff, secrecy was crucial for it enabled them to ignore proposals that were politically infeasible. Recommendations could be adopted or rejected without having to expend political resources defending the choices made. The range of options was not only maximized, it was kept open longer and at very little

---

* None of the respondents offered a concise definition of radical viewpoints or persons. In the context of the interviews, the term usually referred to prescriptions for sweeping changes in the educational system, e.g., abolition of the public schools, or to individuals associated or identified with the so-called New Left.

cost. Secrecy also prevented opposition to task-force proposals from developing until a much later stage in the policy process.

The principal sources of ideas for the task forces were the members and the staff. The members, of course, drew upon their backgrounds and their particular expertise. Accordingly their suggestions reflected philosophical, professional, and experiential considerations.

There seems almost unanimous agreement among persons familiar with the task forces that competent staffing was essential to the success of their operations. The three education task forces were staffed with Bureau of Budget personnel. They tended to prod the task forces to be venturesome. Their activities included preparing or assigning the conduct of background studies, acquiring data, drafting reports, and providing liaison with the White House.

HEW and USOE played a peripheral role in the operation of the outside task forces in education. Since the manifest intent in using outside task forces was to bypass the bureaucracy, departmental and agency officials tended to distrust task forces and minimize their significance. As Samuel Halperin, deputy assistant secretary of HEW for legislation remarked, "The reports are kept so secret that they don't really pollinate anything." [14]

In interagency task forces, the primary department or agency dominated the proceedings. For example, Commissioner Howe was the key figure in the work of the 1967 inside task force in education. That group developed the administration's 1968 legislative program on the basis of recommendations of the Friday Task Force and agency submissions; however, the Friday Task Force report was not made available to all members of the inside group. At least part of the reason for the creation of the interagency group and the limited access given its members to the Friday Task Force report appears to have been the administration's negative evaluation of the latter document.

The evaluation of the reports of outside task forces was a somewhat unstructured process. After being sent to the President and deposited with the Budget Bureau's Office of Legislative Reference, the reports went to the Bureau's examining divisions, other units in the Presidency, and the agencies for comment. The role of the agencies was minor, however, compared with that of the Bureau of the Budget and the White House staff. Significantly, the same personnel from the Bureau and the White House who served on the task-force staffs and sat with them as liaison men were usually involved in evaluating the reports.

The dual role of the Bureau and the White House staff meant that the reports had an Executive Office bias which was not openly acknowledged. One HEW official charged that "there is an incestuous relationship between the task forces on the one hand and the Budget Bureau and the White House on the other." [15] The Bureau was aware of its dual role and the problems inherent in it. According to the staff director for the Gardner and Friday task forces, "I leaned over backward to be fair, but I did feel like I was meeting myself coming back." [16] Or, as William Carey, the assistant director in charge of the Human Resources Division, observed, "We are involved at the Bureau with task forces as participants and as critics." [17] But the dual role was perplexing and frustrating for those outside the Presidency who were affected by its actions.

It is, of course, impossible to measure directly the effects of task-force reports on education policy. They had only a limited impact on the development of the budget which proceeded in customary fashion and was altered mainly by the introduction of PPBS. But there is little question that the independent advice and suggestions provided by the task forces helped to shape the broad outlines of President Johnson's legislative program and provided some specific proposals as well. One of the most innovative programs of ESEA, Title III, clearly originated with the Gardner Task Force, and Title IV received a major push from it. Most of the recommendations of the 1966 Early Childhood Task Force were adopted, although at lower funding levels than recommended. On the other hand, only a few recommendations of the 1967 Friday Task Force, principally the Networks for Knowledge and the Partnership for Learning and Earning proposals, appeared in the administration's 1968 education bills. The muted impact of the Friday Task Force report can be explained in part by its focus on long-range rather than immediate problems and by political and budgetary constraints imposed by the Vietnam war.

There are indications that the flexibility and adaptability of the task forces in education had begun to decline as their operations became increasingly systematized toward the end of the Johnson administration. They were tending to become elaborate instruments of incremental adjustment rather than catalytic agents of change. A leadership technique designed to produce policy innovation worked so well initially that overuse was rendering it counterproductive. It also appears that the substantive innovations resulting from the task forces may have been less than their advocates claimed. As a Bureau of the Budget official acknowledged, "they tended to pull together existing things instead of coming up with new ideas." [18]

To the extent that task forces were made representative through their membership, tendencies toward innovation may have been mitigated. This appears likely since consensus was the fundamental decision-making rule and final agreement tended to represent compromise rather than creative thinking. However, the fact that task forces may not have been as inventive as their proponents claimed does not mean that essentially the same courses of action would have been followed without them. The ideas they promoted may not have been entirely new, but they were not yet embodied in the presidential policy agenda, nor, in most cases, were they supported by the bureaucracy. Without the Gardner Task Force, for example, it is not likely that the supplementary educational centers and regional education laboratories would have been pushed by the administration and authorized by Congress as part of ESEA.

But more important than the immediate substantive results of the task-force operation in education were the procedural consequences for policy formulation. The Presidency acquired a steady input of new ideas from nontraditional sources which afforded a maximum range of options that could be kept open over a long period of time with minimal energy required to defend presidential choices. This was a substantial, but immeasurable advantage to an innovation-minded President. However, it entailed substantial costs in the form of resentments engendered in the bureaucracy and among powerful clientele groups. It also appears to have contributed to heightened expectations of a steady flow of new programs and benefits which could not be met as the costs of the Vietnam war increasingly limited nondefense spending. Such unfilled expectations reduced presidential support among education clientele and other interest groups. Whatever its costs and benefits, the Johnson task-force operation was a major new tool of presidential leadership that profoundly influenced the policy formulation stage of the educational policy process. Its failure to survive in the Nixon administration reflects the different leadership style and policy objectives of Johnson's successor and not the insignificance of the task forces as they functioned between 1964 and 1969.

Policy formulation in the educational policy process centered, then, in the Presidency. The key participants were the President, the White House staff members, and Budget Bureau officials. Acting in response to explicit presidential directives or in accordance with their interpretations of more general presidential objectives, the central decision makers set educational policy priorities within the parameters imposed by budgetary constraints and other external considerations. Also included among the central decision makers were the commissioner of education and selected HEW officials. Their involvement, while frequent and often intensive, was regulated by the Presidency. They were necessarily included as leaders and representatives of the bureaucracy and they wielded substantial influence in consequence of their positions. Additional influence and involvement were based on their standing with members of the institutionalized Presidency. Both Commissioner Howe and Secretary Gardner, until his departure, were held in high regard and exerted considerable influence on personal rather than positional grounds.

Equally significant in examining the policy formulation stage were the kinds of participants who were not included. Not surprisingly, there was little direct congressional participation during the 90th Congress. Congressional leaders were informed of the content of the legislative program before it was made final, but they were not consulted during its development. The major legislative innovations of the 89th Congress were not repeated in the 90th, although the administration continued the search for new ideas and attempted to give the appearance of creativity in its legislative proposals by authorizing small programs which could later be expanded. There was no need for early or sustained congressional involvement in what was basically a non-innovating period. Loyal administration spokesmen on the Hill could be relied on to push the ESEA, HEA, and voc-ed extension bills through along with the eye-catching but minor new programs and, most importantly, to ward off opposition attempts to redirect the basic legislation, e.g., the Quie Amendment. Congressional considerations under such conditions could be effectively incorporated during the adoption stage. The education establishment groups were accorded limited access to the formulation stage through their White House contact, Douglass Cater. The education association officials who spoke to the matter complained of their lack of access to the Bureau of the Budget. Non-education groups, including labor, civil rights, and other black organizations, were conspicuous by their absence during the formulative stage.[19]

Although priorities were determined and the policy agenda set by a group of central decision makers operating in the Presidency, there were effective limits to the scope of their action. For example, in spite of a strong preference in the Presidency for imaginative programs that would change American education, some highly innovative proposals, such as the EOB, were kept off the policy agenda by strong opposition from certain higher education groups and from key members of Congress. The prospect of conflict with some major supporters of the administration's education policies prevented the EOB from receiving serious consideration. Anticipated reaction accorded strategic interests a veto without a fight. Once the Land Grant College Association attacked it publicly, the EOB was a dead letter.

Much of the decision making regarding the policy agenda did not take place in public, however. Task-force reports and, to a large extent, agency submissions, were the subject of debate and negotiation inside the institutionalized Presidency. Direct congressional and interest-group input was readily available, but generally it was obtained indirectly through brokers. The principal brokers in the educational policy process were HEW's legislative liaison officials, Ralph Huitt and Samuel Halperin. Both were highly regarded by the establishment associations, and both had the confidence and support of top HEW officials. Halperin in particular had developed extensive contacts in Congress, most of which were favorable to him. Huitt and Halperin were able to assess the viability of salability of various proposals "on the Hill" and with the lobby groups. Those assessments were of critical importance in program formulation. Because of his active style of operation, Halperin appeared to be a powerful mover of ideas. This visibility had its costs, however, for Budget Bureau and White House staff participants in the policy process tended to regard him skeptically. What they failed to recognize was that his value to the Presidency stemmed from his wide reputation in the policy process as an honest broker.

In spite of the constraints imposed through anticipated congressional and interest-group reactions and indirect external influence exerted through brokers, the formulation stage of the policy process remained under the effective control of the institutionalized Presidency. The effectiveness of the Presidency in establishing priorities and setting the agenda for action is reflected in the hostility that several respondents expressed to the Bureau of the Budget and the White House staff. Of 33 responses to a question which asked if the major elements involved in making and implementing education policy ought to be more or less powerful, 12 called for a reduction in the power of the Budget Bureau or the White House Staff (see table 7-2).

Table 7-2
Perceptions of Power Distribution in Policy Process by Policy Role

Role	Generally Satisfied	Generally Dissatisfied	BOB White House Too Powerful	Foundations Too Powerful	Own Group Requires More Power
Bureaucrat	2	2	5	1	3
Legislator			1	1	
Legislative staff	1		3		1
Lobbyist		3	3	3	1
Expert	2	1			
Total	5	6	12	5	5
N = 33					

Although these data cannot be regarded as accurate reflections of the participant's perception of the policy process, they do indicate the presence of extensive dissatisfaction with the perceived balance of power in the process. The Bureau of the Budget was the focus of much of that dissatisfaction. Bureaucrats, legislative staff members, and lobbyists particularly tended to regard it as too powerful. Their complaints were directed toward the Bureau's role in developing legislative proposals and establishing basic policy goals rather than its budgetary role. A recurring theme was the Bureau's lack of expertise in education. Typical of the Bureau's negative image among other policy makers were the comments of a bureaucrat:

> The Budget Bureau strikes me as moving a bit too far into content questions which they aren't competent to carry through. Here and there, because of the frenetic pace, many thoughtful program people are at the mercy of the Budget Bureau people who don't know what is in the black book.[20]

A legislator:

> The Budget Bureau is far too powerful. It is much too influential in
> setting national priorities. More so than any other element in the process.
> This is especially disturbing since the Budget Bureau people have no
> special competence or expertise in education. They are generalists who
> have no knowledge of the real needs and problems.[21]

A legislative staff member:

> The Budget Bureau is exercising too much control. It plays two roles.
> Before OE and HEW can come up with legislative proposals, the Budget
> Bureau must approve. I don't know where they get the competence to do
> it. . . . Secondly, when appropriation requests are being made I have less
> quarrel.[22]

And a lobbyist:

> The Bureau of the Budget ought to be deemphasized. They don't know
> enough about education. They have a transitory staff and the directors
> are laymen.[23]

Objections to the foundations and expressions of general discontent were
much less explicit.

For a sizable number of educational policy makers, then, too much
control over policy was lodged in the institutionalized Presidency. The
problem was not so much that the President with the help of his supportive
staff aides and units defined goals, established priorities, and set the agenda, but
that access to that critical stage of formulation was limited and tightly
controlled. As the NEA's principal lobbyist, Dr. John Lumley, remarked in
discussing the Bureau of the Budget, "It is the one place in the system which is
closed to us. Other than trouble getting access to the Budget Bureau, we have
our day in court everywhere else." [24] Yet, it was that very lack of open access
to congressional, clientele, bureaucratic, and other interests that enabled the
Bureau to serve the President so effectively and which has led Presidents since
Franklin Roosevelt to rely so heavily on its judgment. The absence of
professional experts in the Bureau and on the White House staff was ideally
suited to the needs of a President whose primary goal for federal educational
programs was to promote change. The absence of education professionals in
the presidency was partially compensated for by the inclusion of Commissioner Howe among the central decision makers, the ready availability of
input from external interests, and the acquired expertise of Bureau of the
Budget personnel. Had President Johnson not been so disposed to promote
change through federal programs, the Bureau's influence would probably have

been considerably less. Even so, if one notes only casually the visible effects or outcomes of the educational policy "innovations" of the Johnson administration it is apparent that the Bureau's impact was somewhat exaggerated. The education programs of the administration contributed more to the maintenance of existing educational systems than to the promotion of fundamental changes. Programs with potential for breakthrough change, e.g., ESEA Title III, were brought under control of the establishment by the end of 1967 despite the protests of the Presidency, the reports of task forces, and the arguments of intellectuals and experts in universities and foundations.

Adoption

The results of the formulative stage of the policy process set the outer limits of prospective actions in the adoption stage. The locus of action moves from the executive branch to Congress. The bureaucracy and the Presidency join forces to secure enactment of the President's legislative program and approval of his budget. Clientele groups and other organized interests enjoy comparatively open access and compete with the departments, agencies, the White House, and each other. The most significant results that can be anticipated are not the emergence of major new policies, but rather the modification or defeat of the presidential program. The congressional impact on policy is more likely to be negative, restraining, and remedial than positive, encouraging, and creative. In the educational policy process during the 90th Congress, however, it was at the adoption stage where bargains were made and compromises struck that provided the authority and the wherewithal for action.

Policy adoption requires approval in committee and then on the floor in each House of Congress. Most of the time that a proposal is before Congress is spent in committee where consideration is extensive and detailed. Floor action, although subject to dilatory tactics, occurs in a limited time period and usually focuses on a few salient issues. Members of the committee which considered and reported the bill are experts in the particular policy area, however, and they tend to dominate proceedings on the floor.

As previously observed (see chapter 5), the House and Senate committees and subcommittees in the educational policy process differed sharply with respect to their levels of partisanship, operational patterns, and the personal styles of their leaders. The House Education and Labor Committee was characterized by a high degree of partisan conflict in hearings and during markup sessions, divided votes in committee, and minority reports on most important legislation. On controversial issues, committee Republicans generally took opposite positions from the liberal Democratic members with the balance of power residing in a small group of moderate Democrats.

Compromises were sufficient to produce minimum winning coalitions, usually among the Democratic majority who, on occasion, were joined by one or two deviant liberal Republicans. The House committee members tended to "do their own legislative work" and relied on staff primarily for information and technical advice. The House committee, being fairly large (33 members) and fragmented, had a set of leaders who reflected its internal divisions. They regarded themselves as spokesmen for partisan, administration, or clientele interests and contended actively with each other to maximize their impact on legislation. Consequently, issues that divided the committee usually were brought up and fought out again on the floor.

In contrast, the Senate Education Subcommittee was characterized by the absence of overt partisanship, extensive use of and dependence on staff, and a consensual decisional pattern accompanied by a single dominant leader. Although substantial ideological and partisan differences existed between various members of the Senate subcommittee, its hearings were seldom acerbic, markup sessions were for bargaining and not advocacy, and it nearly always produced a unanimous report. The leadership style of Senator Morse appears to have been a major factor contributing to the sublimation of partisanship. Morse sought to build unanimity, or at least obtain acquiescence, in the committee by according any senator who wished it "a piece of the action" and by making compromises whenever necessary. He attempted to take legislation to the floor that carried total committee backing.

The contrasts between the House and Senate appropriations subcommittees were equally striking. The House subcommittee conducted extensive hearings that probed the details of HEW and USOE operations and program administration. House subcommittee members sought through the hearings to effect changes in policy implementation by the bureaucracy. And the House subcommittee manifested a strong cutting bias with respect to the administration's budget requests. The Senate subcommittee's performance was quite perfunctory in comparison. Only its chairman and ranking minority member participated in the brief hearings. Its major effect was to restore partially the House-imposed cuts.

Although the differences between House and Senate committee operations were quite striking, there were also many similarities. The procedural routines were almost identical. More importantly, education associations, institutions, and individual educators as well as numerous other interests had open and readily available access to committee members and staff. Groups that lacked effective access to any of the key participants in the formulative stage, e.g., labor, civil rights, and other black organizations, encountered little difficulty making their views known and obtaining advocates in Congress. Additionally, in spite of operational differences, the range of policy goals, social attitudes, and values was quite similar in both the House and Senate committees.

The differences that were so salient in the committee phase of the adoption process did not characterize floor action. At first blush it seemed likely that floor action in the House would be more sharply partisan than in the Senate. An examination of the debates as reported in the *Congressional Record* and the descriptive summaries in *Congressional Quarterly* indicated that this was not the case. Unlike the analysis of the committee stage, which because of a lack of data was necessarily qualitative, it is possible to analyze floor action quantitatively using roll-call votes which are a readily available source of data.

The votes included in the analysis were all the contested roll calls involving substantive education issues in the 90th Congress. These included bills on final passage, amendments to bills, and amendments to appropriation bills. The determination of substantive education issues was necessarily a subjective judgment, but it seemed more appropriate to resolve all cases of doubt in favor of inclusion. Final votes on the Labor–HEW appropriation bills were not included, however, as they embodied non-education issues. (The context in which the votes occurred is described and discussed in chapter 4.) There were a total of 10 roll calls in the House and 18 in the Senate in the two sessions of the 90th Congress. The smaller number of roll calls in the House appears to have been due more to the disposition of issues by voice votes in committee of the whole rather than to less contentiousness on the floor.

A few caveats on roll calls are in order before proceeding with the analysis. Roll calls are an essential but not necessarily determinative aspect of the policy adoption process. They are often preceded by unrecorded decisions and agreements that affect the outcome. In spite of these limitations, roll calls have one indisputable advantage: they "represent a record of the principal congressional actions." [25] They provide firm data on how congressmen voted. Although such data do not establish the causes of congressional voting, they do give evidence of the importance of various reference groups and individuals as sources of voting cues.

In most studies of congressional voting, party is an important, if not the primary reference group.[26] Other factors that have been found to have an important relationship to voting include region, committee colleagues, state delegations in the House, constituency, and leaders. The contrasting levels of partisanship, decisional patterns, and leadership styles in the House and Senate education committees direct the focus of this analysis of floor voting. Its objective is to examine the impact on the voting of party, legislative committee, region (among Democrats), ideology (as manifested in the so-called conservative coalition), and committee leaders.

The reference groups that will be examined include Republican and Democratic party members in the full chamber, northern and southern Democrats, the conservative coalition comprised of Republicans and southern Democrats, all committee members, and committee Democrats and

Republicans. The importance of these groups as sources of voting cues will be measured through use of the index of cohesion. A measure of intragroup agreement, the index of cohesion is computed by taking the number of votes cast by the members of the group in a majority on a roll call and dividing it by the number of group members who voted, subtracting 50 from it, and multiplying by 2.[27] Thus, $IC = 2(100(m/t) - 50)$, where m = votes cast by the majority and t = the total group vote. The higher the level of cohesion, the greater the probable importance of the group as a referent for its members.

An additional indication of the importance of the various reference groups can be obtained by examining the extent to which they serve as a basis for structuring cleavages. This will be determined by measuring the difference on roll-call votes between various pairs of reference groups with the index of dis-likeness. The index of dis-likeness is computed by subtracting the percentage of yes votes cast by one group from the percentage of yes votes cast by the other. Thus, $IDL = \%Y_1 - \%Y_2$. The index is an absolute value, i.e., the greater it is numerically the greater the dissimilarity between groups regardless of algebraic sign. Consequently, all IDL scores will be reported as positive integers. The IDL has been selected in preference to the more familiar index of likeness[28] because intergroup differences are the object of concern.

On the basis of the analysis of the legislative committees, it was anticipated that full chamber and committee party groups might manifest substantially higher internal cohesion in the House than in the Senate and that there would be more conflict between the members of pairs of opposed groups in the House than in the Senate. There was no basis for predicting whether the regional and ideological reference groups would have greater intragroup agreement in one chamber than in the other or if they would appear as stronger forces than party and committee groups. It was assumed that party, region, and ideology would serve as a basis for some intergroup conflict in both chambers. Only a portion of these expectations were filled (see tables 7-3 and 7-4).

The most striking aspect of these data is the high degree of similarity in the patterns of reference-group influence in the House and Senate. All committee members, committee Republicans, all Republicans, and the conservative coalition had approximately equal levels of internal agreement in each chamber. Committee Democrats, all Democrats, and northern Democrats manifested a higher degree of cohesion in the House than their Senate counterparts did, but southern Democrats were more cohesive in the Senate.

In both chambers, regional reference groups within the Democratic party appeared to have the strongest influence on their members. Region was an important cue source for all Senate Democrats and for northern Democrats in the House. The lower level of cohesion among southern Democrats in the House may reflect a division between members with predominantly urban

Table 7-3
90th Congress. Reference Group Cohesion on Education Roll-Call Votes[a]

House Education and Labor Committee			House of Representatives					
Members	Dems.	Reps.	Members	Dems.	N.Dems.	S.Dems.	Reps.	Conservative Coalition
55.9	85.9	49.3	35.0	50.6	84.7	36.1	47.3	39.7

Senate Labor and Public Welfare Committee			Senate					
Members	Dems.	Reps.	Members	Dems.	N.Dems.	S.Dems.	Reps.	Conservative Coalition
55.9	70.4	47.8	30.0	40.4	69.6	57.8	45.7	41.9

[a] Mean index-of-cohesion scores on 10 House and 18 Senate roll calls.

constituencies and those with more rural districts. As the South becomes more urbanized and congressional districts are reapportioned according to population distribution, the traditionally high voting cohesion of its Democratic congressmen on domestic policy issues no longer prevails. Its heavily urbanized districts elect more liberal congressmen while continued election of fairly conservative Democrats rather than Republicans in many non-urban congressional districts helps to reduce voting cohesion. The higher cohesion level among southern Democratic senators can be explained, at least in part, as a consequence of the senators' statewide constituencies. They tended to be more responsive to the traditional pressures and concerns of their region and to be somewhat less affected by socioeconomic change than their House counterparts. However, that they were subject to some intragroup tensions is apparent when they are compared to their party colleagues from the North.

The relatively low level of cohesion among Republicans in both chambers probably stems, at least in part, from the internal contradictions that beset the party. It also reflects the party's out-of-power status during the 90th Congress. Republican congressmen were not under pressure to rally behind their President's program. They were more free to push their own projects and those of other reference groups.

In spite of operational differences between the House and Senate committees, they performed similar functions for their members as cue sources in floor voting. It was somewhat unexpected that the Senate committee members manifested no more internal agreement in floor action than members of the House committee. It was also mildly surprising to find that Senate Democratic committee members were a less cohesive voting block than House committee Democrats. Apparently Senator Morse's carefully engineered committee consensus was subject to breakdowns on the floor. Agreement to report a bill from committee did not necessarily commit a member to support it on the floor. That there was a relatively high degree of agreement among committee members on education roll calls in both houses suggests that committee partisanship and decisional style are not strongly related to or determinative of committee members' voting behavior on the floor. The somewhat lower level of cohesion among Senate than House committee Democrats may, however, be a consequence of less partisanship in the Senate committee. Its Democratic members may feel less compelled to maintain committee positions on the floor which had not previously been sharply contested with committee Republicans.

Table 7-4
90th Congress: Reference-Group Conflict on Education Roll-Call Votes[a]

House of Representatives						
All Dems. vs. All Reps.	Comm. Dems. vs. Comm. Reps.	Comm. Dems. vs. All Dems.	Comm. Reps. vs. All Reps.	N.Dems. vs. S.Dems.	S.Dems. vs. All Reps.	N.Dems. vs. C.Coalition
26.9	34.9	25.5	11.4	49.0	21.3	46.6
Senate						
27.4	32.7	16.3	14.8	50.8	25.8	41.1

[a] Mean index of dislikeness between reference-group pairs.

The role of reference groups in organizing cleavages in floor voting provides another perspective on their function as cue sources for their members. Again, we find more similarities than differences between the two houses of Congress (see table 7-4). In each House, the sharpest differences were between northern and southern Democrats and between northern Democrats and the conservative coalition. Straight party conflict was sharper among committee members than among all members of each house. Apparently divisive issues could be perceived more clearly by policy experts than by non-experts. The greater difference between committee Democrats and the rest of their party colleagues than that which existed among Republicans in each chamber probably reflects a greater ideological dispersion among congressional Democrats.

The differences between reference groups in education roll-call voting reveal the combined importance of party, region, and ideology. Neither party alone nor the committees were as important in structuring conflict as the classic split between northern democrats and the conservative coalition or the regional division among congressional Democrats. In this respect, congressional action in education policy adoption resembles that in other policy areas.[29] Nor does the role of the reference groups examined here as cue sources vary markedly between the two houses.

Another potential source of cues in congressional voting are those members who have acquired leadership roles. In the educational policy process the principal leadership roles in the adoption stage were filled by committee leaders. The elected congressional party leaders did not take an active part in floor debate. Some measure of the importance of committee leaders as cue givers in roll-call voting can be obtained by ascertaining the extent to which members of various reference groups agreed with each leader. It should be recognized that the leader-group agreement scores cannot demonstrate influence relationships. Influence can move in either direction:

$$group \longleftrightarrow leader$$

I am assuming that leaders give direction to reference groups and that they consciously seek to affect the actions, in this case roll-call votes, of group members. I am also assuming that leaders respond to cues or signals from relevant reference groups.

As previously indicated, there were four distinctive educational policy leaders in the House and three in the Senate (see chapter 5). The House leaders included: Representative Carl Perkins, who as committee chairman found himself acting as spokesman for the administration; Representative John Brademas, principal spokesman for the committee's liberal Democrats on education; Representative Edith Green, self-styled spokesman for the education profession and unofficial leader of the moderate Democrats; and Representative Albert Quie, the Republican leader and spokesman. On the other side of Capitol Hill, the education policy leaders were Senator Wayne Morse, chairman of the Education Subcommittee, administration spokesman, leader of the Senate's liberal Democrats, and "Mr. Education" to the press; Senator Jacob Javits, official Republican spokesman; and Senator Peter Dominick, the unofficial voice of senatorial conservatives. The reference groups are those examined above.

The data reflect the ascribed leadership roles quite accurately in both houses (see table 7-5). Perkins, as committee chairman, had the highest agreement score with Democratic members and northern Democrats in the whole House. He was in agreement with the full membership on almost two-thirds of the roll calls and with both elements of the conservative coalition over half of the time. His scores suggest an effort to maintain the committee and the administration position in floor voting accompanied by a willingness to compromise. Perkins appears to have a style fairly typical of the brokerage leadership exercised by committee chairmen, including Senator Morse whose scores closely resembled Perkins'. The only notable difference between the two committee chairmen was Morse's higher level of agreement with his northern Democratic colleagues and greater disagreement with members of

Table 7-5
Leader-Reference-Group Agreement on Education Roll Call Votes[a]

Leaders	Education and Labor Committee			House of Representatives					
	Members	Dems.	Reps.	Members	Dems.	N.Dems.	S.Dems.	Reps.	Conservative Coalition
Perkins	70.1	81.6	57.6	63.0	68.7	75.2	51.0	53.0	52.3
Brademas	79.5	92.6	59.1	57.9	61.2	68.5	42.2	51.6	44.3
Green	67.8	68.7	68.2	65.0	64.9	68.1	56.2	59.4	58.4
Quie	69.5	66.7	73.2	60.0	55.4	56.5	52.5	68.2	63.1

Leaders	Labor and Public Welfare Committee			Senate					
	Members	Dems.	Reps.	Members	Dems.	N.Dems.	S.Dems.	Reps.	Conservative Coalition
Morse	75.7	82.6	64.8	61.5	68.8	83.0	40.9	49.2	44.8
Javits	72.0	85.8	52.0	55.5	62.6	81.2	26.1	42.6	36.4
Dominick	43.6	28.7	51.1	55.8	48.6	38.5	68.7	67.6	68.0

[a] Percentage of agreement between individual leaders and reference-group members.

the conservative coalition. The larger proportion of northern Democrats in the upper chamber apparently made compromise less imperative for Morse.

Representative Brademas and Senator Javits, as liberal spokesmen, manifested similar but not identical patterns in their agreement scores. Brademas was in agreement with committee colleagues more than his chairman, a consequence of his nearly unanimous agreement with fellow Democrats. Perkins apparently accepted a higher level of disagreement with committee members in the interest of extending his influence with other members. Brademas's low agreement scores outside the committee, especially with the conservative coalition, reflect the ideological distance between the liberally oriented committee and the rest of the House. Javits appears as a maverick Republican superliberal. He agreed with his Democratic committee colleagues slightly more than his chairman, disagreed with all Senate Republicans somewhat more than Morse, and was at odds with southern Democrats three times in four. He managed to agree with the full membership of the Senate more often than not only because of very high agreement with northern Democrats. His agreement scores suggest that on education matters he was but a nominal Republican. He does not appear to have maximized the influence potential of his formal position as ranking Senate Republican in the area of education. The pattern of Javits' scores suggests that congressional committee leadership is constrained by party reference groups. Of course the data do not discount the possibility that Javits may have influenced northern Democrats substantially, although that seems unlikely given the assertive and skillful brokerage role played by Morse.

The two other Republican leaders, Quie in the House and Dominick in the Senate, were more in accord with their fellow Republican and southern Democratic reference groups. However, Quie was far more in harmony with his committee colleagues than Dominick was with his. Also, Dominick tended to agree more with southern and less with northern Democrats in the full chamber than did Quie. These differences reflect Quie's more liberal posture and his more extensive involvement in committee decision making. Dominick, much less a leader in committee than Quie, confined his activity primarily to the floor. The strong liberal orientation of the Senate Education Subcommittee and Morse's leadership style in committee apparently left little room for an active conservative voice.

The Senate did not contain an analogue to the fourth House leader, Representative Green. Mrs. Green's agreement scores reflect her efforts to maximize her influence by sacrificing some agreement with committee colleagues and appealing to all major reference groups. Her success is apparent in her relatively high agreement scores with both northern Democrats and the conservative coalition and the highest level of agreement by any leader with all House members. Among committee members, she agreed at an equal level with both party groups and minimized her disagreements with the full-chamber reference groups. Whether this reflects an independent leadership role committed to the pursuit and defense of principle or a calculated personal aggrandizement of influence is a matter of disputed conjecture. No doubt both explanations are partially valid.

The pattern of congressional education policy leaders' roll-call voting was largely as expected in terms of the extent to which they agreed with various reference groups. But the approximately equivalent degree of partisanship on the floor of each House was not anticipated. Senator Morse's consensual style of committee leadership led to a pattern of floor conflict similar to that produced in the highly partisan and personal competition of the House committee. Also, the internal cohesion of the major partisan, regional, and ideological reference groups was not appreciably greater in the House than in the Senate, nor was the pattern of intergroup conflict markedly different.

It is possible that the perceptions of observers and participants of the respective committee proceedings were biased. This prospect must be discounted, however, by the extensive evidence of partisan conflict in the House committee, e.g., miniority reports and amendments and substitute proposals offered by committee leaders on the floor. Another possibility is that the House committee's partisanship and the combative rather than consensual style of its leaders merely reflected the actual systemic conflicts over policy. In the Senate, however, the deft compromises fashioned in committee by Senator Morse tended to break down on the floor as the cleavages asserted themselves. Committees proved to be less potent sources of cues in floor action than full-chamber reference groups based on party, region, and ideology.

In any event, roll-call voting on education issues in the 90th Congress tended to follow a partisan-regional-ideological cleavage and appeared to be relatively unrelated to sharp differences in the pattern of legislative committee operations and the leadership styles of education policy leaders in the two chambers. Policy adoption appeared to be most substantially influenced by Senator Morse and Representative Green. Those two leaders facilitated agreements, arranged compromises, and represented educational interests. But the adoption stage was the point at which the political executive defended its program against all comers, where the claims of a myriad of interests in education, government, and society were pressed and considered, and where the major societal forces of party, region, and ideology came together in the struggle over policy.

In the context of such macro-level activity, the effects of individual actors are difficult to estimate let alone measure. In policy adoption, as in the case of a ship at sea, the congressional leader like the helmsman does not function independently of other individuals nor are his actions unaffected by environmental factors. In the educational policy process, the adoption stage functioned substantially but not wholly as President Johnson wished thanks, in part, to the help of his congressional "helmsmen," Morse and Perkins. But the establishment associations representing education professionals, the USOE bureaucracy, intellectual critics of education, labor and business interests, and civil rights groups managed to make their input with the aid of other leaders, e.g., Mrs. Green, Brademas, and Dominick, and to gain at least "a piece of the action," if only in a negative sense.

Implementation

The importance of the implementation stage of the policy process is a basic axiom in the literature of public administration. The achievement of the objectives developed in the formulation stage and legitimized in the adoption stage is dependent on the execution of programs in the agency. As Bailey and Mosher observed in their detailed analysis of the process of implementing ESEA, the formulation and adoption "activities simply set the conditions and the framework within which the overwhelming majority of the agency's personnel fulfill their operating functions." [30] Those functions encompass the exercise of discretion in the development and promulgation of rules and guidelines; the receipt, evaluation, and approval of grant applications and plans for program administration; the gathering and analysis of data on problems and programs; and the adjustment of policy along with the formulation of requests for changes in the statutes that authorize the programs. All this activity occurs as "an administrative dialectic—a series of promulgations . . . preceded, accompanied, and followed by inputs and feedbacks from affected clientele." [31] Implementation and feedback go hand in hand and must be considered together.

However, it is not my purpose to reexamine a process explored in depth and with considerable insight elsewhere. [32] Rather, I shall analyze the implementation stage of the educational policy process as an organizational process conducted by USOE's basic operating units, the bureaus. The analysis is based primarily on open-ended interviews conducted with 6 bureau chiefs and 22 division directors during the first six months of 1968. It examines some of the more salient features of the implementation stage, the major problems encountered in implementation, and the external relationships of USOE in policy implementation. The analysis will be summarized in two models of USOE's operating bureaus. Although the models are primarily descriptive and their function is to facilitate explanation and understanding of the observed phenomena, they may have limited predictive value for other agencies.

Policy implementation was clearly the function of the bureaus. USOE's top officials and their supportive staff personnel were engaged primarily in developing broad policy goals and securing their enactment in legislation. They tended not to become involved in the more mundane aspects of implementation unless it produced negative feedback. Complaints from the field about administrative operations and the decisions of middle- and lower-level bureaucrats, when sufficient in number and directed to appropriate policy makers in Congress and the education lobbies, eventually would come to the attention of the commissioner, or perhaps the HEW hierarchy, and result in some corrective action. That action could take the form of a directive to alter the offending condition or it might entail an effort to modify the appropriate statute. Generally, as one moved downward in the hierarchy, officials were increasingly concerned with questions and problems involving program execution.

The bureau level constituted the critical juncture. Bureau chiefs were the highest-ranking officials who maintained regularized direct contact with individuals and groups in the field. They were responsible for coordinating and rationalizing a set of interrelated programs in a way that gave them an overall focus or thrust. At the same time, however, the bureau chiefs were the lowest-ranking political executives in the agency. They had to consider the impact of their decisions on the activities of the other bureaus and the agency as a whole. The bureau chiefs operated under conflicting pressures; national objectives vs. parochial interests, political obligation vs. professional loyalty. Their perspectives were thus subjected to both expansionary and confining forces. The chief of the Bureau of Adult, Vocational, and Library Programs expressed the bureau's dilemma in this manner:

> We have great conflict with the planning group in government. Their viewpoint, which is national in concept and origin, runs head-on with the belief in state and local control and operation. There is a real problem here for the operating bureau.[33]

Moving further downward, the tension tended to ease. Division directors supervised and managed the operation of a set of closely related programs or a single major program. Their concerns were with the pragmatic question of how to translate statutory directives into operating programs. They dealt directly with individuals in the field and with clientele groups in negotiating the structure of programs. Appointed primarily for their professional expertise and experience either from the ranks of USOE careerists or from practitioners in the field, they were not subject to intense political scrutiny. The division directors' policy impact was substantial because they largely determined the operational shape of legislation. They constituted the last hierarchical level at which officials were not forced to think and act in organizational terms:

> This is as high in the bureaucracy that people get and still remain in contact with reality. [Go] beyond our level and you are in the realm of theory and abstraction.[34]

Division directors did take political considerations into account, however, and several of those in the Bureaus of Elementary and Secondary Education and Higher Education engaged in extensive political bargaining with congressional participants in the policy process. The extent to which division directors interacted with congressional and lobby-group personnel appears to be roughly related to the nature of their programs. Directors supervising "big money" formula-grant programs appeared to be more active participants in the policy adoption stage than those with smaller, project-grant programs. The branch chiefs, located at the next lower echelon, tended even more to be "pure" professional types. Their focus was on individual programs or a set of projects within a program. They made decisions more on the basis of objective criteria than political and clientele pressures. The branch chiefs and their subordinates linked USOE to the broad, complex social system which is American education. Their perspectives were not organizational, but were framed in terms of specific programs and projects. Goldhammer and his associates regarded the branch chiefs as the key people in the policy implementation process.[35] Although the branch chiefs constituted the agency's "face" to the public, they did not make the crucial decisions that determined the ultimate success or failure of USOE's programs. Those decisions were usually passed "up the line" for resolution.

In order to gain some insight into the locus of critical decisional authority, I asked the division directors whom I interviewed the following questions:

> Where do you think the really critical decisions are made which ultimately make or break your programs?

And,

> Granted that developing the budget is a complex process, at what level of decision do you think your influence stops?

The sixteen responses revealed sharply contrasting differences in the division directors' perceptions of their influence in decisions crucial to their programs and their influence in budgetary decisions (see table 7-6).

The directors tended to have a much greater sense of control over decisions affecting their programs than over budget decisions. They regarded their programs as falling primarily within the jurisdiction of the Office of Education. The budget, however, seemed to be determined at a remote distance from the agency and its principal officials. The three division directors who expressed a high sense of efficacy in the budgetary process indicated that their divisions fared quite well, but even they had no illusions concerning the locus of critical choice. The tendency of the division directors

Table 7-6
USOE Division Directors' Perceptions of Influence in Program and Budgetary Decisions

Locus of Critical Choice	Program Decisions	Budgetary Decisions
Division	5	0
Bureau	4	0
USOE	2	0
HEW	0	7
BOB–White House	3	4
Congress	1	2
Other	1	0
Total	16	13

Table 7-7
Division Directors Perceptions of Policy Impact

	None	Some	Extensive
Programs	1	10	8
Legislation	2	12	8
N = 22			

to feel efficacious about USOE's control of its programs undoubtedly reflects the discretion accorded them. It is also possible that their responses reflect a certain amount of self-justification and ego-gratification. But there is no mistaking their strong conviction that the size of their divisional budgets is subject to minimum influence by them. Budget decisions are recognized as being made in a broad context, departmental or governmental in scope. Program decisions, as distinguished from legislative decisions, are set in the much more limited context of the divisions and bureaus.

The division directors did not express much dissatisfaction over the limited extent of their influence in budgetary decisions. They recognized and accepted the coordinating and consolidating role played by HEW and BOB further "up the line." Most of them felt that they had had at least some impact on the content and operation of programs in their areas and they reported light to extensive involvement in legislative development (see table 7-7). The impact that they thought they had on programs and legislation may have helped to compensate for their limited sense of control over the budget.

The division directors may also have derived some feeling of importance and some sense of accomplishment in this work from their location at the source of each of the three major decision-information streams within USOE. Those streams included the regular budgetary process, the program planning and budgeting system (PPBS), and the legislation-program policy decision system. These streams flowed in parallel beds with little contact or crossover between each stream except through the coordination provided by the bureau chiefs, the commissioner, and ultimately the Bureau of the Budget. Information flowed both upward and downward in these hierarchical streams. Upward-flowing information consisted mainly of reports, requests, and recommendations while the downward flow contained primarily directives and decisions. The streams produced national education policy when they converged at the upward end of their flow and gave effect to that policy when they met at the downward terminus. Division directors and their subordinates made program decisions relating to regulations and guidelines, the approval of projects and award of grants, and the approval of state plans and the distribution of funds under them. On the basis of their experience and feedback from their clienteles, they formulated budget requests, recommended legislation, and developed planning documents. Above the division level these sets of information were processed by staff units with their specialized personnel. The bureau chiefs, the commissioner, and the secretary coordinated the flow of information in the streams but for the most part they moved independently of each other above the operating level (see figure 7-1).

The planning stream was established in 1966 when President Johnson ordered the government-wide installation of the PPB system that had been developed in the Pentagon under Secretary McNamara. It brought to USOE a conscious, systematic effort to integrate the tools of cost-benefit analysis, systems analysis, and operations research with the regular budgetary and policy-making processes.[36] Its principal features in USOE were a program budget conceived in terms of output categories defined as programs, a five-year plan which projected program objectives, and annual program memoranda which assessed progress toward the objectives and related the governmental budget to the plan.

In USOE, the integration of the planning and budgeting processes had not been accomplished in 1968. In addition to a lack of communication between budgeting and planning personnel there was a timing problem. The program memoranda appeared in the fall after the budget was completed.[37] A further obstacle to the development of the PPB system in USOE was the skepticism and, in some instances, opposition of many long-time officials who found it strange, confusing, and threatening. They also objected to the heavy demands for information made by the planning and evaluation staff whom they charged were concerned only with cost effectiveness and not with values and political factors. But with strong support from the President, the secretary, and the commissioner, USOE's PPB system did lead to the development of new methods of defining and categorizing information, it

Figure 7-1
**Decision-Information Streams in the
Educational Policy Process**

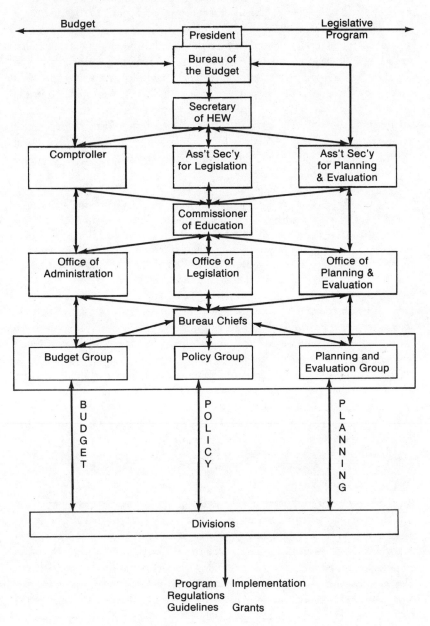

expanded the scope of data gathered, and it led to an increased emphasis on evaluating the effectiveness of the agency's programs and the nation's educational system. However, the impact of planning and evaluation on budgeting and policy making was not significantly felt until 1970 [38] and three years later it had been abandoned.[39]

The regular budget process functioned in the incremental fashion that characterized line-item budgeting throughout the federal government.[40] The decisions were made in terms of incremental adjustments to the previous year's appropriation which served as a base. The budget was prepared in the context of the overall fiscal situation. Budgetary decision makers in the bureaucracy assessed competing requests for funds within financial parameters set by the Bureau of the Budget. They were guided by tactical political considerations rather than achievement of program goals. As HEW's principal budget officer described the process:

> . . . we review the budget proposals of the commissioner and assist the secretary in developing a salable budget. . . . In putting the budget together we try to develop tactics that will prevail on the Hill. . . . You have to be aware of the tactical reality of what you can sell. There are sacred cows in various programs [and] the President should know these things and avoid recommending precipitous changes.[41]

Although the budget is undoubtedly a policy document that reflects the administration's priorities, it is heavily influenced by immediate political concerns. Its orientation is necessarily pragmatic whereas the program memoranda produced by the PPB system were designed to be more theoretical and idealistic. The problem facing USOE and most other agencies in 1967–68 was that officials had not learned how to employ planning and analysis to positive advantage in the harsh environment of incremental budgeting. The regular budget process did have an occasional impact on substantive policy, other than the funds available for various programs, as in 1967 when the House Appropriations Committee forced the transfer of the enforcement of Title VI of the Civil Rights Act from USOE to the Office of the Secretary of HEW.

The policy decision stream relating to programs and legislation operated with limited regard to questions of cost and cost effectiveness. The major concern was putting together a legislative program that would win the support of various clientele and gain acceptance in the Bureau of the Budget and in Congress. Program administrators, having asked for the funds they believed they needed, were concerned primarily with gaining and maintaining the support of their clientele who, recognizing the limits of their influence on the budget, did not hold them accountable for what both agreed was an inadequate level of funding. Furthermore, most educational policy makers blamed budgetary constraints and budget officials for whatever failures and limitations were apparent in programs. From the division through the departmental level, officials expressed the conviction that much more could be accomplished if only programs were funded at 100 percent of the amounts authorized. This mode of thinking was notably absent in the Presidency where conflicting departmental claims for funds were resolved and legislative aspirations were reconciled with the reality of finite resources. Perhaps the tension and conflict in the bureaucracy between budget and policy people and the antipathy that both felt toward the planners and evaluators was inevitable as long as demands exceeded resources and effective coordination of the three decision-information streams did not occur until the presidential level. It may also be argued that even though such conflict was frequently unsettling and somewhat inefficient, it had beneficial consequences in the form of increased inventiveness and greater political competence, although there is no way to test these hypotheses.

The implementation of programs, although supervised by bureau chiefs and reviewed by their superiors, was the function of the divisions and their branches. The mechanical aspects of implementation, e.g., development of regulations and guidelines and the expenditure of funds, occurred at this level. Contacts with "the field" by division and branch officials produced much of the feedback that led to eventual policy modification and were instrumental in generating support for USOE and its programs. Also, the problems encountered in implementation were experienced initially at this level.

Among the primary mechanisms of policy implementation are regulations and guidelines. Regulations are sets of formal rules promulgated in accordance with the Administrative Procedure Act. They are published in the *Federal Register* and have the status of law. Guidelines have no official status and in USOE the term refers to a variety of published program materials including memoranda, manuals, pamphlets, and booklets that explain statutes and regulations.[42] There was no uniform format for USOE's guidelines nor were there any procedural requirements for developing them. Regulations were developed and promulgated following the enactment of legislation. Guidelines were usually issued shortly afterward and were reviewed and modified on an irregular basis. The absence of uniformities in format and procedures resulted in considerable variation in the utility of USOE's program guidelines. Some were current, others outdated, some were sketchy, others extensively detailed, and none of them were embodied in convenient regularly revised manuals. This prompted the Green Report to recommend a standardized guideline format and the adoption of procedures to keep guidelines up to date.[43]

In spite of the chaotic state of the guidelines, the division directors regarded them as important policy documents. As one director remarked, "our main influence on policies comes in the course of drafting the guidelines." [44]

However, the flexibility of the guidelines and the absence of formal procedures for drafting them facilitated modifications resulting from experience. Regulations, in contrast, were seldom changed unless statutory amendments made it necessary. Nineteen of twenty-two division directors interviewed had either drafted or revised their guidelines, but none reported any work on regulations.

The general procedure for working on guidelines was to appoint a committee or a task force of USOE program personnel and representatives from the HEW General Counsel's office. The task forces usually had some consultation with the field. Of thirteen division directors who described their work on guidelines, nine submitted drafts to state or local officials or to advisory groups and the remaining four had involved outsiders in drafting the guidelines. Consultation, although not systematized, appeared to be frequently and widely employed. The degree to which feedback affects revisions in the guidelines was not ascertained. But the guidelines did to varying degrees reflect USOE's interpretation of statutory goals and contain statements of criteria for the award of grants and the approval of state plans for spending money. If there is conflict between USOE and people in the field, the content of the guidelines will be one of the principal focal points.[45]

In addition to developing guidelines, program administrators have an impact on policy through the exercise of discretion in the interpretation and application of statutes. Eleven of fourteen division directors responding to a question asking if they had made or suggested substantial changes in their programs gave affirmative answers. Two reported that they had proposed new legislation, five cited substantive changes in the content and goals of programs, and four described procedural changes affecting program administration. All those who had made procedural changes were in charge of large formula grant programs located in the Bureaus of Elementary and Secondary Education and Higher Education. The procedural changes all involved coordinated or consolidated administration of a division's programs in a single "package." Interestingly, the negative respondents were also administrators of heavily funded formula grant programs. The division directors who had developed new legislation or made substantive changes in their programs tended to be located in the Bureau of Education for the Handicapped and the Bureau of Research. Their programs involved modest funding levels and were administered on a project grant basis.

The distinction between formula and project grant programs also appeared to be related to the division directors' perceptions of their statutory authority. The directors tended strongly to feel that they had flexible statutes to administer, but where they regarded themselves as constrained, they dealt more with formula than project grants (see table 7-8). Typical of the administrators of project grants was this comment of the director of the Division of Research in the Bureau for the Education of the Handicapped:

Table 7-8
**Division Directors' Perceptions of Statutory
Authority by Form of Program Administration**

	Statutory Authority		
Programs	Confining	Mixed	Broad
Project grant	0	1	9
Formula grant	5	1	4
Total	5	2	13

> Our legislation is quite broad. Congress has expanded our authority. . . .
> We can support a wide variety of activities. . . . There is no earmarking
> of funds. We set our own goals. But we don't have a lot of money, only
> $11 million.[46]

On the other hand, the director of the Division of College Facilities, who had
sizable funding for his programs, gave a response typical of those who felt
confined by statutes:

> Most of our programs are quite well hemmed in. The major programs,
> undergraduate construction grants and equipment grants, involved
> mandatory grants under state plans. We have some discretion in
> establishing criteria for approval of state plans.[47]

Perhaps the best description of how the form of grant administration
affects the implementation of programs was provided in this response:

> In the Adult Basic Education Program we have $40 million funding of
> which $30 million goes to the states. We have little control over it. But of
> the $10 million we have we can make grants for various projects over
> which we have full control.
> The Community Service and Continuing Education program, Title
> I of the Higher Education Act, has no set-aside for innovative programs.
> It is a straight formula grant program. Our influence occurs through
> persuasion and not decision. Most of our energy goes to improving the
> competence of state directors and their program people.[48]

The concern of USOE officials in charge of large formula-grant
programs with the effectiveness of state and local administration was only
partly due to their own lack of discretionary authority. Congress had
delegated to USOE responsibility for approving state plans and supervising
their operation. In addition, there were serious problems in USOE's

administration of its large formula-grant programs. The Green Report cited major problems involving the operation of regional offices, the timing of funding for programs, and the participation of persons in the field in the agency's decisional processes.

Established in 1950, the regional offices originally gathered data, disseminated information, and provided professional advisory services. Following passage of ESEA, and in keeping with President Johnson's commitment to a "creative federalism" based on a greatly decentralized federal bureaucracy, USOE's regional offices were given expanded authority over substantial programs. By 1967, the regional offices had acquired authority over several state grant programs including Titles I, II, and V of ESEA, NDEA Titles III, V-A, and V, arts and humanities state grants, Title I of the Higher Education Act, the three major vocational education acts, adult basic education, and library services and construction.[49]

The regional offices, located in Boston, New York, Charlottesville, Atlanta, Chicago, Kansas City, Dallas, Denver, and San Francisco, were placed under assistant commissioners and their staffs augmented, although not to the degree necessary to implement all their contemplated functions. Those functions included "delegated responsibility for reviewing and approving state plans and projected programs and for project approval in certain others" and "primary responsibility for grant awards maintaining prime records, and reporting on the use of grant funds." [50] The Green subcommittee conducted extensive hearings on USOE's administrative decentralization program and found two specific objections to it on the part of people in the field; regional office personnel were not as competent or experienced as those in Washington and the regional offices lacked authority to make final program decisions and thus constituted but another layer of bureaucratic red tape.[51] The subcommittee endorsed the concept of decentralization, but recommended that it be accompanied by clearly defined decisional authority and that it occur only when "a sufficient number of competent staff could be assigned to the regional offices."

Strong objection to the expanded role of the regional offices was voiced by the Council of Chief State School Officers, the American Association of School Administrators, and the National Education Association. Higher education associations and institutions were generally satisfied with decentralization. These reactions appear to have been due to the different relationship of elementary and secondary officials and higher education administrators to their national associations and to state education agencies. The national elementary and secondary organizations were closely tied to state education agencies. Part of their strength was derived from the state agencies. Regional administration of USOE programs threatened to dilute the power of state agencies by enabling local schoolmen to deal directly with USOE. This would, in turn, weaken the national associations.

In contrast, administrators in higher education had always dealt directly with USOE. Strong state agencies did not exist in the higher education system. Consequently, the national associations which drew their strength directly from institutions had no basis for opposing expanded regional offices. The decentralization of program administration was a welcome convenience for most college and university officials. The opposition of the Council of Chief State School Officers and its allies to decentralization received sympathetic consideration from the Senate Appropriations Subcommittee. The Council and the American Association of School Administrators, aided by Herman Downey, the subcommittee clerk, managed to obtain language in the fiscal 1968 appropriation restricting decentralization.[52] Although no action was taken at that time, in September 1968 the two organizations and the NEA pressured USOE into reversing the decentralization program.[53] In a confidential memorandum, Commissioner Howe agreed that there would be no further decentralization and that administration of Title I of ESEA would be returned to Washington at once, with other elementary and secondary education programs to follow over time.

If administrative decentralization created political problems for USOE, the political considerations involved in the appropriations process were responsible for major administrative difficulties for the agency and for people in the field. The principal problem was the late funding of USOE's programs. This resulted from the disparity between the timing of the educational planning and budgeting process and the congressional appropriations process. Educators planned in the spring for the forthcoming academic year which would begin in September. Congress appropriated funds on the basis of the July 1–June 30 fiscal year; however, final passage of appropriations bills usually occurred in the summer or fall, long after the completion of educational planning and budgeting. As long as federal funds constituted only a small portion of the operating budgets of the public schools and institutions of higher education their operations were not seriously disrupted by late funding. But with the increased flow of federal money into education the uncertainty of the level of support produced conditions that were variously described as "disastrous" and "chaotic" and which seriously inhibited the achievement of congressional objectives in the authorizing legislation.

The Green subcommittee received more complaints about late funding than any other aspect of USOE's operations. The subcommittee considered the problem to be of such a critical nature that released a separate report on it in advance of its full report. The subcommittee called for development of a solution to the problem by a joint committee of legislative and appropriations committee members in both houses of Congress[54] President Johnson recognized the seriousness of the problem in his 1967 Health and Education message and called upon the secretary of HEW to work with Congress to make the federal legislative calendar more compatible with the academic calendar. Secretary Gardner appointed a task force to study ways and means of improving the timing of federal appropriations for education programs.

The task force, under the chairmanship of HEW Comptroller James Kelly, reported to Gardner on September 14, 1967. Its principal recommendations called for five-year authorizations for educational assistance programs, advancement of appropriations by one year so as to give notice to officials in the field of the amounts which will become available to them at the beginning of the next fiscal year, and the allotment of planning funds on a continuing basis.[55] As a consequence of pressures from school and college officials, education associations, the administration, and the recommendations of the Green Report, an advanced funding provision was included in the 1967 ESEA amendments. It authorized the appropriation of funds for ESEA programs a year prior to the year in which they would be obligated. Similar authorization was extended to all USOE programs in the Vocational Education Act amendments of 1968. However, Congress has since been unwilling to appropriate funds in advance.

The Green subcommittee's concern over the extent of external participation in USOE's planning processes was manifested in recommendations calling for a broadening of the planning operation "so that State entities, major professional associations, and all other user groups may participate more fully" and for "more active participation by OE field staff and by State and local educational officials" in the legislative planning process.[56] The subcommittee did not indicate how this increased participation might be accomplished nor did it express any awareness of the potential threat to presidential and congressional control over USOE's programs that expanded involvement of politically nonaccountable external interests might entail.[57] In fact, the subcommittee acknowledged that outside access to USOE was very open. The problem apparently stemmed from a desire on the part of persons in the field who testified before the subcommittee to be a part of the formal planning and decisional process. Such educators expressed a feeling of uncertainty "as to whether the[ir] recommendations and suggestions received consideration beyond their initial point of entry, irrespective of the merits of the proposals." [58] In spite of its openness to the public and professionals in the field, USOE was apparently not successful in convincing its clientele that its feedback processes significantly affected program implementation and legislative development.

This apparent discontent with USOE's external relations is difficult to understand, especially in view of the wide scope and variety of contacts with individuals and groups in the education community as well as its central position in the education policy system. The contacts included state and local officials, college and university administrators, classroom teachers, fellow professionals, representatives of clientele groups, non-education lobbyists, and members of Congress and their staffs. In addition, USOE officials interacted extensively among themselves and regularly with officials in HEW, BOB, and other agencies dealing with education. Almost all the division directors I interviewed explicitly mentioned that they had extensive contacts with "people in the field" and with clientele groups in their program areas (see table 7-9).

Table 7-9
Division Directors External Contacts by Bureau

Bureau	The Field	Clientele Groups	Con-gress	Budget Bureau	Other Agencies	N
Education of the Handicapped	3	2	1	—	—	4
Research	4	4	1	2	1	4
Personnel Development	2	2	1	—	—	2
Adult, Vocational, & Library Programs	2	3	2	—	—	3
Higher Education	4	4	4	—	—	4
Elementary & Secondary Education	4	4	3	—	—	4
Total	19	19	13	2	1	21

Contacts with congressional personnel, although frequent, tended to be confined to divisions in the bureaus with "big money" programs, specifically, Elementary and Secondary Education, Higher Education, and Adult, Vocational, and Library Programs. Contacts with individuals in the Bureau of the Budget and other agencies were limited, at least as reported in my interviews, to division directors in the Bureau of Research.

The principal means of obtaining advice and of conducting external relations was the advisory council. Fifteen of the division directors indicated that they employed statutory or ad hoc advisory bodies on a regular basis.[59] As reported in a study which I conducted with Thomas E. Cronin, USOE's twenty-six advisory councils were elitist and not broadly representative in the composition of their membership. They performed supportive and legitimizing along with advisory and critical functions for USOE. Their major policy impact was on implementation rather than new legislation, and the impact tended to take the form of incremental adjustments rather than major innovations. USOE officials obtained valuable feedback on their programs through the councils, but there were difficulties associated with their operations such as the desire of some council members to assume an active managerial role and the costs, in terms of time and money, of informing and staffing the councils.

Other mechanisms employed by program administrators in the conduct of their external relations included technical review panels that helped to decide on competing applications for project grants, site visits, attendance at professional meetings, presentation of testimony in congressional hearings, and informal conversations and consultations. The pattern of the division directors' external contacts tended to vary between the bureaus. In those bureaus which administered small, project-grant programs with an experimental or research orientation the division directors expressed a preference for ad hoc advisory mechanisms and they did not develop elaborate formal networks of contacts in Washington or with the field. They expressed concern over the low frequency and inadequacy of their interaction with officials in other bureaus and with the USOE hierarchy. In the bureaus administering heavily funded, formula-grant programs, division directors had a broad network of formal contacts and they limited employment of advisory councils to statutory bodies. Their extensive interaction with Congress reflects the politically sensitive as opposed to professional nature of their external relations.

This discussion of USOE's external relations would not be complete without noting the survey of public school superintendents conducted by the House Committee on Education and Labor in late 1968. The responses revealed a predictably ambivalent attitude toward the federal role in education.[60] The superintendents believed overwhelmingly that ESEA was inadequately funded (70 percent) and that the federal government was not doing its share to support education (65 percent) but they were even more strongly convinced that the new federal programs of the 1960s had been of concrete assistance to them (74 percent). Committee Chairman Perkins concluded that the survey demonstrated that "the benefits derived from the programs clearly outweigh the problems" experienced during the "early years of program implementation." [61] Among the greatest needs perceived by Perkins' respondents were: "personnel" (2,657 citations); research, curriculum development, and special programs for disadvantaged and handicapped children (1,929); solution of "problems associated with funding" (1,897); "facilities" (1,344); and "supplies" (1,238). Three of these need categories, personnel, facilities, and supplies, could be dealt with by increased funding.

Most participants in the educational policy process were fully aware of the inadequacy of funding levels in the fiscal 1968 and 1969 budgets and they were quite conscious of and frustrated by the federal government's inability to provide additional funds. An effort was made to solve the problems associated with funding by the authorization of advance funding for educational programs. The need for research, curriculum development, and special programs to aid the handicapped and the disadvantaged could not be met by administrative reform or an immediate increase in funds. It reflected the inability of American education to respond effectively to the unique educational needs of children handicapped by poverty and physical disability. The superintendents' perceptions of their needs reflects both the importance of money as a solution to the problems of education and also its limitations.

The program administrators in USOE also cited inadequate funding as a major obstacle to effective operation of their divisions. In addition, they complained of staffing problems caused by federal personnel procedures, time pressures, and the difficulty of coordinating their programs with those in other divisions and other bureaus. In particular, research program administrators felt their efforts did not mesh with the administration of the "big money" programs. Some problems in the administration of formula-grant programs appear to have been eased by the development of coordinated "single package" applications on a state-plan basis, but undoubtedly a considerable amount of "red tape" remained to frustrate state and local education officials, college and university administrators, and USOE personnel.

The implementation stage of the national policy process in education is unbelievably complex and this discussion has necessarily been limited to a few of the most salient features of it. One aspect of implementation that stood out was the central importance of the bureaus. Programs, which were administered singly or in small sets by the divisions, were grouped together in the bureaus around an integrating concept. (The sole exception was the Bureau of Adult, Vocational and Library Programs, a residual collection of unrelated programs not sufficiently important to entitle them to bureau status.) The bureau chiefs stood at the interface between the micro-policy makers who implemented programs and the macro-policy makers who developed broad goals and objectives. The bureaus were the largest program operating units and they were the lowest units in the hierarchy possessing separate staff support for budgeting, planning, and legislative policy development. The bureaus set the tone, determined the style, and prescribed the form of policy implementation.

In USOE there appeared to be two distinct models of bureau operations. One, which may be labeled the research and development (R&D) model, was typified by the Bureau of Research and the Bureau of Education for the Handicapped. The other, which may be designated the educational support model, was exemplified by the Bureau of Elementary and Secondary Education and the Bureau of Higher Education. The Bureau of Education Personnel Development fell closer to the R&D model and the catchall bureau, in spite of its divergent programs, approximated the support model.

The characteristics of the two models are summarized in figure 7-2. The bureaus can be conceived of as falling on a continuum running from the Bureau of Research, the best example of the R&D model, to the Bureau of Elementary and Secondary Education, the closest approximation to the support model. The models differ substantially with respect to several characteristics. The officials under the R&D model tend to be professionals who are serving in government for a relatively limited period of time. Support-model officials are more likely to be governmental careerists. The decisional pattern under the R&D model is collegial with professional

Figure 7-2

Characteristics of USOE Bureaus by Models of Operation

BR BEH BEDP	Bureaus	BAVLP BHE BESE
Research and Development	Models Characteristics	Educational Support
Professionals-short term	Officials	Careerists-long term
Collegial	Decisional Pattern	Hierarchical
Broad-innovative	Statutes	Circumscribed-conservative
Project grant	Form of Programs	Formula grant
Research	Focus of Programs	Operations
Low–politically nonsensitive	Political Involvement	High–politically sensitive
Extensive-informal	External Participation	Limited-formal

colleagues collectively making choices. Decisions in support-model bureaus tended to be made independently by persons in authority. The statutes which governed R&D model programs were more flexible than those under which support-model programs operated. The programs administered by the R&D model bureaus were predominantly research-oriented project grant programs with limited funding while those of the support-model bureaus provided extensive support on a formula-grant basis for educational operations of schools and colleges and to students. The support-model bureaus were extensively involved in politics and highly sensitive to political considerations. The R&D model bureaus were less politically involved, but they encouraged more extensive outside participation in their decision-making processes.

Although the R&D model was clearly more compatible with the innovative thrust that President Johnson, Secretary Gardner, and the Bureau of the Budget wished to impart to USOE, the higher budgetary priority accorded the support-model bureaus was persuasive evidence of the agency's actual character. It was a mission-oriented organization that closely approximated the negative "old-line agency" image held by White House staff members and Budget Bureau officials. Implementation was an intensely political process that was for the most part operated for the benefit of, if not openly controlled by, the education establishment. The goal of introducing qualitative improvements into American education was not likely to be achieved as long as the R&D model bureaus and their programs continued to be subordinated to the support-model bureaus. As this analysis of the educational policy process has attempted to demonstrate in various ways, such a development did not appear likely at the end of the Johnson administration nor has it occurred since then, the creation of the NIE notwithstanding. In the next and final chapter, I will review the findings that led to this conclusion in an assessment of the structure of power and the determinants of influence in the educational policy process.

Notes

1. Adam Yarmolinsky, "Ideas into Programs," *The Public Interest*, no. 2 (Winter 1966): 73.

2. See Richard E. Neustadt, "The Presidency and Legislation: The Growth of Central Clearance," *American Political Science Review* 48 (1954): 641–70; and his "The Presidency and Legislation: Planning the President's Program," *American Political Science Review* 49 (1955): 980–1018.

3. Quoted in William E. Leuchtenberg, "The Genesis of the Great Society," *The Reporter*, 21 April 1966, pp. 36–39.

4. See Norman C. Thomas and Harold L. Wolman, "The Presidency and Policy Formulation: The Task Force Device," *Public Administration Review* 29 (September/October 1969): 459–71.

5. A sharp differentiation of the functions of policy planning and legislative liaison occurred on the Johnson White House staff with the policy planners enjoying greater influence and status. See Thomas E. Cronin, "The Presidency and Education," *Phi Delta Kappan* 49 (February 1968): 295–99. This was an interesting and somewhat surprising development given Johnson's reputation as a legislative wizard.

6. Interview, Harold Howe II, 9 January 1968.

7. Confidential interview.

8. Confidential interview.

9. Louis B. Koenig's prediction, made in 1964 at the outset of the Johnson Presidency, that the White House staff would play a reduced and the old-line departments a greater role in policy-formulation did not prove correct. The reverse occurred. *The Chief Executive* (New York: Harcourt, Brace, and World, 1964), pp. 182–83.

10. This description is based on interviews. See also the description of the preparation of the 1968 State of the Union message in "Formulating Presidential Program Is Long Process," *Congressional Quarterly Weekly Report*, 26 January 1968, pp. 111–14.

11. See James M. Burns, *Presidential Government* (Boston: Houghton Mifflin, 1966), p. 143. Burns cites the highly relevant comments of Arthur M. Schlesinger, Jr., based on his experiences in the White House during the Kennedy administration: "Nothing in my recent experience has been more chastening than the attempt to penetrate into the process of decision. I shudder a little when I think how confidently I have analyzed decisions in the ages of Jackson and Roosevelt, traced influences, assigned motives, evaluated roles, allocated responsibilities, and, in short, transformed a disheveled and murky evolution into a tidy and ordered transaction. The sad fact is that, in many cases, the basic evidence for the historian's reconstruction of the really hard cases does not exist—and the evidence that it does is often incomplete, misleading or erroneous." From "The Historian and History," *Foreign Affairs* 41 (April 1963): 491–97.

12. Wilbur J. Cohen, "Education Legislation 1963–68 from Various Vantage Points" (Paper presented at the LBJ Library, Austin, Texas, 24 January 1972).

13. Confidential interview.

14. Interview, Samuel Halperin, 11 December 1967.

15. Confidential interview.

16. Interview, William Cannon, 30 April 1968.

17. Interview, William Carey, 23 January 1968.

18. Confidential interview.

19. See Harold L. Wolman and Norman C. Thomas, "Black Interests, Black Groups, and Black Influence in the Federal Policy Process: The Cases of Housing and Education," *Journal of Politics* 32 (November 1970): 875–97.

20. Interview, Paul Miller, 10 January 1968.

21. Interview, Edith Green, 23 February 1968.

22. Interview, John Forsythe, 16 January 1968.

23. Interview, Edgar Fuller, 7 February 1968.

24. Interview, John Lumley, 12 March 1968.

25. Malcolm E. Jewell and Samuel C. Patterson; *The Legislative Process in the United States* (New York: Random House, 1966), p. 415. This discussion is based on their excellent explanation of legislative voting behavior in chapter 17.

26. Ibid. See especially David B. Truman, *The Congressional Party* (New York: John Wiley & Sons, 1959).

27. Ibid., p. 533.

28. Ibid. $IL = 100 - (\%Y_1 - \%Y_2)$.

29. Cf. H. L. Wolman, *Politics of Federal Housing* (New York: Dodd, Mead and Company, 1971).

30. Stephen K. Bailey and Edith K. Mosher, *ESEA: The Office of Education Administers a Law* (Syracuse: Syracuse University Press, 1968), p. 98.

31. Ibid., p. 159.

32. Cf. ibid., chap. 4; and Keith Goldhammer, John E. Suttle, William D. Aldridge, and Gerald L. Becker, *Issues and Problems in Contemporary Educational Administration* (Eugene, Ore.: Center for the Study of Educational Administration, 1967), chap. 3. These and other related works are reviewed in my "Politics, Administration, and American Education," *Public Administration Review* 30 (November/December 1970): 646–54.

33. Interview, Dr. Grant Venn, 19 December 1967.

34. Interview, Dr. Donald Bigelow, director, Division of Program Administration, Bureau of Education Personnel Development, 8 May 1968.

35. Goldhammer, Suttle, Aldridge and Becker. *Issues in Contemporary Educational Administration*, pp. 60–62.

36. Two excellent collections of materials on PPBS are Fremont J. Lyden and Ernest G. Miller, eds., *Planning Programming Budgeting: A Systems Approach to Management* (Chicago: Markham, 1968); and Robert H. Haveman and Julius Margolis, eds., *Public Expenditures and Policy Analysis* (Chicago: Markham, 1970), pts. 4 and 5.

37. See John E. Brandl, "Education Program Analysis at HEW," in Haveman and Margolis, *Public Expenditures*, pp. 549–61.

38. Ibid. Brandl credits HEW Secretary Robert Finch with initiative and direction that established a planning-budgeting process which reflected explicit, albeit controversial objectives. However, the value of that achievement was unclear "since little *analysis* was available to bolster the arguments for change."

39. See Allen Schick, "A Death in the Bureaucracy," *Public Administration Review* 33 (March/April 1973): 146–56.

40. See Aaron Wildavsky, *The Politics of the Budgetary Process* (Boston: Little, Brown, 1964).

41. Interview, James Kelly, comptroller of HEW, 9 January 1968.

42. See the discussion in the "Green Report," U.S. Congress, House of Representatives, Special Subcommittee on Education, Study of the United States Office of Education, House Document No. 193, 90th Congress, 1st sess. (1967), pp. 401–20.

43. Ibid., p. 420.

44. Interview, Chalmers Norris, director, Division of College Facilities, Bureau of Higher Education, 10 May 1968.

45. Cf. Bailey and Mosher, *ESEA*, p. 114.

46. Interview, James W. Moss, 12 June 1968.

47. Interview, Chalmers Norris, 10 May 1968.

48. Interview, Paul Delker, director, Division of Adult Education Programs, 14 May 1968.

49. See James A. Turman, "Decisions from the Field," *American Education*, July/August 1967; and "Decision Power Moving to USOE Regional Offices," *Education USA: Washington Monitor*, 8 December 1966, p. 89.

50. Turman, "Decisions from the Field."

51. Green Report, p. 393.

52. Confidential interview, education association lobbyist, 5 September 1968.

53. "Office of Education Acts to Centralize Programs," *Washington Star*, 4 September 1968.

54. Green Report, p. 446.

55. "HEW Unveils Task Force Report for Fund Distribution," *College and University Business* 43 (November 1967), p. 25.

56. Green Report, pp. 436–37.

57. Cf. Theodore J. Lowi, *The End of Liberalism* (New York: Norton, 1969). The subcommittee's recommendations are an open invitation to additional "interest group liberalism," the phenomenon so thoroughly criticized by Lowi.

58. Green Report, p. 435.

59. In early 1969, Thomas E. Cronin and I conducted a questionnaire survey of the members of the 26 advisory councils and committees then counseling USOE. The results of that survey, to which 72 percent of the members of those advisory groups responded, are reported and analyzed in T. E. Cronin and N. C. Thomas, "Educational Policy Advisors and the Great Society," *Public Policy* 18 (1970): 659–86; and "Federal Advisory Processes: Advice and Discontent," *Science* 171 (26 February 1971): 771–79.

60. The committee chairman, Rep. Carl Perkins (D.-Ky.), entered tabulated results of the survey in the *Congressional Record* and discussed the committee staff's analysis of them on four occasions in early 1969. See *Congressional Record*, daily edition, 30 January 1969, pp. H-607–11; 6 February 1969, pp. H-811–15; 18 February 1969, pp. H-996–1002; and 3 March 1969, pp. H-1358–61.

61. *Congressional Record*, daily edition, 6 February 1969, p. H-815.

IV
CONCLUSION

8
THE EDUCATIONAL POLICY PROCESS
IN RETROSPECT

This analysis has sought to increase understanding of national educational policy making in terms of the issues, activity, and policies involved. A summary of the major findings in terms of the questions posed in chapter 1 will help to set the study in an appropriate theoretical context.

Demands and Issues

In education as in other policy areas, there is no way to answer precisely the question of where ideas come from. Occasionally an idea can be traced to a specific individual, e.g., the basic elements of the Educational Opportunity Bank proposal of 1967 and the educational voucher system suggestions of recent years first appeared (to the best of my knowledge) in a 1955 essay by Milton Friedman,[1] but most of the time ideas seem to emerge in several places at once with multiple parentage claimed for them. Some ideas originate in leading universities or with lay critics and commentators. Others come from foundations or "think tanks" established by the government or foundations. Still others are the result of experience gained in the operation of the educational system and are suggested by practitioners in the field or by governmental officials.

Ideas move into the policy process at many points in the federal bureaucracy, Congress, and the Presidency. In the educational policy process, the national associations played a major role in moving ideas and marshaling

221

support for them, but they did not contribute substantially to the development of new ideas. There is an important distinction to be made between the inventor, who creates new ideas; the innovator, who moves new ideas into the policy process where they become part of the structure of demands; and the broker, who arranges the terms and conditions that permit ideas to move through the conversion process and become embodied in programs. In the educational policy process, most inventors were located outside the federal government in the elite world of major universities, foundations, and intellectual periodicals. The innovators tended to be concentrated in the Presidency and in the upper echelons of the bureaucracy. Brokers occupied strategic positions in Congress, the bureaucracy, the Presidency, and the national associations. In most instances, there was a long gestation period between the spawning of an idea by one or more inventors until it was successfully embodied in a program through the efforts of a succession of innovators and brokers.

In an administration deeply committed to domestic policy innovation, as was that of President Lyndon B. Johnson, the means used to obtain and evaluate ideas were of crucial importance. In the Johnson administration, task forces played a major role in performing this function. This systematic attempt to obtain new ideas and proposals from other than the traditional bureaucratic sources proved highly successful initially, but institutionalization of the device and subsequent overuse reduced its value. Still, the task-force device did, at least in education, accord educational inventors access to high-level policy formulation which they did not enjoy before and have not had since.

The evaluations and preparation of ideas was a function of a special presidential assistant for education (Douglass Cater), an ad hoc domestic policy staff under Joseph Califano, and Bureau of the Budget personnel. In addition, Commissioner Harold Howe and high-ranking HEW officials played key roles in shaping presidential legislative proposals. The final element involved in generating and evaluating new ideas consisted of the twenty-six advisory councils to USOE. These units were comprised primarily of education professionals and members of other social and political elites. Their function mainly involved the approval rather than the development of new policy proposals. Although the councils did expand the range of demands acted upon by the policy process, they were primarily instruments of elite rather than mass participation.[2]

For the most part demands were made by organized interests. Chief among them were the national associations representing the established profession in elementary and secondary education and various types of institutions in higher education. These groups were joined by organizations representing labor, business, the Catholic church, and citizens committed to such goals as the separation of church and state and improvement of the public schools. Organized groups had access to the policy process principally through Congress and the bureaucracy. Their demands were known to policy makers in the Presidency, but access to that institution was controlled and the groups, for the most part, felt excluded from it. The Presidency did accord easier access, however, to the "new establishment" intellectuals and academics who were the major proponents of change in American education. The access of all these groups, although not equally distributed, was readily obtainable and highly effective at one or more locations in the educational policy process.

This cannot be taken as a full confirmation of the pluralist model, however, as there were interests with a manifest stake in the federal educational policies that did not enjoy effective access to the policy process. These groups, primarily the poor and members of racial and ethnic minorities (especially blacks), made only limited demands. They tended to concentrate on overt questions of desegregation and civil rights enforcement and to seek access through congressional lobbying and litigation. Although they had spokesmen in the policy process who provided a form of surrogate representation, they did not enjoy full participation in the crucial formulative stage of the process where agendas are determined or in the implementation stage where programs are translated into action.

The differential effectiveness among interests in obtaining access and in the scope and volume of demands stemmed from three factors. Access to the formulative stage centered in the Presidency appeared to depend principally on the nature of the ideas espoused and the demands made. However, an interest had to possess a minimum degree of resources and knowledge in order to utilize the opportunity for access. For example, the poor and the minorities were largely unable to capitalize on the sympathetic attitude of the Johnson administration toward them because they lacked leadership, political sophistication, organization, and the substantive knowledge required to suggest proposals for qualitative educational improvements. Consequently, their interests were primarily represented in the formulative stage by surrogates. (Even the professionals and the intellectual and academic critics were groping for ways in which to improve the education of the economically disadvantaged, however.)

The effectiveness of interest-group participation in the adoption and implementation stage depended more on resources and knowledge than on the substance of their ideas. The professional interests were the most effective nongovernmental participants. They articulated a set of demands primarily in monetary terms which could clearly be understood, their leaders organized them to press the demands, and they were more than sufficiently sophisticated to modify and adapt their demands to other interests and participants in the policy process. Interests representing the poor and the minorities, although they were lacking in expertise, enjoyed substantially greater impact at the adoption than the formulative stage because of their substantial political resources—votes. This reflects the reactive rather than innovative character of the congressional role and the representational function of Congress. Professional interests were also highly effective participants at the implementation stage. USOE's needs for clientele group support and the groups' stake in the agency's programs lead to the mutually beneficial relationships that characterize the policy process in the national government and which Lowi has labeled "interest group liberalism."

The substantive issues that the demands presented reflected both continuity and change. Issues that had been current since the late 1940s remained controversial, but with new dimensions added to them. Also, new issues emerged as the federal role in education expanded. The continuing issues included the extent of federal control of education, church-state relations, and racial equality in education. The major newer issues were the extent and form of federal support for higher education and the role of vocational education.

The federal control issue involved two related questions: general vs. categorical aid, and whether the federal role should be supportive or innovative. The basic question of the 1950s, whether the federal government should assume any role in education, had been resolved affirmatively in the legislation of the mid-1960s. Some federal control was accepted as inescapable; the issue was how much there should be and what form it should assume. The established educational interests tended to prefer general aid, awarded in block grants to the states and administered under state plans drafted with minimal federal controls. This position was also subscribed to by congressional conservatives and most business interests. The Johnson administration and its educational policy makers tended to favor categorical aid and an innovative federal role. Congressional opinion encompassed both positions and tended to compromise on large categorical programs administered on a formula-grant basis. The positions of policy process participants on this crucial issue were in flux, and by 1972 the NEA had moved to strong support of categorical aid.

The church-state controversy involved mainly the demands of sectarian elementary and secondary schools (predominantly those operated by the Roman Catholic church) to participate in federal programs and the insistence of separationist and civil libertarian groups that they not do so. Other policy makers were less concerned with the fate of the establishment-of-religion clause than with the maintenance of adequate support for education, and they continually sought accommodations acceptable to both parties.

As the financial crisis of public and private elementary and secondary education worsened in the 1970s, the church-state issue remained on center stage in the educational policy arena. Given the intractable stance of the separationists and the clarity of the constitutional language, it seems even more likely now, in 1974, than it did six years ago that the matter will ultimately be resolved in the courts in favor of the separationists or through a constitutional amendment engineered by sectarian interests. Even though most other educational policy-process participants would like the religious issue quietly to vanish, it is unlikely to do so; ultimately they will be unable to avoid confronting it directly. The fragile accommodation between the sectarians and the separationists that produced the legislation of the 1960s is essential to the maintenance of the federal educational role, yet it has come under increasing stress since then. At the same time, the federal role has expanded to the point where it is a vital element in the structure of educational finance in all areas of the nation.

The issue of racial equality affected most national educational policy making during the 90th Congress. The controversy over the elimination of de jure dual school systems which followed the Supreme Court's 1954 ruling in the *Brown* decision was definitively settled by passage of the Civil Rights Act of 1964 and judicial invalidation of freedom of choice, the last formal attempt to preserve some form of segregation. The focus of conflict shifted, during the 1966–68 period, to administration efforts to enforce Title VI of the Civil Rights Act and to the question of the status of nonsouthern school systems that were de facto segregated as a result of housing patterns, zoning, and economic factors.

The drive against de facto segregation was only in its initial stages at the end of the Johnson administration, but it had already sparked intense controversy. The Johnson administration was strongly integrationist and the congressional position tended to be lukewarm toward racial balance and more positive toward compensation. The established education clientele groups remained aloof from the battle except in instances, such as the community control experiment in New York City's Ocean Hill–Brownsville slum district, where the career interests of education professionals appeared threatened. By the outset of the Nixon administration in 1969, the racial issue in education was highly confused. The easy ordering of conflict along liberal-conservative and black-white lines that had prevailed until 1965 was no longer possible. Respectable (or nonrespectable depending on one's perspective) supporters could be found for most alternatives.

The increasing financial difficulties of higher education presented a new issue to the policy process. It was widely assumed in 1967 and 1968 that some form of expanded continuous federal support for higher education was inevitable in the not too distant future. (It was authorized in the Higher Education Act of 1972.) The principal bone of contention was whether the bulk of the aid should be provided directly to the institutions for general operating expenses or whether it should be channeled through students.

The institutions and their associations advocated some form of institutional aid coupled with an expansion of assistance to students. The basis of institutional aid provoked controversy within higher education. Prestigious, elite schools argued for the incorporation of qualitative criteria in any formula whereas the two- and four-year colleges which catered to the mass of undergraduates preferred a straight quantitative, per capita approach. The strongest supporters of direct student aid were the critics of higher education. It was generally agreed that student aid should be based more on need than ability and that its purpose should be to expand opportunities in higher education. There was also disagreement over the form of student aid. The Johnson administration, because of budgetary constraints, wished to minimize scholarships in favor of loans, and to shift the lending from USOE to banks. Higher education associations opposed this move on the grounds it would discourage students from attending college.

In vocational education the major issue was the quest of that segment of professionals for greater recognition in the federal educational effort. Vocational education's major backers were in Congress; it faced opposition from the Presidency and the upper echelons of the bureaucracy. This issue turned on the amount of money provided rather than the objectives and content of vocational education programs.

The Policy Process

The individual participants in the policy process were a highly elite group that consisted primarily of educators, career politicians and civil servants, and prominent laymen. Their influence appeared to be derived from three factors: institutional position, individual achievements in education or related areas of activity, and personal ambition and effort. Institutional position emerged as the most important determinant of participation and influence in the policy process. Most policy roles were institutionally defined, and only a few individuals were able to have a pronounced impact on educational policy without an organizational base of operations. Those few individuals who managed to have an impact without occupying a strategic position did so on the basis of high status acquired through recognition of their achievements or because they had become prominent while in an important post in the past. What could be accomplished, however, by most policy-process participants, say, a bureau chief in USOE or a subcommittee chairman, was to a substantial degree determined by the behavioral expectations which they and the other participants held for those offices. Within those institutionally defined limits individuals appeared to be able through the exercise of effort born of ambition and commitment to alter somewhat the content of the policies shaped at various stages in the policy process.

Even though it is not possible to measure the extent to which individual differences account for differences in policy, it is obvious that some positions afford greater opportunity to shape the course of events than others and it is quite possible, as this study shows, for individuals to define and act out their policy roles in a manner that gives effect to specific substantive goals and more general values. That educational policy makers varied in the extent to which they did so reflects the effect of differences in personal style, intensity of commitment to certain objectives, and accountability perspectives.

Beyond the limits imposed by institutional factors and individuals' perspectives, the behavior of the policy makers was affected by environmental factors. The principal environmental factors at work during the 90th Congress were the limited size of public-sector resources; strong claims advanced for defense, military operations in Southeast Asia, and other domestic policy sectors; the degree of public support for education and for federal educational spending; and presidential policy objectives. Budgetary constraints arising from the costs of the Vietnam war and inflation prevented full funding of authorized education programs and made unlikely any new policy departures.

There was, however, substantial public support for education as an important societal function along with a tendency to look to the federal government as a source of relief from the increasing financial pressures which state and local governments encountered in funding education. Public support for education was attenuated by a growing sense of disappointment in the apparent inability of elementary and secondary schools to fulfill the expectation of creating social mobility for everyone (which it obviously cannot do), to meet the special needs of disadvantaged children, and by resentment over the ferment on college campuses. These conditions in the environment of the policy process restricted the alternatives that were realistically available. They also may have had the effect of stimulating criticism of the educational system for not making effective use of the substantial resources allocated to it and of generating proposals for change.

President Johnson's policy objectives for education and his reform-oriented Great Society program constituted a major environmental factor. His position enabled him to play what was potentially the most important role in the policy process. His goals, which happened to be expansive and innovative, and the time and energy he devoted to achieving them, were an important determinant of the conditions under which the other participants in the policy process operated. Having committed himself to a major emphasis on education and having mobilized the resources of the Presidency to achieve this end, he preempted center stage, thus lessening the chances of other participants to pursue their own objectives. If, however, the President had limited his goals in education and placed his emphasis elsewhere, thus reducing the involvement of the Presidency in the educational policy process, other participants in it would have enjoyed greater freedom of action but with less chance of successfully diverting more resources to federal education programs. The President's policy objectives and his domestic policy orientation are an environmental factor because they involve the entire ambit of governmental activity. What the President wants for defense or health programs affects what he can accomplish in education.

One of the hallmarks of President Johnson's Great Society was a strong commitment to innovation with a heavy emphasis on education. He wanted the federal role in education to produce qualitative improvements and he wished to be remembered as a President who accomplished a great deal for education. Even as budgetary pressures forced a reduction of the ambitious funding levels visualized in the legislation of 1964 and 1965, he maintained the aspirations which underlay his commitment to education. As a consequence, the Presidency remained centrally involved in the education policy process throughout the Johnson administration. The activities of the other policy-process participants in formulating, adopting, and (to a somewhat lesser extent) implementing policy reflected that domination.

In contrast, President Nixon had no extraordinary commitment to or interest in the educational policy sector. From the outset of his administration he gave it limited attention and did not accord it special recognition in organizing the White House. He had no ambitious desires to introduce major new legislation and his primary concern for education programs was that they operate more effectively, hence an emphasis on program evaluation and a concern that costs be held down. Only when an aspect of national educational policy became a major issue, as in the busing controversy of 1971–72, did President Nixon and the Presidency assume a central role in the policy process, and then it was a reactive rather than an innovative role.

The Johnsonian thrust of innovation leading to qualitative improvement required that the Presidency assume a major role in the formulation stage of the policy process. The usual flow of demands through Congress and the USOE continued, but the innovativeness which the President sought could not be obtained, so it was believed, if the bureaucracy remained the primary source of legislative proposals and other policy suggestions. The result was the establishment of a special means of generating new ideas, the task-force device, and the integration of that mechanism with traditional agency submissions of legislation and the annual budget preparation cycle. Policy makers in the Bureau of the Budget and on the White House staff, in collaboration with a few selected officials from HEW and USOE, set the agenda for new actions. Items that did not get placed on the agenda stood little prospect of adoption and implementation. In setting the policy agenda for education, the Bureau of the Budget and White House staff participants in the policy process sought to safeguard the presidential emphasis on education. This led them to adopt a highly critical view of USOE and its supportive clientele groups, a view which was met with considerable resentment and hostility in those quarters. The administration did not exclude established groups from policy formulation, but it made clear its preference for individuals and organizations with new ideas who were committed to change.

In policy adoption the locus of action shifts to Congress, first to the subcommittees and committees with jurisdiction over education bills and appropriations and then to the House and Senate floors. Representatives of the education associations, other groups with an interest in education, and bureaucrats from HEW and USOE, especially those with legislative liaison responsibilities, played major roles in the adoption stage.

Responding to pressures from interest groups, their constituencies, and the White House, congressmen dealt with the policy agenda prepared in the formulative stage and embodied in the President's education messages and the federal budget. Those interests whose demands were not fully incorporated in the products of the formulative stage articulated them, often with some measure of success, in the adoption stage. However, opportunities for altering presidentially imparted policy directions at this point were rather limited. The principal opportunities to influence policy were negative rather than positive. They arose from the ability of a few key individuals or groups to thwart presidential intentions by withholding their approval. In exchange for concessions or compromises, that approval would be granted. The result would be the adoption of the presidential policy agenda with modifications.

The sharp differences between the House and Senate education subcommittees with respect to the level of conflict and partisanship and the styles of their leaders along with differences in the size and procedures of the two chambers did not appear related to floor action in terms of roll-call voting patterns. Party, region, and ideology had similar apparent effects in structuring cleavages in each house. The House did in the case of the 1967 ESEA Amendments, the one instance where there were major substantive differences in a bill sent to conference, force a substantial retreat from the administration's position. The Senate tended to be somewhat more supportive of administration desires, although not slavishly so.

The involvement of the Presidency and Congress in the implementation stage was quite minimal. The principal participants were the operating bureaus in USOE. Interacting with "the field" (defined as individual school administrators, university faculty and officials, institutions of higher education, and associations representing academic disciplines as well as the "establishment"), the bureau chiefs and their subordinates attempted to translate legislative objectives into programmatic realities. Their ability to do so successfully was hampered by an inadequate level of funding (a chronic complaint which, I suspect, will be uttered by bureaucrats as long as there are governments) and by the absence of clearly defined program goals.

The USOE program directors felt that they had adequate statutory authority, but they lacked resources to perform their missions effectively.*

* It should be apparent that educational effectiveness has been an elusive and ill-defined concept as used in this study. Although many persons interviewed spoke in terms of the effectiveness or ineffectiveness of the educational system and of federal education programs, no clear and

Even if they had had the resources, it is doubtful that effective performances would have been recognized, because few programs had goals that could be measured. Either the objectives were specified in qualitative terms, e.g., improve the education of disadvantaged children; or they were defined in quantitative terms that did not reflect the presidential goal of qualitative improvement, e.g., turn federal funds over to state and local officials; or they required a long lead time before their effects could begin to be ascertained, e.g., grants for basic research and development. In all instances, evaluation of program results was a difficult task which was either done infrequently or not at all. Accompanying the lack of evaluation of program results was the absence of systematic monitoring of the implementation stage by the Presidency or Congress. Most of the monitoring that did occur was conducted by "the field" through advisory councils, and "bird-dogging" of the bureaus by lobbyists and other Washington operatives.

Implementation is the least exciting stage of the policy process but it is equally as important as the formulation and adoption stages, if not more so. Organized interests, especially education clientele groups and the bureaucrats, recognized this as did some members of Congress, most notably Representative Edith Green, and the careerists in the Bureau of the Budget. But the failure of Congress to exercise more careful and exacting oversight, and the inability of the Presidency to mount effective monitoring of the bureaucracy,[3] resulted in a considerable amount of slippage in the achievement of policy objectives once programs had been authorized and funded. Much of this slippage occurred because of the symbiotic relationships that existed within the policy triangles between the agencies, congressional subcommittees, and clientele groups which Lowi has characterized as "interest group liberalism."[4]

The educational policy process received continuous feedback of new demands resulting from the impact of programs following implementation. Difficulties encountered in the course of implementation and changes in the environment which occurred as federal funds moved into the education system led to suggestions for amendments to the authorizing legislation, revisions in administrative guidelines and regulations, new programs, and more money. Feedback was received mainly by the bureaucracy and Congress and transmitted by individual educators, organized groups, and educa-

---

generally accepted definition of effectiveness ever emerged nor, I suspect, did one exist. Critics of American education and high-level policy makers in the Presidency appeared to believe that the schools were failing as agents of social mobility and economic democratization because of rigidities resulting from excessive professionalization and bureaucratization. This condition could be corrected by federal programs that stimulated change. But, the critics and the presidential policy makers did not develop operational criteria for assessing the success or failure of these efforts. In retrospect it seems that their goals were somewhat unrealistic and that they overestimated the capacity of education to solve the complex problem of economic dependency and underestimated the strength of the forces committed to the maintenance of the status quo. Effectiveness, a very ambiguous term when employed in this context, became an all-purpose standard that meant quite different things to the various participants in the policy process.

tion critics. The primary devices for picking up feedback, in addition to direct communications initiated by individuals and groups in the field, were advisory councils and congressional hearings.

It is difficult to distinguish feedback from new demands, but a prime example of its presence in the policy process during the period covered by this study can be cited in the successful drive to obtain authorization of advance funding of federal programs so as to coordinate the timing of school and college financial planning with the federal budget cycle. While it is not necessary to make an operational separation between feedback and new demand, it is important for analytical purposes to recognize that there is interaction between new ideas and those resulting from the effects of current policy.

Policies and Their Objectives

The products of the educational policy process were the statutes and appropriations enacted by Congress and implemented in the programs operated by USOE. Two of the most important characteristics of the programs were focus or orientation and form of administration. Programs were focused at: educational levels, e.g., elementary/secondary or higher education; sectors or problems, e.g., federally impacted areas, vocational education, libraries, adult education, and education of the handicapped; and functions, e.g., research, dissemination of information, and personnel development. The focus of a program usually reflected response to a set of demands advanced by organized interests, although sometimes programs developed through recognition of a special problem after which an interest organized itself around the program, as in the case of impacted-areas aid. The tendency to orient programs in response to organized interests, the most influential of which were education clientele groups, was another manifestation of interest-group liberalism. It was a major factor contributing to the frustration of presidential intentions and of presidential efforts to control policy implementation.

Educational programs were administered on a formula-grant or a project-grant basis. Formula-grant programs received the lion's share of federal funds. They were supportive of the operations of the existing educational system and its institutions and were highly sensitive politically due to the proprietary regard that powerful clientele interests had for them. Project-grant programs were more research-oriented and concerned with developing solutions to nonfinancial problems. They had greater flexibility due to less rigorous and less potent clientele-group scrutiny, but they had far less money with which to work, a factor undoubtedly associated with their lower political sensitivity.

I have not attempted to examine policy outcomes in this study, nor had the effects of major education programs been evaluated systematically within the policy process. Initial evaluations of Title I of ESEA, for example, were qualitative in character and were attacked as valueless by persons such as the late Senator Robert Kennedy. The attempt to evaluate the overall effectiveness of American education, the National Assessment, produced extensive opposition and was mounted only after its design was modified to avoid identifying individuals and school systems.[5] The results of the assessment do not, however, enable policy makers to determine the effects of federal programs. The need for accurate program evaluation received recognition from Johnson administration officials,[6] but the problems involved in determining "what works" are difficult methodologically and sensitive politically. The Nixon administration apparently made substantial progress in this direction; however, much still remains to be done by governmental officials and by social scientists if outcomes are to be included in policy analysis.

General Observations

The educational policy process was a fairly closed elite activity which, however, was internally quite diversified. National educational policy making closely approximated the pluralist model of American politics. An elite representing the great diversification of interests found in American education made policy through a bargaining process of compromise and mutual adjustment. Except for infrequent major changes of a redistributive character, e.g., ESEA and the other statutes enacted in the mid-1960s, national educational policy making involved the incremental distribution of resources.

Although the system was not characterized by monolithic elite domination, it was highly elitist in composition and provided an inhospitable environment for substantial policy changes. This inhospitality occurred not because the proponents of radical change were excluded from participation—intellectual and academic critics were systematically sought out and consulted and unorganized interests received attention through surrogate representation—but because American politics affords a considerable advantage to defenders of the status quo. The sequential approvals required to move an idea from proposal to program affords a multiplicity of access points at which organized interests can modify or exercise a veto over policy change. Consequently, power is exercised as much through the thwarting of initiatives and the frustration of action as through the positive mobilization of support from policy initiatives.[7]

Although I have not examined the negative or defensive exercise of power in the educational policy process in any detail, it is apparent that not all demands called for positive action and that some of the most influential participants were the establishment groups—education professionals, state and local officials, and higher education administrators—who exercised power by virtue of the veto they shared with key individuals in Congress and the bureaucracy.

The plurality of interests in education and the importance of negative checks in the policy process produced a fragmentation of power in the educational policy process. Although the Presidency had the greatest potential to shape policy, it shared influence with other institutional participants. Even with presidential influence strongly applied, as it was in education during the Johnson administration, other policy-process participants had to be reckoned with as they derive their influence from different sources than the President.

In education, one of the most important sources of power for the purpose of influencing national policy was professionalism as manifested in the national association. Professional interests were well organized, they had competent leadership, they possessed expertise which was needed by the government (both to implement programs and to build support for them) and which was used to strengthen their own demands, and they have entered into the symbiotic relationships with congressional committees and the operating agency that are characteristic of interest-group liberalism. The major objective of the professionals was to obtain increased public-sector resources for education. They sought to obtain funds on an unconditional, discretionary basis, making for a federal role that was supportive rather than innovative. Professionalism was thus one of the strongest forces at work in the educational policy process.

The consequences of professionalism were conservative rather than reactionary, however, as education professionals had some norms favorable to change and they were highly adaptive. They accept change, indeed they often promote it themselves, or coopt it when others initiate it, but their strong preference is for incremental change that can be controlled and turned to their advantage.

The conservative impact of professionalism in the educational policy process was counterbalanced to some extent by the constant criticisms and suggestions emanating from intellectuals and reformers located in elite universities and foundations. This loosely structured group exerted its influence primarily through printed forums open to them in academic journals and semipopular and elitist periodicals. Although these individuals and the institutions with which they were associated were a force for educational change, they did not engage in open combat with the national associations. In fact, many of the critics and innovators moved in establishment circles. They regarded themselves as collaborators rather than competitors of the established profession. Their task was the generation, development, and dissemination of new approaches and techniques.

Because they were relatively few in number and their involvement in the policy process was by invitation (from the Presidency, the bureaucracy, or congressional committee) they had but limited immediate impact on policy. Over a longer time their efforts may prove to be more consequential, but in the short span of a presidential administration, their direct influence on federal policies was limited.

The most important force for change in the educational policy process was unquestionably the Presidency. The strong emphasis that President Johnson placed on new domestic legislation and on programs having an innovative impact created an atmosphere congenial to the advocates of change. But even a friendly President could not overcome many of the built-in obstacles to comprehensive policy changes. The effect of personality, in the group sociological sense, was rather limited. Institutions and forces operating in the policy process appeared to be more important determinants of action (or inaction) and policy.

Institutions were a major factor shaping policy roles and accountability perspectives. Role expectations and behavior tended to be defined in a frame of reference based on official position. The parameters of individual action were, to a considerable extent, institutionally prescribed. External factors such as professionalism and public opinion further restricted the impact of personality. Professionalism provided a set of norms and values that serve as guides to behavior and a reference for accountability perspectives. Public expectations and the intensity of public support for or opposition to various demands that become substantive issues further circumscribed the capacity of individual policy makers "to make a difference."

Even though this is not a longitudinal study, events in the educational policy process since January 1969 provide further evidence of the limited impact of personality in the group sociological sense. Institutional and environmental factors have continued to operate even though individual policy makers have departed. President Nixon did not maintain his predecessor's high priority for education; there is no longer a presidential assistant with primary responsibility for education like Douglass Cater; and the policy makers who seemed to dominate the action during 1967 and 1968—Howe, Gardner, Halperin, and Morse—have all departed. In addition Charles Lee moved from his staff role in the Senate to the direction of a multigroup lobbying operation (The Committee for Full Funding), James Allen and Sidney Marland have served as commissioners of education, and Edith Green moved from the House Education and Labor Committee to the Appropriations Committee where she serves on the Labor–HEW subcommittee. Funding for federal education programs has not dropped precipitously, the basic issues and demands have changed only slightly, and the policy process has continued to function in much the same fashion as in the previous administration.

The impact of individuals in the educational policy process can perhaps be more clearly understood if considered in terms of Greenstein's distinction between "action dispensability" and "actor dispensability." [8] Greenstein argues that the question of when the actions of individuals affect events (action dispensability) is quite different from the question of when different actors similarly situated vary in their behavior (actor dispensability). So far in this discussion, I have treated these questions together. The question of action dispensability encompasses all the individual participants in the policy process and is the one with which I have been most concerned.

According to Greenstein, the impact of an individual actor on political outcomes varied with three factors: (1) "the degree that the environment admits of restructuring"; (2) "the actor's location in the environment"; and (3) "the personal strengths or weaknesses of the actor." [9] The environment of participants in the educational policy process during 1967 and 1968 did not permit much restructuring. The instability which had facilitated the redistributive legislation of 1964 and 1965 and the subsequent reorganization of USOE had crystallized in a new and relatively stable equilibrium of distributive policy making. Scarce public-sector resources and a widely apparent belief that the major challenge was to achieve the objectives of existing legislation rather than to enact major new statutes combined to reduce the manipulability of the environment.

Unquestionably certain policy makers, e.g., the President, the secretary of HEW, the commissioner of education, and congressional committee and subcommittee chairman, were more strategically located and thus had more opportunity to influence policy decisions. President Johnson, Secretary Gardner, Commissioner Howe and Senator Morse all had substantial impacts on policy by virtue of their key locations. But, and this is the final element of action dispensability, some policy-process participants appeared to have greater personal impact and some less than their positions and the degree of environmental manipulability would lead one to expect. The greater influence of, say, Representative Green as compared with most of her colleagues on the House Education and Labor Committee can only be explained in terms of her superior parliamentary skill, high ambition and motivation, and comprehensive substantive knowledge. The failure of other policy makers (who will remain nameless) to achieve a comparable impact on policy is likewise due to personal attributes, but of a more negative character, e.g., ineptitude and lack of energy.

This leads, then, to Greenstein's second question of actor dispensability or the conditions under which personal variability affects behavior. If individual actors are placed in a common situation, and in this respect we are limited to considering a set of bureau chiefs or congressional committee members, or lobbyists, under what circumstances do variations in their personal traits affect their behavior? Greenstein discusses the conditions in terms of the familiar paradigm of $E \rightarrow P \rightarrow R$ (Environment, Predispositions,

Response.)[10] He cites eleven propositions which I have summarized in slightly reformulated fashion (see table 8-1). In addition to the propositions in his paradigm, Greenstein states that to the extent that individuals perform policy roles that are not circumscribed by "elaborate expectations of fixed content" personal variation in their traits will affect their actions.

Table 8-1

Conditions Under Which Personal Variability Affects Actors' Behavior (adapted from Greenstein)

A. Environmental
   1. Ambiguous situations
   2. No sanctions attached to alternatives
   3. Actor is not in a group context
B. Predispositional
   1. Actor lacks mental sets which help to structure perceptions of situations and resolve ambiguities
   2. Given sanctioned alternatives, actor has strong dispositions in a contrary direction
   3. Actor is not disposed toward conformity
   4. Actor has high emotional involvement in policy situation
C. Responses
   1. Peripheral rather than central
   2. Demanding rather than conventional
   3. Spontaneous rather than premeditated

Although this analysis has not touched directly on all these propositions, it is possible and useful to examine actor dispensability in the educational policy process in terms of Greenstein's paradigm, bearing in mind that the seventy-seven actors were not similarly situated. The environmental elements, whether we are considering bureau chiefs, presidential staff members, or the incumbents of other roles, appeared for the most part to increase actor dispensability, i.e., to reduce the effect of individual variability on policy-making behavior. Most situations were fairly well defined rather than ambiguous. The primary sources of cues were known—the Presidency and the professional association—and there were few complex decisional situations in which contradictory and confusing cues were present. (The changing attitude of certain interests toward school integration was the most notable exception.)

Secondly, many policy alternatives had a recognized set of sanctions and reward attached to them. Few policy-process participants had difficulty determining the costs and benefits that would ensue, say, from opposing the Fountain Amendment or supporting the Quie Amendment. Nor did they lack knowledge of the sources of the sanctions and rewards. It should be observed, however, that the magnitude of the costs and benefits varied with the issues. Opposition to the administration or the NEA, or to other power groups, on a crucial measure, e.g., the 1967 ESEA Amendments bill, was likely to be more costly than on a lesser measure, e.g., EPDA.

Finally, most policy makers made their decisions in a group context of some sort—a congressional subcommittee, USOE, the Presidency, or the ACE Secretariat—so their views were known and subject to scrutiny. To the extent that these actors were disposed toward conformity, i.e., they took their cues from others, the impact of individual differences on their actions was lessened. While I did not assess the predispositions toward conformity of the individuals whom I interviewed, there were strong expressions of group expectations of loyalty that constituted what appeared to be highly effective normative constraints on behavior. Individuals were reluctant to act contrary to such reference groups as "the administration," "the leadership," "the profession," and "the field."

The effect of the predispositional element of actor dispensability was less pronounced since I did not systematically measure individual members' attitudes along the four dimensions. There did not appear, however, to be many mavericks with strong dispositions to ignore or resist sanctions manifest in policy alternatives and several individuals seemed partially to perceive their roles and the issues and problems they faced in the context of mental sets structured around the norms and expectations of professional educators, attorneys, or governmental careerists. Many respondents conveyed through public statements, policy actions, and interview comments a high emotional involvement in the policy process. Persons such as Samuel Halperin, Representative John Brademas, and Senator Morse had deep personal stakes in the education programs and policies of the federal government. Their emotional involvement may explain, at least in part, their highly active and effective performances.

The actions of the policy makers constitute the third element of Greenstein's paradigm. Here, the educational policy process conforms to his propositions. The "peripheral" aspects of action, e.g., personal style, varied widely between individuals as was manifested in the differences in leadership exercised by Representative Perkins and Senator Morse or in the contrasting patterns of administration manifested by the six USOE bureau chiefs. The "central" aspects of action, congressional voting, clientele group statements to congressional committees afforded little room for individual differences to affect action. The bulk of the actions called for in the policy process were demanding rather than conventional in that they required some investment of analytical effort and could not be conducted by prescribed routines. They were more heuristic than programmed and in this regard they tended to vary with individual differences. This decrease in actor dispensability arising from the heuristic character of action was counterbalanced by the absence of opportunities for spontaneous acts. Most policy-making activity was conducted in complex predetermined sequences that required no spur-of-the-moment decisions and afforded ample opportunity for careful consideration.

The final factor Greenstein discusses, roles, also contributes to an increase in actor dispensability in the educational policy process. As this study has emphasized, most of the policy roles were sharply defined by their incumbents in terms of their expectations of their duties and by the other participants in terms of their expectations of the role incumbents' behavior. These institutionally derived expectations and the accompanying accountability perspectives restricted the extent to which role behavior varied with individuals.

Although no measurements can be devised, it seems safe to assay that action dispensability was somewhat greater than actor dispensability in the educational policy process, but neither appeared large enough to assign determinative explanatory weight to personality.

Furthermore, even though many policy-process participants who were interviewed for this study described its operation primarily in terms of alliances based on personal relations, it is clear that personality was only one of several factors that influenced policy making and policy content. In my judgment, institutional and environmental factors were, collectively, more important than personality. One of the most active policy makers during the Johnson administration who espoused a personality oriented explanation, Samuel Halperin, recognized the effects of other factors from the perspective of four years:

> Morse and Lee shaped the operation in the Senate and the new guys haven't changed it much. The continuity is pretty great. . . . On the Hill the same kinds of people tend to get on the committees. Liberals predominate in both the House and Senate.[11]

Halperin maintained that people still "make a difference," but there were major situational changes since his involvement ended:

> The main difference now is that the questions are different. Now they ask: why this and not that? How do we know this [program] works? These are tougher questions than we had to deal with . . . [and] the NEA is in a weaker position now. They have become staunch defenders of categorical aid. They have lost a lot of credibility, like all of professions.[12]

Halperin's comments still reflect the personalized perspectives of a participant, but they also suggest that much of the continuity and change in the policy process are the product of nonpersonality factors.

Another observation concerns the central role of the operating agency,

USOE, in a policy arena typical of interest-group liberalism. Although educational policy formulation centered in the Presidency, policy adoption was the manifest function of Congress, and implementation was the task of the bureaucracy, the agency's involvement extended deeply into the other two stages of the policy process. It was the only institutional participant actively involved in all stages. It was the central node in the communication network and the main locus for the interaction of the individuals and interests who made national educational policy. Its involvement extended to all substantive issues, and the ultimate achievement of policy goals was more dependent on the agency's performance than on any other component in the process.

Finally, the educational policy process can be assessed in terms of Lowi's interest-group liberalism. Lowi argues that interest-group liberalism represents a bankruptcy of the democratic process that results in the breakdown of popular control of public policy, the creation and maintenance of "centers of privilege," and conservative policies.

The absence of clear statutory directives accompanied by substantial grants of discretionary authority led officials in USOE's bureaus and divisions to seek support and cues from key members of Congress, their clientele and other reference groups. Although they had no strong or overt desire to thwart presidential objectives, survival imperatives[13] severely restricted the degree of their responsiveness to the Presidency. The costs to the Presidency, in terms of time, energy, and political resources, of reducing agency and bureau autonomy and increasing their responsiveness to presidential policy goals were too great to pay on a continuous basis. This particular case represents a breakdown in popular control if such control is conceived of as being exercised primarily through the Presidency. If, on the other hand, popular control can also be considered to occur through administrative responsiveness to Congress and to organized interest groups, then the breakdown is not so severe.

It is clear, however, that the elitist character of the educational policy process accorded the "establishment" groups and the competitive "new establishment" critics a privileged position. Access to decision makers in the process was open to other interests but on a differential basis depending on political resources and expertise. There was substantial disagreement over policy, but the alternatives fell within recognized and generally accepted limits. Whether the policies and their outcomes can be called "conservative" depends on the values and policy preferences of the commentator. Certainly changes occurred in the educational system and in federal education policies, but they were more of an incremental than comprehensive nature.

The question, then, is whether the interest-group liberalism of the educational policy process was as bankrupt a phenomenon as Lowi's generalized description indicates. I think not, but it is a matter of degree. Popular control, through Congress and the Presidency, operated imperfectly; the value of representativeness was served but with an elitist bias; and policies tended more to preserve than to alter the status quo although in improved form. Moreover, Lowi's proposed solution to interest-group liberalism, a "juridical democracy" entailing the explicit statement of congressional objectives in statutory language,[14] does not appear to be practical in an area such as education where even among experts there is disagreement over concepts, theories, and goals. Neither have other attempts at solution, e.g., direct presidential intervention in policy implementation and short circuiting of the bureaucracy in policy formulation, been successful in education or other policy areas.[15] There are problems with the policy process of interest-group liberalism, but so far a workable solution has not been fashioned that falls within the framework of the constitutional system.

Notes

1. Milton Friedman, "The Role of Government in Education," in Robert A. Solo, ed., *Economics and the Public Interest* (New Brunswick: Rutgers University Press, 1955), pp. 123–44.
2. See Thomas E. Cronin and Norman C. Thomas, "Educational Policy Advisors and the Great Society," *Public Policy* 18 (1970): 659–86; and their "Federal Advisory Processes: Advice and Discontent," *Science* 171 (26 February 1971): 771–79.
3. For a perceptive discussion of the obstacles to such monitoring, see Thomas E. Cronin, *The State of the Presidency* (Boston: Little, Brown, 1975).
4. Theodore J. Lowi, *The End of Liberalism* (New York: Norton, 1969).
5. See Martin T. Katzman and Roland S. Rosen, "The Science and Politics of National Assessment," *The Record* 71 (1971): 571–86.
6. See, for example, Alice M. Rivlin, *Systematic Thinking for Social Action* (Washington, D.C.: Brookings Institution, 1971).
7. See the interchange on the "two faces of power" concept between Raymond Wolfinger and Fred Frey, "Nondecisions and the Study of Local Politics," *American Political Science Review* 65 (1971): 1063–1104.
8. Fred I. Greenstein, "The Impact of Personality on Politics," *American Political Science Review* (1967): 629–41. See also his *Personality and Politics* (Chicago: Markham, 1969).
9. "Impact of Personality on Politics," p. 634.
10. Ibid., pp. 636–39.
11. Interview, Samuel Halperin, 12 June 1972.
12. Ibid.
13. For a discussion of the difficulties of bureaucratic survival, see Herbert A. Simon, Donald W. Smithburg, and Victor A. Thompson, *Public Administration* (New York: Knopf, 1950), chaps. 18, 19.
14. Lowi, *End of Liberalism*, chap. 10.
15. Cronin reaches this conclusion. His extensive discussion of the frustration of presidential intentions confirms my more limited findings and is the basis of the following remarks.

INDEX

Accountability perspectives, 114, 149–50
Administrative decentralization, 208–9
Advisory councils, 177, 211, 222
Alford, Albert, 123n.
Allen, James, 147, 234
American Association for Higher Education, 142
American Association of Junior Colleges (AAJC), 55, 142, 144
American Association of School Administrators (AASA), 42, 138–39, 173, 208–9
American Association of University Professors (AAUP), 142
American Association of University Women (AAUW), 82, 140
American Civil Liberties Union (ACLU), 44, 46
American Council on Education (ACE), 34, 55, 97, 141–43, 181
American Federation of Labor–Congress of Industrial Organizations (AFL–CIO), 79, 85–86, 137–38, 140–41, 180
American Federation of Teachers (AFT), 85, 137–38
American Jewish Congress, 46
American Library Association, 85, 135, 140
Americans United, 44, 46
American Vocational Association (AVA), 65, 99, 139
Appropriation acts for the Department of Health, Education, and Welfare (HEW Appropriation)

fiscal year 1968, 12, 100–4
fiscal year 1969, 12, 100–4
fiscal year 1970, 105
fiscal year 1972, 105
Assessment. *See* National assessment of educational progress
Association of American Colleges (AAC), 55, 145–46
Association of American Universities (AAU), 54, 144
Association of State Colleges and Universities (ASCU), 55, 57, 145

Barden, Graham, 25
Basic opportunity grant (BOG), 59
Big Six. *See* Education establishment, Education interest groups, Elementary and secondary education
Block grants, 40, 74, 79, 116
Bailey, Stephen K., 3n., 19n., 20n., 22n., 29n., 31, 32n., 33n., 44n., 47, 48n., 73n., 118n., 119n., 198
Beckler, John, 59, 64n.
Board of Education of Central School District No. 1 v. *Allen* (1967), 45n.
Brademas, John, 63, 131, 168n., 194–96, 198
Bradley v. *Milliken* (1972), 50n.
Bradley v. *School Board of City of Richmond, Va.* (1972), 50n.
Brown v. *Board of Education* (1954), 8n.
Budget decisions, 200–2, 204

Bureaucracy, 160, 162–66, 169, 175, 184, 188–89, 239
Bureaucrats, 158, 160, 229–30
Bureau of the Budget (BOB), 7, 73, 1'5, 127–29, 175, 178, 180, 182, 185–88, 201, 204, 214, 228, 230
Bureau operation models, 213–14
Bureaus. See USOE, Bureaus
Burkett, Lowell A., 139
Burns, James M., 178n.
Busing, 50, 52, 88, 103, 105–6, 228

Califano, Joseph A., 176–77, 222
Campbell, Roald F., 39n.
Cannon, William, 73n., 183n.
Carey, Hugh, 77, 130
Carey, William G., 117, 128n., 183
Carlin, Paul, 139
Carnegie Commission on Higher Education, 53–54
Carnegie Corporation, 41–42, 53, 147
Cass, James, 41n.
Categorical aid, 28, 38–41, 52–53, 74, 76, 104, 116, 128, 224
Cater, Douglass, 7, 126–27, 185, 222, 234
Child-benefit theory, 43–46
Citizens for Educational Freedom, 46
Civil Rights Act of 1964, 27, 48–50, 73, 78, 80, 83, 88, 101, 225
Civil rights enforcement, 78, 83, 88–89, 101, 204, 225; see also HEW, Office of Civil Rights
Clientele groups, 101, 149, 184, 187–88, 199, 210–11, 230; see also Interest groups
Cochran v. Louisiana (1930), 44n.
Cohen, Wilbur, 28, 82, 91, 173, 179
Collective bargaining, 138
Committee for Public Education v. Nyquist (1973), 47n.
Communication, 154–55, 168–70
Communication network, 158–62
Community colleges, 144
Comprehensive Health Care Planning and Services Act, 40
Conference committee, 90–91
Congress, 8, 30, 34, 129–35, 160–61, 165–66, 169, 174, 184, 188, 239
    90th Congress, 11, 34, 39, 65–66, 72, 74, 95, 101, 104, 130, 155, 168, 174, 184
Congressional committees, 6, 8, 191–93
Congressional committee staffs, 131–34, 166
Congressional leaders, 194–97
Congressional parties, 190–91, 197
Conner, Forrest, 139
Consedine, William P., 81, 140
Conservative coalition, 83, 85, 190
Cooperative Research Act, 23

Cronin, Thomas E., 211, 222n., 230n., 240n.
Council of Chief State School Officers (CCSSO), 44, 76, 79–89, 137, 208–9
Council of Graduate Schools, 142

Desegregation. See Racial issue, Segregated schools
Dirksen, Everett M., 88
Dominick, Peter, 87, 94, 132–33, 194–96
Donohue, James C., 46n., 80–81, 140
Donovan, Bernard, 76, 81
Downey, Herman, 135, 209

Education Amendments Act of 1972, 55, 59
Education associations. See Education interest groups
Education Commission of the States, 43
Education establishment, 139, 142, 148, 168, 181, 185, 239
Education Facilities Laboratory, 147
Education interest groups, 8, 34, 39, 128, 137–46, 168, 173, 181, 184–85, 187–89, 208–9, 221–24
    elementary and secondary education, 137–41, 160–61, 208
    higher education, 56, 141–46, 160–61, 209
Education of disadvantaged children, 28–30, 33, 117; see also ESEA, Title I
Education of the handicapped, 101, 120
Education Opportunity Bank (EOB), 57–58, 116, 143, 173, 185
Educational Policies Commission, 138, 173
Education Professions Development Act (EPDA), 11, 91–95, 120
Educational research, 59–64
Eidenberg, Eugene, 40n., 43n., 44
Eisenhower, Dwight D., 3, 23, 138
Elementary and Secondary Education Act (ESEA), 4, 27, 28–33, 43–44, 74
    Title I, 29–30, 33, 38, 43–45, 72–73, 77–82, 84, 86–87, 90, 209, 232
    Title II, 30, 43–45
    Title III, 28n., 30, 76–77, 82, 84, 86–87, 89–90, 179, 183
    Title IV, 28n., 30, 179, 183
    Title V, 30, 39, 84, 89–90
    1966 Amendments, 33, 72–73
    1967 Amendments, 11, 73–91
Elitism, 232, 239
Elliott, Emerson, 128n., 37
Ervin, Sam J., 44, 45n., 88
Estes, Nolan,101, 123n., 167
Everson v. Board of Education (1947), 44n.
Executive Office of the President, 32, 73, 160–62, 165–66; see also Presidency

Federal control issue, 30, 37–43, 75–80, 104, 224
Federal role in education, 3, 19–20, 27, 40, 77, 104–6, 115, 224
Feedback, 91, 198–99, 206, 210, 230–31
Fenno, Richard F., 5n., 6, 10n., 19n., 100n., 129n., 134n.
First Amendment, 44–45
Fischer, John H., 147
Flast v. Cohen (1968), 45n.
Flood, Daniel, 101–3, 134
Ford Foundation, 42, 147
Formula grants, 200, 206–8, 213, 231
Forsythe, John S., 133–34
Forward funding, 78, 86, 209–10
Foundations, 40, 146–47, 165–66, 168, 186–88, 221–22, 233–34
Fountain amendment, 73n., 83, 85, 88, 90
Freedom of choice plans, 48–49
Freeman, J. Lieper, 6, 168
Friday, William G., 115, 147, 149
Friedman, Milton, 57n., 221
Froomkin, Joseph, 123n.
Frothingham v. Mellon (1923), 44n.
Fuller, Edgar, 31, 46n., 76, 139

GI Bill of Rights, 20, 55
Gallagher, James, 167
Gardner, John W., 25n., 39–40, 52n., 74, 78, 82, 89, 125, 181, 184, 214, 234
Gaul, William, 131
General aid, 20–22, 28, 38–39, 116, 173, 224
Gergen, Kenneth J., 9n.
Gibbons, Sam, 78, 84–85, 89, 130
Goodell, Charles, 90, 130–31
Goodlad, John I., 42
Gores, Harold, 147
Gorham, William, 125n., 167
Green, Edith, 44, 60–61, 77, 82–84, 89–91, 93–97, 105, 130–131, 140, 167, 194–98, 230, 234–35
Green Report, 61n., 205, 208
Green v. County Board of New Kent County, Va. (1968), 49n.
Greenstein, Fred I., 11n., 235–38
Griffith, Ernest S., 6

Halperin, Samuel W., 29, 62, 82, 92–93, 104n., 126n., 182, 185, 234, 238
Headstart, 96, 99–100
Health, Education, and Welfare, Department of (HEW), 7, 40, 125–26, 161, 165, 181–82, 201, 206, 228–29
    Office of Civil Rights, 49–50, 73, 78, 80, 83, 89, 204
Hechinger, Fred M., 38n., 39n., 62n.
Higher Education Act, 4, 27, 32

1966 Amendments, 33–34
1968 Amendments, 11, 74, 95–98
Higher education aid, 52–59, 106, 115, 225–26
Higher Education Facilities Act, 4, 26
Hill, Lister, 132, 135
Hochwalt, Frederick C., 25, 29
Horace Mann League, et al. v. Board of Public Works of Maryland et al. (1966), 45n.
House Appropriations Subcommittee, 59, 101, 134–35, 189
House Education and Labor Committee, 25–26, 74, 93, 129–32, 188–89, 229
House Rules Committee, 26, 31
House Special Education Subcommittee, 60, 79, 92, 96
Howe, Harold, 39n., 42, 63, 74–76, 81, 96, 101, 105, 122, 166–67, 176, 181, 184, 187, 222, 234
Huitt, Ralph K., 11n., 82, 117, 185

Ideas, origin of, 172–74, 183–84, 221–22
Impacted areas aid, 20, 22–23, 101
Income tax credits, 47
Incrementalism, 5, 22
Individuals, impact on policy making, 11, 149, 226–27, 234–38
Information sources, 162–70
Ink, Dwight, 32–33
Innovation, 39, 115, 119, 128, 166, 174, 178, 183, 187–88, 214, 222, 228, 233–34
Institutional affiliation of policy makers, 154, 158, 163, 165, 169
Institutional grants to colleges, 54, 115
Institutions, impact on policy making, 113–14, 149, 154–55, 162, 165, 168, 226, 234, 238
Interest group liberalism, 62, 224, 230–33, 239–40
Interest groups, 101, 135–37, 165, 185, 223–24
International Education Act of 1966, 96, 101, 103, 179

Jasper, Herbert, 128n.
Javits, Jacob K., 65, 87, 132–33, 135, 194–96
Johnson, Lyndon B., 4, 26–29, 38–39, 73, 81, 89–91, 98, 105, 126, 176, 178, 187, 202, 214, 227, 234
Judicial review amendment, 44, 88, 90

Kaufman, Herbert, 120n.
Kelly, James, 204n., 210
Kennedy, John F., 26
Keppel, Francis, 25n., 29, 34, 39n., 42–43, 118–19, 173, 181
Keyes v. School District No. 1, Denver, Colo. (1969) (1973), 50n.
Krettek, Germaine, 139
Kursh, Harry, 118n.

Laird, Melvin, 103, 134, 167
Lambert, Sam M., 139
LaNoue, George R., 46*n*.
Lee, Charles, 120*n*., 133–34, 173
Legislative development, 92–93, 127, 143, 174–75, 186, 204
Legislative liaison, 161–62, 168, 185
Lemmon v. *Kurtzman* (1971), 47*n*.
Leuchtenberg, William E., 28*n*., 175*n*.
Libassi, F. Peter, 78, 83
Liberal arts colleges, 145–46
Library Services and Construction Act, 4, 26
Lingoes, James C., 156*n*.
Lobbies, 163, 165–66, 168
Lobbying, 136, 138–45
Lowi, Theodore J., 7*n*., 62*n*., 230, 239–40
Lumley, John M., 62, 139, 187

Mallan, John P., 54*n*., 58*n*., 144
Manley, John F., 11*n*.
Manpower development and training, 65
Marland, Sidney P., 76, 78, 121, 147, 149, 234
Mattheis, Duane, 76, 78
Meade, Edward J., 147
Megel, Carl, 138
Meranto, Philip, 28*n*., 29*n*., 30, 30*n*., 43*n*.
Millenson, Roy, 133–34
Miller bill, 54–55
Miller, Paul, 125–26
Mitchell, Clarence, 85
Morey, Roy D., 40*n*., 43*n*., 44
Morgan, Richard E., 45
Morrissett, Lloyd N., 147
Morse, John F., 143
Morse, Wayne, 28, 85–91, 94, 98, 105, 132–34, 173, 189, 194–98, 234
Mosher, Edith K., 3*n*., 19*n*., 20*n*., 22*n*., 29*n*., 31, 32*n*., 33*n*., 44*n*., 47, 48*n*., 73*n*., 118*n*., 119*n*., 198
Moyer, Robert, 134, 135*n*.
Muirhead, Peter, 101, 123*n*.
Munger, Frank J., 19*n*., 129*n*.

National Academy of Education, 148, 167
National assessment of educational progress, 40–43, 101
National Association for the Advancement of Colored People (NAACP), 82, 85–86, 180 Legal Defense Fund, 49
National Association of College and University Business Officers, 142
National Association of School Boards (NASB), 137, 139
National Association of State Boards of Education, 137, 139
National Association of State Universities and

Land Grant Colleges (NASULGC), 54, 57, 143–44
National Audio-Visual Association (NAVA), 137, 141
National Catholic Education Association, 47, 137
National Catholic Welfare Conference, 25, 28, 34, 43, 45
National Commission on Accreditation, 142
National Committee for Public Schools, 140
National Congress of Parents and Teachers, 82, 137, 139
National Council of Churches, 43
National Defense Education Act (NDEA), 3–4, 23–26
National Education Association (NEA), 3, 23, 29, 34, 41–43, 62, 80, 82, 86, 89, 128, 137–39, 173, 181, 208
National Institute of Education (NIE), 64, 121–22, 214
National Science Foundation (NSF), 22, 60
National Security Industrial Association (NSIA), 61–62
Neustadt, Richard E., 175*n*.
New Establishment, 39, 42, 148, 223, 239
New Guard. *See* New establishment
Nixon, Richard, M., 47, 50–51, 105, 228, 234

Office of Economic Opportunity, 65, 96, 130
Office of Management and Budget. *See* Bureau of the Budget
Office of Science and Technology, 57, 73, 180
O'Hara, James, 83, 90, 130
Orfield, Gary, 48*n*.
Outside experts, 146–49

Parochial schools, 21, 26, 43–47
Perkins, Carl, 28, 74, 82–83, 90–91, 130–31, 194–96
Personality. *See* Individuals, impact on policy
Pfeffer, Leo, 46*n*.
Pifer, Alan, 53, 147
Pluralism, 232–33
Policy, 4–5, 7, 113
Policy adoption, 188–98, 224, 229
Policy agenda, 174–75, 183, 185–86, 229
Policy analysis, 5–7
Policy formulation, 172–88, 224, 229
Policy implementation, 198–215, 223, 230
Policy makers, 114–15, 149, 226
Policy process, 7–8, 113, 154, 158, 160, 169–70, 172, 174, 197–98, 226–31
Policy roles, 114, 122–26, 131, 133–34, 141, 146, 149–50, 155, 162–63, 166, 169, 226–27
Poverty, 27–29, 173
Powell, Adam Clayton, 25–26, 130
Power, 186–87, 232

Presidency, 126–29, 165, 174–75, 184–86, 205, 223, 227–29, 234, 239
Presidential staff. *See* White House staff
President's Science Advisory Committee (PSAC), 57
Professionalism, 233–34
Program administration, 189, 198–201, 204–5, 213–14, 230–32; *see also* Formula grants and Project grants
Program evaluation, 232
Program Planning Budgeting System (PPBS), 183, 202, 204
Project ARISTOTLE, 61–62
Project grants, 200, 206–7, 214, 231
Pucinski, Roman, 65, 74*n.*, 130, 173

Quie, Albert H., 65, 76, 78–85, 130, 194–96
Quie amendment, 79–84, 116

Racial issue, 21, 26–27, 48–52, 74, 78, 83, 88–89, 105–6, 225
Radcliffe, Charles, 79, 131
Redford Emmette, 113
Reed, H. D., 131
Reed, Wayne, 123*n.*
Regional educational laboratories, 30, 60
Regulations and guidelines, 202, 205–6
Religious issue, 21, 26–27, 30, 43–48, 74, 78, 80–82, 117, 224–25
Research and development contracting, 61–62
Research strategy, 10–12
Roles, 10–12, 113–14, 238; *see also* Policy roles
Roll-call vote analysis, 190–91
Roll-call votes, 191–94
Russell, Richard B., 88–89

Salisbury, Robert H., 5, 6*n.*, 136
Sanford, Terry, 148
Schultze, Charles, 127, 177
Segregated schools, 21, 48–50, 104–5, 225
Segregation. *See* racial issue
Senate Appropriations Subcommittee, 101, 135, 189, 209
Senate Committee on Labor and Public Welfare, 32, 94, 98, 132
Senate Education Subcommittee, 85, 94, 97–98, 132–34, 189, 229
Senate Select Committee on Equal Educational Opportunity, 52, 105–6
Separation of church and state. *See* Religious issue
Sloan v. *Lemmon* (1973), 47*n.*
Smallest space analysis (SSA), 156–62
Sociometric techniques, 156
Southern Regional Education Board (SREB), 56

State education agencies, 30, 39, 77, 86–87, 139
State plans, 79, 202, 207
Student aid programs, 34, 55–59, 95, 98, 116
Student disorders, 96–98, 103–4
Sullivan, Graham, 123*n.*
Supplementary education centers, 30, 60
Supreme Court, 47–48, 50
Survey of school superintendents, 212
Swann v. *Charlotte-Mecklenburg Board of Education* (1971), 50*n.*

Task forces, 28, 32–33, 95, 147, 175–77, 180–84
Task forces on education, 25, 28–29, 95, 147, 175–83
Teacher Corps, 32, 73, 75, 78, 84, 91–94, 101–3
Thackery, Russell, 25*n.*, 143–44
Thomas, Norman C., 5*n.*, 28*n.*, 73*n.*, 185*n.*, 211*n.*, 222*n.*
Tiedt, Sidney W., 19*n.*
Tilton v. *Richardson* (1971), 47*n.*
Title I allocation formula. *See* Elementary and Secondary Education Act, Title I
Truman, David B., 135
Tuition grants, 47
Tyler, Ralph W., 41–42, 148

United States Catholic Conference, 46, 74, 81–86, 137, 140
United States Chamber of Commerce, 82, 137, 141, 180
United States Office of Education (USOE), 7, 32–33, 41, 59, 73, 104, 113, 116–25, 160, 181–82, 198–99, 202, 206–9, 214, 228–29, 239
    branch chiefs, 200
    budget, 102–3
    bureau chiefs, 124, 160, 229
    Bureau for the Education of the Handicapped, 119–20, 167, 206, 213
    Bureau of Adult, Vocational, and Library Programs, 119–20, 213
    Bureau of Education Professions Development, 95, 119, 213
    Bureau of Elementary and Secondary Education, 119–20, 206, 213
    Bureau of Higher Education, 119–20, 126, 213
    Bureau of Research, 60, 119–20, 126, 213
    bureaus, 119–21, 160, 168, 198–99, 206, 213–14, 229
    division directors, 199–201, 229–30
    divisions, 199, 206
    external contacts, 210–12
    regional offices, 119, 208–9

reorganization of, 32–33, 118–19, 121
staff offices, 121
Universities, 163, 165, 173, 188, 222–23
University research, 63–64
Upward Bound, 96–97

Venn, Grant, 123–24, 199n.
Vietnam war, 63, 72, 103, 117, 183, 227
Vocational education, 64–65, 99–101, 139, 226
Vocational Education Act, 26–27, 64, 74, 99
Vocational Education Amendments of 1968, 11, 74, 99–100
Vouchers, 48, 173

War on poverty. *See* Poverty
Ward, F. Champion, 147
White House Conference on Education, 42
White House staff, 7, 73, 175, 178, 180, 182, 186–87, 214, 228
Wildavsky, Aaron, 5n., 6, 100n., 204n.
Wilson, Logan, 142–43
Wolman, Harold L., 28n., 73n., 172, 185n.
World War II, 20, 22
Wright, Deil S., 38n.

Yarborough, Ralph, 89
Young, Kenneth, 79, 83, 140